'The writing is perfectly poised and seductive, luminous, an earthy immersion into the granular dark of place. The prose has an intense, porous quality, inhabiting the reader right from the stunning start with the voices of rock, earth, wood and water. This is a truly elemental read from which I emerged subtly changed. The writing has a shamanic quality; Benjamin Myers is a writer of exceptional talent and originality . . . it has all the makings of a classic' – Miriam Darlington, author of *Otter Country* and *Owl Sense*

'One of the many joys of *Under the Rock* – this absorbing, compelling, moving book – is its language; it trickles like a rivulet, thunders like a cataract, and sticks to you like mud. It is full of crannies and dips and peaks wherein wonders hide; explore it for a lifetime and you will not exhaust its mysteries. Unafraid of blood-drenched history and the darkest of despair, this is nonetheless a defiantly life-praising book; it accompanied me to bed and bar, train and plane, and each situation was enriched and brightened by its presence . . . It is utterly vital' – Niall Griffiths, author of *Grits*, *Sheepshagger* and *Stump*

'I really, really loved *Under the Rock* . . . it truly stands out and confirms Ben as one of the most original and engaging British authors currently writing about landscape. He describes brilliantly the emotions that nature and place trigger in us, and the endless fascination we have with them. It's a bone-tingling book about both a beautiful location, and about the nature of our engagement with our environment' – Richard Benson, author of *The Valley* and *The Farm*

'What distinguishes *Under the Rock* is Myers' unshakeable commitment. He writes at all times with rock-solid conviction, fashioning a book which is less a work of simple description than a new contribution to the mythology of Elmet' – Will Ashon, author of *Strange Labyrinth*, *Clear Water* and *The Heritage*

'Place-writing at its most supple: both deeply considered, and deeply felt' – Melissa Harrison, author of *Rain: Four Walks in English Weather*

'Richly layered, densely and elegantly structured, discursive, elegiac and beautiful. *Under the Rock* is a stunning exploration of place, mind and myth' – Jenn Ashworth, author of *Fell* and *The Friday Gospels*

'I have become a Benjamin Myers junkie in the last 12 months . . . Myers' place-writing is as good as anything being scrawled in Britain today' – Horatio Clare, author of *Down to the Sea in Ships* and *Orison for a Curlew*

Praise for *The Gallows Pole*:

'Fierce, gale-driven prose that speaks to and of the northern English landscape . . . much admiration' – Robert Macfarlane, author of *Landmarks* and *The Lost Words*

'Terrific: illuminating, gripping and deeply rooted in its setting' – Amy Liptrot, author of *The Outrun*

'Myers is the master of English rural noir' – Paul Kingsnorth, author of *The Wake* and *Beast*

'Starkly beautiful prose' – Alex Preston, the *Guardian*

UNDER
THE
ROCK

UNDER
THE
ROCK

THE POETRY OF
A PLACE

BENJAMIN MYERS

First published 2018 by
Elliott and Thompson Limited
27 John Street
London WC1N 2BX
www.eandtbooks.com

ISBN: 978-1-78396-362-1

Picture credits:
Photography © Benjamin Myers with the exception of page 100 (top), from PDHA –
HB Local History.

Text permissions:
Page 4, 27, 33, 59, 60–1, 62: Extracts taken from 'The Rock', Copyright the Estate of Ted Hughes and
Reproduced by permission of Faber & Faber Ltd; Page 6: Extract taken from *Difficulties of a Bride Groom*,
Copyright the Estate of Ted Hughes and Reproduced by permission of Faber & Faber Ltd; Page 13: Extract
taken from 'The Pike', Copyright the Estate of Ted Hughes, first appeared in *Ted Hughes: Collected Poems*.
Reproduced by permission of Faber & Faber Ltd; Page 35: Extract taken from 'The Door', Copyright the
Estate of Ted Hughes, first appeared in *Crow: From the Life and Songs of the Crow*. Reproduced by permission
of Faber & Faber Ltd; Page 53: Extract taken from 'Sacrifice', Copyright the Estate of Ted Hughes, first
appeared in *Wolfwatching*. Reproduced by permission of Faber & Faber Ltd; Page 58: Extract taken from 'Crag
Jack's Apostasy', Copyright the Estate of Ted Hughes, first appeared in *Lupercal*. Reproduced by permission
of Faber & Faber Ltd; Page 60: Extract from unpublished letter, from Smith College Plath papers, series 6,
Hughes correspondence, Copyright the Estate of Ted Hughes and Reproduced by permission of Faber &
Faber Ltd; Page 66: Extract taken from *Remains of Elmet*, Copyright the Estate of Ted Hughes and Reproduced
by permission of Faber & Faber Ltd; Page 107: Extract taken from 'Widdop', Copyright the Estate of Ted
Hughes, first appeared in *Remains of Elmet*. Reproduced by permission of Faber & Faber Ltd; Page 107: Extract
taken from 'West Laithe Cobbles', Copyright the Estate of Ted Hughes, first appeared in *Remains of Elmet*.
Reproduced by permission of Faber & Faber Ltd; Page 115: Extract taken from 'Six Young Men', Copyright
the Estate of Ted Hughes, first appeared in *The Hawk in the Rain*. Reproduced by permission of Faber &
Faber Ltd; Page 117: 'Hill' from *No Map Could Show Them* by Helen Mort. Published by Chatto & Windus,
2016. Copyright © Helen Mort. Reproduced by permission of the author c/o Rogers, Coleridge & White
Ltd., 20 Powis Mews, London W11 1JN; Page 134: Extract taken from 'Prometheus on his Crag', Copyright
the Estate of Ted Hughes, first appeared in *Prometheus on his Crag*. Reproduced by permission of Faber &
Faber Ltd; Page 161: Extract taken from 'Leaf Mould', Copyright the Estate of Ted Hughes, first appeared in
Wolfwatching. Reproduced by permission of Faber & Faber Ltd; Page 162: Extract taken from 'The Horses',
Copyright the Estate of Ted Hughes, first appeared in *The Hawk in the Rain*. Reproduced by permission of
Faber & Faber Ltd; Page 163 Extract taken from unpublished letter to Donald Crossley, Copyright the Estate
of Ted Hughes and Reproduced by permission of Faber & Faber Ltd; Page 168: Extract taken from 'The
Thought-Fox', Copyright the Estate of Ted Hughes, first appeared in *The Hawk in the Rain*. Reproduced
by permission of Faber & Faber Ltd; Page 170: Extract taken from 'The Warm and the Cold', Copyright
the Estate of Ted Hughes, first appeared in *Season Songs*. Reproduced by permission of Faber & Faber Ltd;
Page 281: 'From My Window, North: Winter' by Dominic Cooper, reproduced with kind permission.

9 8 7 6 5 4 3 2 1

A catalogue record for this book is available from the British Library.

Typesetting: Marie Doherty
Printed in the UK by TJ International Ltd

Contents

Introduction

Picture a hill half blasted into history.

Imagine one side of this great hill torn away, hewn and cleaved, quarried and pillaged, dumped in and raked over, hacked and scarred, its face forever disfigured, like that of a Passchendaele survivor.

Now fill this blackened space with seeds and spores. Slowly, now. Let things settle. Let trees reach downwards, their curling roots grasping deep into the underworld. Let weeds wander, and life crawl and colonise and entangle.

Let the seasons set the pace. Months, not minutes. Decades, not days.

See a century that feels like a second. Let life breathe.

In time creatures will come. All the indigenous species of the North Country: the deer and the fox, the badger and the squirrel. Rabbits too, though far fewer than you would imagine.

And birds, of course. Here birds will find a haven in the upper reaches of the looming cliff face, or create crowns of thorns in the tops of trees that in the wet and windy months sway like the masts of ships. Birds of many varieties will pass through the thick woodland's clotted corridors, some feeding and flitting, others in full-throated joyous song.

Willow warblers and chiffchaffs.

Woodpeckers and wagtails.

Goldcrests and nuthatches.

Blackcaps and red kites.

In the trees there will also appear owls, exploding from branches like white fireworks, their magnesium feathers shimmering beyond the reaches of the old tallow candles, the oil, gas and kerosene lamps that illuminate the ages, before finally, silently, crossing the searching beams of alkaline-powered torches and the dipped headlights of distant growling cars.

This way ghosts were born: in wooded dells, down dark lanes of hedgerow and holloway, across clodded fields, when drunk men took fright at the unblinking brilliant xanthous eyes of an ice-white barn owl in flight, its talons stowed, wings beating a rhythm into the night, and had to create a new mythology to save face. Centuries later the nocturnal call of the owl runs the length of the woods and permeates the dreams of those of us who live close by, prone under duck down, the night world at our window.

Insects thrum and hatch and hover before filling the beaks and bellies of the bird life, and so the circle spins.

NOW IMAGINE MAN coming here.

Imagine man coming with pickaxes and chisels.

Imagine man coming with jackhammers and flak jackets.

Imagine man coming with dynamite and diggers and drills.

The crows take their temporary leave as industry makes its mark. The deer too will tread lightly through the mud and sandstone colluvium and rise to the top slopes, carving a new path up, up and away to the moor beyond.

In time they will return. In time they will all return, the wild creatures of this unknown place. The mammals, the birds, the insects. New burrows and dens and setts will be unearthed, latrines dug out and nests lined. The cycle will start again, and again. But not before the land has been blasted and quarried, dug and drained and filled, tipped into, dumped on and polluted with the death-making products of the accelerated industrial age. Fence it then, they will say. Shut it down and block it off, and create a cursed mythology of toxic soil and bottomless mineshafts and cliff-diving suicides and unexpected landslides in the night. Fence off this scar across the pocked face of the curiously named Mytholmroyd in the Upper Calder Valley, West Yorkshire, a piece of England sliced away.

Imagine this wild place. Summon it from the thousands of colours that swirl and merge in the prickling abyss behind your eyelids. See it now as the sun rises and sets behind this sparkling bluff of stone, and then open your eyes and there it is once again: Scout Rock. Here I sit now within its creeping shadow, a dark presence blackening my bitter coffee darker still. I drink it in.

Sometimes – especially in the depths of another dank, dreek autumn or on a sunless winter day too sallow even to grant us the thinnest of frosts, or perhaps at the dizzy height of summer, when the sun rises victoriously over its ragged crest to win the push-and-pull battle between light and dark – it feels as if The Rock is guiding my every movement. It is dictating my moods, my emotions. Steering hand and mind in every word I write.

It's there looking over my shoulder now – see it, always? – a folded shroud for the town, a black dog stalking the sleep of all who lie below it, a tombstone erected in memoriam of old sky creatures unseen.

Tomorrow the sun's rays will reach the lower canopy of this fenced-off green cathedral, and the nettles and balsam and rag-wort and hogweed will reclaim their kingdom once again. The deer will dance, the badgers will snitter and the single pair of nesting ravens will kite the warming updrafts, their full-throated croak, like a digital chuckle full of malice, will echo down the valley, and though no locals would consider entering this place, which they deem cursed down the centuries, I will vault the sagging wire and take to the slopes, home again.

PART I

Wood

Chapter One

Unremarkable places are made remarkable by the minds that map them.

Carved from the south side of the Calder Valley at Mytholmroyd, Scout Rock is a sheer slab of crag overlooking wooded slopes and undulating, weed-tangled plateaus. To most, it is unremarkable, a fleeting backdrop gone in a slow blink from a passing train or car window, or perhaps more akin to a dirty grounded iceberg if seen from a slow-gliding canal boat; an umbral form flitting briefly across the mind's eye. Subliminal, almost.

To others The Rock might serve as a marker for the widening out of the dale between the more heavily populated conurbation of Halifax to the east and a narrowing at Hebden Bridge to the west. Here great wooded walls harbour hidden ante-valleys, ruined mills and the ghostly remains of hamlets, which appear to squeeze inwards, restricting daylight and shortening the breath for just a few hard miles to the valley town of Todmorden and, beyond it, the hinterlands of Lancashire (as an old saying goes: 'Yorkshire is all hills and moors; Lancashire is all mills and whores.')

For some of the more mature generation Scout Rock is a doomed place. Foreboding mythologies took seed in the fertile imagination of childhood and made it a no-go area, where eighteenth-century thieves hid out, where the town tip once was, and later where industrial refuse was dumped without forethought or environmental consideration.

Charles Dickens passed through the area in 1858 and later wrote of it in a lengthy piece entitled 'The Calder Valley'. Dickens charted the rich history of the area in fascinated detail. Of Scout Rock he wrote: 'Beyond Mytholmroyd by the precipitous crags of Hathershelf Scouts – a rampart-like range of weather-worn rock, very conspicuous in the neighbourhood, and in places the sides are richly wooded. This place was the head of a feudal district, the forest of Sowerbyshire.'

Too doomed to be a playground for the modern valley's children, Scout Rock was yet significant enough to imprint itself upon the memory of a master of words who came of age facing this very arboreal stage, Edward James 'Ted' Hughes, described on his death by Seamus Heaney as 'a great arch under which the least of poetry's children could enter and feel secure'. This man is remembered in blushed recollections and with a reading voice like thunder rolling down off Midgley Moor; his life is commemorated with a Westminster slab, and with him rest the fading memories stored in muscle and bone of the black-stone scarp that haunted his adolescence, the 'memento mundi over my birth; my spiritual midwife at the time and my godfather ever since'.

Scout Rock is remarkable in the eyes of those who have decided it is so. Anything can be if it is willed into being: a pebble shaped by centuries of tumbling in the oceanic backwash, a single falling feather so light it barely succumbs to gravity, a mysterious gash in the landscape dense with trees, now fenced off and left to rewild itself.

Today The Rock still inspires dark utterances from the tongues of elders, their weather-worn faces creasing in admonishment at my confession that I like to explore this place that is, officially at least, hazardous and out of bounds to all members of the public: *stay away from the Rock, lad*, they say in voices as deep as ancient wells. *Nothing good ever happened up there.*

WE LEAVE LONDON early one June morning, Della and I. It is a decade ago and all our combined possessions have been crammed into a removal van that left the night before. What remains is shoved into the back of my car.

The last item we pack is half a tin of treacle, whose lid, almost inevitably, will be prised open during the journey by the dumb-bell that it is pressed up against. We will arrive at a new life dripping sticky syrup and curses.

Before we set off, one of the removal men, whose limbs give the appearance of having been elongated from years of lifting, tells us that his team had recently helped a mother and her four children relocate to 'that neck of the woods'.

'It was a house somewhere up on the tops,' he explains, lifting a filing cabinet beneath one arm. 'Same valley. Remote. She said it would be a new start for her.'

I nod. He sniffs.

'She killed herself after two months.'

We hit the morning traffic and an hour later are still edging along Vauxhall Bridge Road into Victoria. Our mood is strained, conversation terse. The stress of a house move is underpinned by the knowledge that once you leave the city it is very difficult to return; one only moves to London when either young or wealthy, and now we were neither.

Twelve years earlier, during the first weeks of Tony Blair's New Labour government, I had tracked a similar journey in reverse, driving a borrowed car full of clothes, books, records and treacle down from the north-east of England to find myself circling Piccadilly Circus at five o'clock on a Saturday evening, Eros looking down at me as I attempted a U-turn, much to the chagrin of the dozen black cabs caught in my slipstream.

Eventually I edged my way south of the river over the same bridge I crossed now, to move into a dilapidated transpontine squat in a labyrinthine Victorian building inhabited by social workers, punks, teachers, Finnish sonic terrorists, drug dealers, Greek artists, council workers, tennis coaches, Irish dissidents, passing backpackers, male prostitutes, an ex-Alpine goat herder, heroin addicts, academics and petty criminals. Here I lived rent-free for four years.

But now it was the height of a recession, and London was no city in which to be poor. Where once it was a dizzying maze to be navigated one day at a time, a playground for constant reinvention, now it was a place owned by the property developers, the oligarchs. The old one-bedroom flat, with its bath on breeze blocks in the kitchen and infestation of mice, abandoned by the local council for thirty years, had recently sold for £800,000.

What pleasure I still found in London for free was the many hours either exploring the overgrown Victorian splendour of Nunhead Cemetery, one of the 'magnificent seven' that circle the city, or tracking the abundance of urban foxes, themselves squatters living beneath the decking in our back garden. I passed hours watching the wild screeching parakeets that soared over Peckham Rye, which were rumoured to have descended from either Henry VIII's menagerie at Hampton Court, or the Ealing Studios set of 1951 film *The African Queen* or – my favourite – liberated by Jimi Hendrix during a moment of clarity on Carnaby Street in the late 1960s.

Nevertheless, I was in danger of becoming parochial, so Della, a fellow Northern exile and herdsman's daughter from a long line of cattle men, and I were doing what many like us had done before: seeking space, silence and the suggestion of financial survival.

We turn off Park Lane and its alien world of wealth, circle Marble Arch, then drive on up the Edgware Road, under the

Westway with all its connotations of Ballard and The Clash, past the Turkish cafés, the old Irish pubs of Kilburn High Road and along Shoot-Up Hill to Cricklewood. As the high-pitched thrum of the city's hive-like centre gives way to the retail parks and unknowable suburban conurbations whose historic names – Burnt Oak, Canons Park – suggest places of musket smoke and great intrigue, we pass through and under the overlapping flyovers like concrete ribbons, and I slither from my old city skin and finally breathe out.

It is June, the month that Pablo Neruda describes as trembling like a butterfly, and the Yorkshire valley is in wild bloom. Whispering fields wave hello, and the river banks are lost beneath blankets of barbed nettles and the soured honey scent of balsam.

The varying shades of green are almost overwhelming, and with the car windows open I hear the cadence of birdsong.

The cottage sits down a narrow lane in a hamlet a mile from Mytholmroyd. It has an old stone inglenook fireplace and original warped beams supporting the ceiling. There are three bedrooms and a garden that is a landscaped, fenced-off corner of a semi-wild meadow, and the water is supplied by a spring up the hill. Rent is affordable, even on the sub-minimum wages of a mature student and freelance writer.

There is a stone water trough out front, and an old man sporting a trilby, a red neckerchief and a sheriff's badge leaning on a five-bar gate, squinting into the sunlight. I will later learn that he is Arthur, a chipper pensioner who likes to dress as a cowboy and take long, looping daily walks from Hebden Bridge, always stopping for a moment of reflection at this favoured view.

The house is a stout weaver's cottage, built from sturdy rain-blackened stone in 1640. The removal lorry cannot make it down the narrow lane so we have arranged a changeover with some local men into a smaller van.

When one of the local guys leans against the drystone wall of our new garden to roll a cigarette I ask him about the silted pond down the lane that I saw when we first viewed the cottage a few weeks earlier.

'That's Stubb Dam, is that,' he says, gesturing towards the hawthorn-lined lane that disappears down into a darkening green tunnel. 'It used to be a lovely little spot. We'd swim in it as kids, and you could fish it too. Plenty of different fish down there. Some nice trout at one point, and giant pike that had been down there years. A few of them. *Beasts.* Aye, it was a lovely place. But then some fella down south bought the land and fenced it off. Put up barbed wire and "Private: No Entry" signs, and what have you. So obviously we weren't having that.'

He pauses to lick his cigarette paper, and then lights it up. He exhales slowly, enjoying the telling of the tale.

'So what happened?' I ask.

'What happened was, me and some of the boys loaded an

old digger that was ready for scrapping with a sack of something nasty and rolled it down the hill and into the pond. Poisoned it.'

'Poisoned it?'

'Aye, chemicals. The fish were floating belly-up by the morning.'

The man pulls on his cigarette and then exhales two plumes, bull-like, from his nostrils.

'Yes, a lovely spot, Stubb Dam. Here, I bet you think we're a right bunch of hillbillies.'

As he says this his phone vibrates. The ring-tone is 'Duelling Banjos'. The theme from *Deliverance*.

THE HOUSE IS the end cottage of three. It is cold, dark and solid, a stone box with small mullion windows set by a stonemason nearly four centuries ago. Two larger houses and an ancient converted barn comprise the rest of what was once a township settlement known as *Saxokakaurhs*.

Habitation in this little collection of homes is believed to date back to the eleventh century: Norman times, when lords ruled over villages and hamlets in the Upper Calder Valley. It then became part of a wooded game park, owned by an earl and managed by foresters. Today's dwellings came later, when they were likely to have been built in a clearing and named Burnt Stubb, meaning a wooded area cleared for cultivation. It eventually became known simply as The Stubb.

Our weaver's cottage was built for £2 10s and it remained unchanged for 250 years. Gas and electricity were installed in the 1920s. According to local historian Steve Murty, who has lived in Great Stubb house all of his life, and whose book *Summat A' Nowt* is a valuable history of the hamlet: 'Some [tenants] didn't want electricity as they simply did not trust it – uneducated people needed to see or smell something to trust it.'

The space where sheep shearings once hung from hooks in the cracked and warped ceiling beams is now an attic room that I use as an office. A Virginia creeper covers the entire face and half the side wall of the cottage, reaching around the windows. Come autumn its waxy leaves will run the full colour chart of decay through to the most brilliant burgundy, but for now our end of The Stubb looks like it is losing a battle with nature. The effect is that of something being consumed and pulled under; drawn back to the root source.

The old lane out the front leads down to the doomed mill pond, Stubb Dam, and once settled I find myself on the water by eight each morning, casting a fishing line baited with sweetcorn into the small and slightly sorrowful murky circle.

Every ten minutes or so a train rattles past my back, transporting valley folk to work in Leeds and Manchester. I see their faces only fleetingly, as they too might get a glimpse through the trees of a man alone as the morning sun lays strips of silver across the water. The sense of freedom and privilege I feel is almost overwhelming. What luck. A new chapter is beginning.

THE POND HAS certainly seen better days.

In the 1870s Stubb Dam provided a head of water to drive wheels that powered lathes in a nearby wood-turning business. Old photographs show a neat, stone-lined basin roughly parallelogram in shape and surrounded by a raised bank. At one end a stone dam controls the overflow. One particular photograph I find in an archive shows clusters of people reclining in the neat grass, and below them in the antique water four children cling to an airbed. It looks like a desirable destination; an upland oasis of sorts. A sunken Arcadia in the West Riding interior.

Today it is a place defined by absence, neglect and decay. The absence of its original industrial purpose, and the decay of its stonework and the slow rusting of the dumped digger that, sure enough, I find submerged in the long grass. The dam itself has collapsed too, so that one end of the pond drains away into a slow-flowing outlet partly clogged by snagged branches, silt, weeds and rocks.

Here and there around it I find dumped beer cans, broken bottles, railway sleepers, black plastic bags containing nothing but the rotten memory of tossed dog shit, and unlabelled oil drums that I would not care to open. I discover a pile of smashed window panes and strips of plastic sealant dumped, perhaps, from a kitchen renovation job. I also discover a tonne of anthracite coal, which I gradually remove bucket by bucket to heat the house.

A passable path runs around the circumference, but it is

surrounded by brambles, snatches of barbed wire and broken, useless fencing. The narrow lane that leads from the cottage is as dark and tunnel-like as the ancient holloways of Dorset and the Downs, and here during one early night's wandering there flashes a huge badger across our path, hunched like an old woman.

Despite appearances, the place is wildly, gloriously alive. In fact, nature is winning here – in the tree trunk that has consumed the line of barbed wire, and the abundance of weeds and roots and creepers that will slowly pull a shed-sized empty metal storage container down to the ground over the coming years. The landscape is erasing man's mistakes and reclaiming the space from its industrial past. This is a process that I will come to see often in the valley.

If the pond was once poisoned, then it has recovered now, for the water is busy with perch and roach feeding on newly hatched flies. I lift out several. Most are only a hand's length or less, and I gently release them back into the murk. Several times I glimpse the long, ridged spine of something far bigger, a muscular tail flick thrashing at my peripherals. It is surely the ancient pike, archetypal as the mythical pike of almost every village pond in England, what Hughes described as being 'of submarine delicacy and horror'. Like other elusive indigenous species – the deer, the badger – the pike is a mystery that stalks the cool and shadowed underworld. It is so briefly seen that it is barely there at all. It exists only for a splinter of a second, a creature that Hughes famously called 'as deep as England'.

Stubb Dam pond was where Ted Hughes learned to swim. In his book *Ted and I*, his older brother Gerald describes the warm summer days spent here between 1927 and 1938 and records their sister Olwyn's recollection of the nascent poet's first dip: 'I was sitting with Mam and Ted was paddling at the edge of the dam – he couldn't swim then – when suddenly he was in quite deep water. Mam tore down to get him out, but he was swimming away happily, doggy-paddle style – his first ever swim.'

Gerald also writes of an incident at this pond in 1937, when Ted was six. The family were enjoying a picnic when, in an act of bravado or wild abandon, their father dived head-first into the water. William Hughes plunged straight into an abandoned bicycle. He surfaced quickly to discover that he had torn his chest and arms on the jagged metal and was bleeding from his injuries.

There is a very good chance that it was here too, on this obscure bowl of water down the lane from my new house, where Hughes also encountered his first pike, and where began a lifelong fascination with the fish that represented to him the essence of the life force.

'Pike had become fixed at some very active, deep level in my imaginative life,' he revealed to Thomas Pero in an interview for American angling magazine *Wild Skeelhead and Salmon* in 1999. 'This recurrent dream was always an image of how I was feeling about life. When I was feeling good, I'd have dreams full of giant pike that were perhaps also leopards . . . They'd become symbols of deep, vital life. That's how I see it. My obsession with pike maybe was my obsession with those energies. It was a psychological thing. This went on for years. A very bad time might produce a nightmare dream of the lake lined with concrete, and empty.'

Hughes went on to describe how the day before his marriage to Sylvia Plath he dreamed of hooking such a pike from a tremendous depth. 'As it came up, its head filled the lake. I brought it out and its girth filled the entire lake. And I was backing up, dragging the thing out.'

In fishing the river, canal and local ponds such as this, Hughes found a focus for his thoughts, in what we would now identify as mindfulness, a practice that he would later apply to poetry. The closest I come, however, is lifting out the palm-sized perch and roach that are said to have consumed the brown trout which once stalked the shallow waters of this mill pond. I am a terrible angler, with little of the skill or desire to catch fish; in fact, in time the guilt I am wracked with at the thought of harming even the smallest bottom feeders will become so great that I will hang up my tackle. But for now, each morning on the water, I enter a sort of becalmed trance that, nearly a decade later, I have begun to identify as a process of decompression. Many anglers will tell you that fishing is rarely about catching fish; instead I was learning to breathe and to think, to master the art of patience and to broaden my horizon.

And I was surely lucky, for most of those June and July mornings the pond was as still as a mirror, a sepia looking glass reflecting my form as I stood and watched and waited to see what shape life would take next, though as A. E. Housman wrote: 'June suns, you cannot store them / To warm the winter's cold.'

The tragedy of summer is that it never lasts.

ONE MORNING EARLY in our relocation to the countryside I draw the curtains and watch a long and slender stoat slink the length of a field's drystone wall. A hunter returning, it moves without urgency or fear, as swaggering in its ownership of the space around it as a solitary bull in a paddock awaiting breeding time.

Scattered like the lines of a net cast out over the North Country, each such drystone wall houses a city. A universe. These veins of the land harbour within them lives unseen.

The dawn stoat's tiny spine ripples like the crest of a low-slung wave riding through the shallows to the shore. From this distance only its size differentiates it from the much smaller weasel, and it wears its sandy-brown summer jerkin; its belly is as white as daisy petals.

Here the wall is an arterial route, the stalking ground of this fearful killer of rabbits and rats, this tree-climbing, nest-raiding sneak thief of eggs. Perhaps it is a mother returning to attend to its litter of squeaking kits.

Two fields over from the house I see a bank above another drystone wall come alive with shrews, the tangle of grass busy with dozens of these scuttling long-nosed mammals working in unison towards some shared common cause – a relocation perhaps, or preparations for a great midsummer party. Shrews are territorial and can be aggressive when their home turf is impinged upon, so it is an unusual sight.

The drystone walls of England are the through-lines of our natural narrative, and home to a variety of fauna that so often goes unnoticed at first glance. Here lowland wagtails seek safety from predators and toads lurk in cool, dark crevices, and wasps build their paper-lantern nests of delicate beauty from an architectural blueprint held deep within their DNA and refined over tens of thousands of years. The nibble marks of these pulp-making machines can often be found on their discarded building materials – an old wooden palette, for example, or the chewed remnants of a cardboard coffee-cup holder.

The eyes of owls, robins and redstarts can be seen watching from cracks and gaps and cavities too.

RURAL LIFE WAS new to me then, a present continually being unwrapped with wonder, though I have since come to recognise that my existence barely qualifies as rural.

Instead this is countryside that is lived in, on and *through*. Perhaps life here in the valley could be described as 'post-rural'

– a world where the cottages of old have fast Wi-Fi connections and the old stone wells out front are nothing but water-filled reminders of other times, portals of the imagination; where the shrinking territories of the deer and the fox and the badger are sliced through by roads, rivers and railways tracks.

Post-rural is an emerging lifestyle choice, one that is slowly reshaping the topography and demographics of Britain's countryside, offering the best of both worlds: the comfort and convenience of modernity coupled with the *otherness* of the hills, woods and moors, and the deep-rooted symbiotic relationship with nature which still lingers within us after centuries of an agricultural existence, despite the accelerated migration that followed.

A census taken in 1801 found that the proportion of the English population living in cities was just 17 per cent, but by the close of that century, as landowners were displaced and industry boomed, the figure had jumped to 72 per cent. At the dawn of the twenty-first century the census found that 83 per cent of us now live in urbanised areas, while a mere 7 per cent of the population live in rural communities that qualify as villages or hamlets.

My own childhood was a suburban one, spent in the clean streets and cul-de-sacs that sprouted from the post-war/post-industrial English soil like mushrooms in an autumnal dawn. The countryside was close by, right where the tarmac oozed to a halt by the fields, lanes and scrublands, but it was nature contained. Beyond this shrinking triangulated space and across the cornfields were more houses, more estates, slowly linking up. I go back there often, and stepping out of the front door of my parents' house into the still summer night of a housing estate in the English suburbs now is like slipping into a warm blue memory pool of longing. The past surrounds me in a swirl of emotions. Everything remains the same – neat, trimmed, ordered – yet somehow different too.

The trees on the small communal patch of grass out front – when did they get so big? I remember them being planted, but now their loftiness is unfathomable.

The cul-de-sacs are each named after an English county, and the similarity between houses and gardens is disorientating enough to strangers to create a maze-like effect. Dropped in the centre of the estate, a visitor might find themselves wandering for a long time down alleyways and cuts, only to arrive Escher-like, back where they started.

I like to walk the streets at night, especially in summer when the flat north-eastern skies stretch wide, and gaze into living rooms illuminated by the cool blue wash from the oversized flat-screen televisions. The estate is silent whenever I walk its velvet pavements, save perhaps for the sound of cars moving at high speed along the A1 only a mile or so away.

To me as a boy, lying in my bedroom, the motorway sounded like the sea, and I envisaged great waves of asphalt rising curling over shores of shifting shale. And now, still, the inland motorway at night is akin to something nautical – as cold and lonely as the vast ocean is to a solitary sailor adrift miles from land, at other times oddly comforting as a landing lamp to a child that is afraid of what might reside in their wardrobe.

Ballard once wrote that 'the future is just going to be a vast conforming suburb of the soul' but never commented on whether this was something to fear or embrace.

Culture paints the suburbs as a drab counterpoint to the visceral thrills of cosmopolitan living, where the city, with its promise of reinvention and anonymity, and endless potential for experience, is given a higher standing in our nation's psyche. Rather than representing community and convenience, for many the suburbs signify a bedding-in, a sense of settling down and therefore, by extension, an acceptance of death. Their uniformity is dismissed by intellectuals.

The countryside, meanwhile, is idealised by some and dismissed as retrogressive by others, a fearful space where death is visible in tooth and claw, where 'old ways' are viewed as 'wrong ways' and all that existential silence and space is insidious, and therefore needing to be filled. Samuel Johnson may have famously said that 'when a man is tired of London, he is tired of life', but I would counter that 'the man who fears the countryside fears himself'.

In the suburbs, nature is kept at arm's length. It has been tamed, existing mainly in a plant pot sitting on a driveway, a hanging basket in a conservatory. A swinging bird feeder, the occasional hedgehog scratching across a dawn lawn. Weeds pushing through gaps. Things dumped in the tangle of the back lanes.

It is a world best portrayed in the artist George Shaw's paintings of Tile Hill, the suburb of Coventry in which he grew up, and which formed the basis for his collections *The Sly and Unseen Day* and *My Back to Nature*. Using cheap Humbrol paint, Shaw captures a place devoid of people, but where the familiar scrublands are invested with meaning, where each stray carrier bag or abandoned stash of pornography is elevated to the status of the iconic, each underpass, alleyway or peephole through a creosoted fence suggesting a portal to another dimension.

The suburbs' creeping encroachment upon our rural landscapes has had knock-on sociological effects: research shows that the behavioural patterns of the young have changed significantly since the 1970s. According to the writer George Monbiot in a *New Statesman* article entitled 'The Age of Loneliness', the 'unaccompanied home range' of children has declined by 90 per cent. 'Not only does this remove them from contact with the natural world, but it limits their contact with other children,' he writes. 'When kids played out on the street or in the woods, they quickly formed their own tribes, learning the social skills that would see them through life.'

Distance from such explorations only breeds a fear and ignorance of the natural world, though the cruel irony is that, having moved away from agrarian life towards urban and suburban living, it is not now the strange natural world of poisonous plants, dirt, death and decay, and the potential for injurious accidents, that parents or their children need fear at all, but the dark and distorted digital world where faceless revenants stalk the most shadowy corners.

Perhaps it will be nature and the natural world in which succour and solace will once again be found by future generations.

And that, perhaps, is why I moved here, to a house by a wood and a moor and a river and a rock. To navigate a new way.

Chapter Two

Walking defines my earlier days in this new terrain. Up hills, into woodlands, along ancient packhorse tracks, through sulphurous bogs, under rocks, down caviar-black banks of slick soil. These lung-burning perambulations are undertaken without direction or a purpose other than to get an overview of the topography. I am doing that which I promised myself I would during a decade of sleepless city nights: I am seeking equanimity.

There is much to see and touch. The gnarly pocked bark of an ancient ash tree; the loaded seed pods of the Himalayan balsam; the moss-covered gritstone needles poking through the soft soil like the pinnacles of deeply buried obelisks. I taste stringent leaves, sour berries and water from a stream that looks like a stained-glass window laid flat across a meadow. I gain my bearings.

From the field that extends beyond our front garden's perimeter, where three grazing horses which smell of warm, wet old socks wander over to snort and nibble at my jumper, I can see a mile east along the valley to a place I have not yet explored in these first weeks of losing myself: Scout Rock.

It is a densely wooded hole in the hillside beneath vertical drops of exposed rock that plunge down like a waterfall petrified by Medusa's glare, and frozen as stone for ever. Viewed along the tunnel of the valley from the small black cottage, it looks like an amphitheatre reclaimed by nature, a lapsed volcano. The suggestion, perhaps, of a lost world.

An old map tells me that this wooded quarry was once known as Hathershelf Scout, unseen from the guts of the valley, but is more colloquially known as Scout Rock. In time, to me at least, it will become known simply as The Rock.

I first walk up there on a still day that smells like freshly sliced cucumber, the sky a rippling banner of blue that hangs over the swaying greens of an Arcadian summer.

SCOUT ROCK LOOMS silently over Mytholmroyd, part-protector, part-illegitimate cousin cast out to the limits of the parish boundaries of a small Pennine town with a population of approximately 4,500 people.

Mytholmroyd is best known as a place with a difficult-to-pronounce name seen from a rain-streaked train window as people pass through on the TransPennine Express route. The book *Yorkshire Past and Present*, published in 1871, claims that 'Mytholmroyd' is a compound of *mey* (girl), *holm* (a meadow) and *riodr* (a clearing), and therefore means 'the girl's meadow clearing'. More likely Mytholmroyd means 'the meeting of two waters', as it was here at this juncture, where Elphin Brook feeds into the shallow-running River Calder, that a town which feels more like a scattered village has spread like moss over the centuries, watched over by the frowning rock that blocks the sky to the south in a valley that John Wesley called 'The most beautiful in England, with the most barbarous people.'

It is also known as the birthplace of Ted Hughes. Sitting on the south side of the valley, Scout Rock glowers down upon 1 Aspinall Street, where Hughes was born in 1930. In the opening lines of his study, *Ted Hughes: The Unauthorised Life*, the biographer Jonathan Bate observes that 'The Rock lowers over an industrial village called Mytholmroyd. Myth is going to be important, but so is the careful, dispassionate work of demythologising: the first syllable is pronounced as in "my", not as in "myth". My-th'm-royd. For Ted Hughes it was "my" place as much a mythic place.' (Hughes might have been amused had he attended the local screening of the 2003 Sylvia Plath biopic *Sylvia*, in which Daniel Craig, as miscast in the role of her husband as Gwyneth Paltrow was as the lead, loudly declared, 'If I close my eyes, I could be back in Mith-mroyd', much to the mirthful vocal disdain of the local filmgoers.)

Mytholmroyd sits a mile or so down the valley from Hebden Bridge, a town of a similar size that is internationally known for having once been voted by a newspaper the 'fourth-funkiest town in the world' and also for having the most lesbian residents per capita in the UK, therefore statistically making it the unofficial gay capital of Britain.

Unlike working Mytholmroyd, Hebden Bridge's population is comprised of a colourful mix of old, deep-rooted Yorkshire families and offcumdens – that transient population of outsiders with a propensity towards bohemia, the arts, free-thinking, dissidence, radicalism and the eco-movement. It is a unique and energetic town where old and new ways merge in a confluence of a thousand ongoing ethical arguments. It is, some have joked, 'a drug town with a tourist problem'. By contrast, Mytholmroyd is more grounded, more stoic. It has few pretensions, and does not flaunt its Hughes connection as Haworth does with the Brontë sisters. Today, 'Royd exists with one foot in a modern era of industrial estates, small businesses, repurposed mills and post-war housing estates, and another in its pre-industrial past.

At the foot of the woods is Scout Road, a street that begins with an imposing Methodist Church perched vulture-like at its base. It's empty now. The grip that this austere strain of Christianity once had on this valley is no more. The worshippers have lost faith or died out.

The road takes in some skulking factory buildings and a series of streets of back-to-back terraces. There's a community-managed park too, with a communal vegetable patch and a pond, before the remaining terraces of houses narrow out to follow the road up to a primary school, an incongruous caravan park tucked away in paddock and then nothing but the trees closing in as you enter Scout Rock Woods.

Here the road rises and winds with The Rock on your right until finally you ascend to the sky, the narrowing road meandering onwards towards the hamlets of Hathershelf and Boulderclough.

Up on the tops, where the valley meets the moors, there still exist tenant farms whose inhabitants have grazed the harsh land for centuries – the soil is no good for cultivation – and scattered around the length of the Upper Calder Valley are the ruins and remnants of eras reaching deeper into Albion: Iron Age, Celtic, Norman, Roman, each piled upon one another, peeling back here and there like the pressed-flat pages of a book, to give a glimpse of past epochs and the lives of our toiling ancestors.

And there like a ghastly curtain, the great slab of plunged earth, Scout Rock, to which no sign points. Though not visible from the valley floor, behind Scout Rock – above it, obscured – is a cloud-world of further farmed fields and brief hamlets and then the unforgiving moors themselves: foreboding and inclement barren plains; a massive flattened mausoleum from which new life springs forth in the cough of a deer or the call of grouse and curlew. Here Hughes's ancestors worked the land, living in a farm 'that seemed to be made wholly of old gravestones and worn-out horse troughs'.

The moods of these West Yorkshire moors swing like those of a stroppy teenager, and art and literature has imbued them with a strong sense of retrospective romance, a canvas on which to project the fancies of office-bound academics. Charlotte Brontë's opinions on the delphs (a delph – or delf – is defined as that which has been dug or excavated, such as a mine, ditch, pit, quarry or even a grave), dingles and cloughs of the area only partially lay claim to the moorlands as muse to the three enamoured sisters. 'The scenery of these hills is not grand – it is not romantic; it is scarcely striking,' she wrote in her prefatory notes to *Selections from Poems by Ellis Bell*. 'Long, low moors, dark with heath, shut in little valleys, where a stream waters, here and there, a fringe of stunted copse. Mills and scattered cottages chase romance from these valleys; it is only higher up, deep in amongst the ridges of the moors, that Imagination can find rest for the sole of her foot.'

The moors stretch away for miles to merge in one direction with the cursed Saddleworth Moor, where the bodies of children were buried in the mire by Ian Brady and Myra Hindley, and then over to the Brontës' stalking grounds of Haworth in the other.

Halfway between sits The Rock, where the moor suddenly drops away to give a glimpse of the black mass beneath it. In his recent guidebook *West Yorkshire Woods – Part 1: The Calder Valley*, local author and cartographer Christopher Goddard describes The Rock: 'Its savage crumbling face was originally formed by an ancient landslip and later scoured out further to build some of Halifax's buildings. It consists of two beds of gritstone separated by 20 feet of loose shale which is why so much of it has fallen into the wood below. Despite the amount of loose rock it was used by climbers in the early twentieth century and there was a viewpoint from the projecting rock in the middle of the Scout.'

Goddard describes this landmark as 'frustratingly inaccessible and it is difficult to get any sort of close-up view of the precipitous face of Scout Rock', noting that 'a couple of foot-paths run through Scout Wood but are closed off due to falling rock in Hathershelf Scout delfs'.

Such hazards ensure that The Rock remains a threat, an enigma, an inscrutable and evasive geological landmark avoided by most, yet its mute malevolence exudes a sort of charisma.

Its true name of Hathershelf Scout derives from the sloping fields above that are now stone-walled into geometric acres grazed in rotation by sedate yet curious cud-stuffed cows. Later the cliffs and woods that sit below came to be known as Scout Rock, 'scout' being a widely used term to refer to a hill or overhanging cliff, and originating from the Norse word *scuti*. *Scuti Rock*. Overhanging cliff.

Norsemen passed through this valley and stayed long enough to bestow etymological epithets that endure today like messages sent from a time when, as now, Britain was an island in transition, a land mass in a state of identity confusion, simultaneously arrogant and fearful, stoic and divided, inward-facing and adrift. Drunk on delusion.

Slice through the four counties of Yorkshire that collectively dominate the North of England and you will find a layer cake of time zones and narratives. We sit upon a massive compressed palimpsest of different strata formed over 500 million years. Britain has been part of a continental shift caused by the continually changing sea floors created by volcanic vents that line a ridge deep in the mid-Atlantic, at the rate of several inches per year. Where once the county was 3,000 miles south of the equator, it is now the same distance in the other direction. And doesn't a Yorkshireman — and it is usually a man — like to remind you of his Northern-ness.

The folded laminations of rock beneath my feet range from sticky clay through cream-coloured limestone to golden sandstone, each holding the fossilised remains of species utterly alien to today's world, skeletal frames buried deep amongst the bedded-down leftovers of steamy tropical rainforests now known as Barnsley, the sandy tough-grit deserts of Doncaster or the dinosaur delta of Scarborough.

Some 320 million years ago in the Carboniferous Period the country was part of a vast granite mountain range whose crenellated crowns were gradually worn down by rainstorms and then washed away in deluges of debris, each new sedimentary layer replacing the previous one, capturing any living thing in its path (fossils of relatives of squid and octopus have been found in gritstone fifty miles or more from any sea). Mainly the stone is comprised of that bejewelled bounty of boyhood explorations, quartz, and rock-forming mineral feldspar – veins of crystallised magma that make up more than half of the earth's crust, and whose name originates from the German compound of *Feld*, meaning field, and *Spat*, a rock that does not contain any ore. *Fieldspat*. Feldspar.

Perhaps the hardest rock is gritstone, or millstone grit as it is known across the Pennines and Peak District, which lies beneath the moorland soil of the West Riding. It is gritstone from which Scout Rock has been sculpted, its great gloomy face an abstract Mount Rushmore carved not by presidential ego but by wind and rain and earth's only true certainty: the irreversible passing of time.

Dubbed 'God's own rock', gritstone defines Calderdale. Inhabitants live in structures built from its hewn blocks, we feel it underfoot in flagstones or we see it, as the late local poet Glyn Hughes (no relation to Ted) put it: 'bonily sticking out of the landscape wherever you look, as the bones press through the flesh of a hungry cow'.

The main gritstone seam of the North runs down from the North Yorkshire Dales through the affluent spa towns of Harrogate and Ilkley, down Calderdale and on towards the flanks of Derbyshire, Staffordshire and Cheshire, periodically rising from the soil where the land has been most weathered, sculpted, quarried, chipped, split and cleaved.

Though robust and insoluble, millstone grit is porous and shot through with vertical joints or lines of weakness that make it susceptible to the long-game attack of the elements, the whistling wind and lashing rain often creating iconic sculptural anomalies of the stone which, if conceived and chiselled by the hand of man, and buffed or polished, would sell for millions on the art market. Both Henry Moore and Barbara Hepworth came from West Yorkshire and the mysterious gritstone playground of Brimham Rocks or the wind-worn forms of the Bridestones of the Upper Calder Valley must surely have left an impression upon both.

Millstone grit also raises itself along a series of dramatic edges beloved of climbers who clamber over the arêtes of the renowned escarpment Stanage Edge and hundreds of other such topographical obscurities. Gritstone, notes M. John Harrison in his novel *Climbers*, has 'a curious spicy odour', but perhaps its most notable trait is its ability to regress from beautiful beginnings to become something altogether more oppressive and surly in appearance. 'The cleanest air will oxidise it from lovely orange and gold, as you see it when it first bursts open, sparkling with innumerable glassy crystals of silica,' writes Glyn Hughes in *Millstone Grit*, 'to the black, black that makes your eyes ache everywhere in West Yorkshire, so that you think of dirt, no matter how clean and bright the day.'

In a landscape further stained by the coughing chimneys of centuries of industry and residential coal-burning, it is hard not to be influenced by the presence of gritstone, especially in the close proximity of this towering rock that sits behind me, casting shadows, dictating moods, probing my peripherals.

In his 1963 essay 'The Rock', Hughes describes the cliff as 'both the curtain and back-drop to existence. All that happened, happened against it or under its supervision . . . It was a darkening presence, like an over-evident cemetery. Living beneath it was like living in a house haunted by a disaster that nobody can quite believe ever happened though it regularly upsets sleep.'

I too began to feel The Rock haunting my dreams, with the one same line chiselled into my subconscious, embedded there and uttered over and over all night long, as if it wanted to explain to me its beginnings, again and again, the one line locked on a reverb-laden loop, until all I could do was rise in the lonely blue pre-dawn stillness and write it down, an exorcism necessary to silence this goading beast.

The Story of The Rock

Ice and fire
fought
until reason
emerged.

From the roadside deep in the tunnel of trees below The Rock, I find the entire place fenced off. It is not a welcoming woodland, but somewhere to be turned away from.

Move along. Nothing to see here.

A drystone wall seems to be straining under the weight of the hillside above it and cheap signage – the modern aesthetic blight – is everywhere, full of veiled threats and negative instructions: *No* and *Don't* promising *Danger* and *Prosecution.*

The road rises winding until I find a way in, cutting right into a clearing where the trees stand tall at the bottom of slopes of leaf and mud and boulder. Above them are the jagged crags of The Rock itself.

There is evidence of an old track, a worn groove in the soil, and I follow it up until I am clambering with my hands over more boulders, and there is moss everywhere.

Already Mytholmroyd, only a half-mile away, feels long behind me as I walk deeper into the woods and The Rock towers like something that has been forced from the earth by its fiery inner workings.

The outside world is entirely obscured from view as I mount a wooded hillock, pulling myself up in places by using the smooth girth of silver birches. Altitude comes quickly when you are young and fearless and don't look back, and The Rock rises taller still.

A squirrel sniffs the air. Twitching, it shakes the leanest boughs, makes a break from a branch and then, with limbs splayed, takes a bold leap onto the limitless ladders of the sky.

Above, crows circle, calling a warning to all the creatures of The Rock: the first human presence in a long time. These creatures have policed this place throughout the ages. The descendants of the same crows that chuntered through Ted Hughes's childhood sleep patterns continue to rule The Rock today. They always commanded top billing in Hughes's 'Crow' cycle of poems: 'There is a doorway in the wall – / A black doorway: The eye's pupil / Through that doorway came Crow.' As intrinsic and immovable as the ravens of the Tower of London, they preside from their vertical-dropped outcrop before fulminating like black confetti flung at a doomed marriage or a funeral for a forest.

The bluebells of April and May are still in evidence, but are flattened down now, wilted and spent, their thin stalks forming a crunchy carpet and their brilliant violet tepals faded in colour, curled into decay. Bracken fronds that smell of childhood have unfolded everywhere. With stealth their branches reach for the sun just as their roots bury quickly into the soil. Fossilised evidence of this pernicious fern, held fast in compacted sediment, has been dated back 55 million years, making it one of the species most adaptable to climate change. I push my way through them and the resistance they offer is like wading through water.

There is an overpowering sense of stillness.

With the throb of blood in my ears I reach the top of the knoll. Here I catch my breath and discover a small circle of stones, perhaps eight or nine feet across, arranged as if to form a fireplace or perhaps the base of a chimney used for some other industrial purpose.

Looking down behind me through columns of trees and the tide of bracken to the wooded plateau below, I sit and eat an apple.

The stone wall of crows above watches on, hard at my back. And so an obsession begins.

I STUMBLE DOWN a diagonal route that follows a general flattening of foliage created not by man but by the daily routines of deer or the nocturnal missions of the badger.

And then I am down on the plateau in the very heart of Scout Rock Woods, and here the atmosphere changes.

Close to the base of the rock face, in an area once quarried for stone, I wander into a small forest of wild plants that tower above me. They stand menacing and triffid-like on wide, hollow stalks, like green cane, their leaves broad and multi-fingered, halfway between nettles and marijuana plants, but stretching to a yard across in places, so much bigger than either plant. The tallest plant easily tops fifteen feet in stature, and it is still growing. Later, when they open up their umbrellas of harmless-looking white flowers that are akin to oversized cow parsley, I will learn that this is a patch of *Heracleum mantegazzianum* or giant hogweed, a plant much feared and avoided.

Originally native to the Caucasus Mountains along Russia's southern border with Georgia, and introduced to Britain as an ornamental plant in the 1800s, giant hogweed's highly toxic sap can cause photosensitivity, and may result in blistering, pigmentation, severe skin burns and, occasionally, when coming into contact with the eyes, blindness.

It is not to be touched.

Immigrant species arriving in Britain and thriving of their own accord, against the odds, it seems, are not welcome ones, and as an alien interloper in Britain's semi-wild spaces the giant hogweed is much denigrated, with many conservationists and almost all gardeners agreeing that it needs to be eradicated.

Recent years have seen newspapers – particularly those prone to playing upon readers' fears of unknown outsiders – continue to run countless stories of injuries caused by the plant, often in language that mirrors that used in pieces on immigrants of a different variety. During June–July I count nine news stories in the *Daily Mail* alone, each written in a tone of indignant outrage.

It is now an offence to plant or encourage the growth of giant hogweed in the UK. Yet here amongst it I find something beautiful and awesome about a plant that can only injure me if I tamper with it some way. The Royal Horticultural Society advises that giant hogweed can grow up to ten feet in height, but, left in isolation away from mankind, these are so much taller, a veritable Mytholmroyd *Übermensch* of the species.

Despite the hatred of hogweed and similar species, recent years have seen an emerging global movement in which invasive plants are to be left alone to flourish; by repurposing disused rural and urban spaces for rewilding they might harbour ailing or endangered plants and animals, increase food supplies, and generally improve the health of the planet – and, in turn, us, its custodians.

In his book *The New Wild: Why Invasive Species Will Be Nature's Salvation*, Fred Pearce points to the exclusion zone the size of Luxembourg that surrounds the Chernobyl nuclear reactor in Ukraine. Devoid of humans and highly radioactive, in the thirty years since the world's worst nuclear power disaster the brownfield site has, against all scientific predictions, seen an area of farmlands, forests, villages and urban areas naturally heal itself.

'An area known as the "red forest" turned rusty brown and died,' writes Pearce. 'After the accident, Soviet authorities removed all humans living within twenty miles of the reactor. The risk of the lingering radiation causing cancers and other diseases was very real. But the immediate damage to the nature they left behind was mostly much less drastic. While the area still sets off Geiger counters, nature has made a huge comeback. Native species have revelled in the absence of humans, and many new species have moved in too.'

I like to think that, following a future apocalypse, the maligned giant hogweed might be one of the first species to move back into an area, expanding its biodiversity. Today's immigrant could be tomorrow's king.

I do not know any of this now, though, as I wander deep into it and feel myself shrink and diminish, a little Gulliver lost in the giant's landscape of Brobdingnag, as even the summer sun struggles to penetrate its dense canopy.

PERHAPS IT IS fitting that this particular patch of giant hog-weed grows in soil contaminated by man's thoughtlessness.

Passing through the patch I come upon a wild garden, but one in which the plants have been replaced by ribbons of plastic sheeting and shards of broken glass, where rusted metal springs and pieces of machinery flower from the earth like crocuses in bloom, and here and there objects surprise the eye, part-rooted relics from another age. I see an ornate, faux-rococo plate where half the pattern is as bright as if it were glazed just yesterday, the other worn away by decades of weather. There's a limbless plastic doll, its eye sockets empty and hair knotted into a chignon of gunk. There are old glass pop bottles with their stoppers wedged in place, yet nevertheless mysteriously full of soil and moss and *life*; two pram wheels joined by a crooked axle; drinks cans from brands that have long since gone out of fashion or business (Top Deck, Skol, Watney's Party Four); a platform shoe sent directly from the glam era, as if tossed from Slade's tour-bus window in the dead of night en route from Ayrshire to Bradford Alhambra.

I am standing on the remains of the dumping ground of Mytholmroyd's household refuse. The old town tip.

For years this beautiful wood saw trucks driving up a track now lost in the undergrowth to dump their waste on the flat plateau at the foot of The Rock. Layer upon layer of it deposited into ditches then buried. But time has drawn back the topsoil like the receding gums of the aged to reveal all that is set within it: hardened sacks of concrete, car parts, cutlery.

Paint tins. Refrigerator components.

Gimcrack trinkets. Useless tools.

Nothing that rots or biodegrades is here. There is no paper, wood, cardboard or fabric, only that which sits in the ground for centuries. Glass, metal and plastic. Lots of plastic. Anything of value was long since taken by those who picked over the tip for bounty, as schoolboys did from the 1950s until the 1980s when it became obsolete (I like to imagine this tip itself one day being dragged away by diggers, to the tip of all tips, where all the ex-dumps of the world gather beneath a cloud of screaming oversized seagulls).

The juxtaposition between this glimpse into a bygone domestic era and nature's reclamation of the space is a thrilling one. It is the domain of beasts once again.

Climbing down a steep bank of soil and cinder I come across an old badger sett, its gaping void pushing straight out through the centre of ribbons of tattered plastic that deck its entrance like a gawdy funfair sideshow.

My eye registers a small rabbit dart across the tip, and then zip in the other direction beyond the hogweed forest. Rabbits are rare here in the Upper Calder Valley. An abundance of pet dogs, a thriving population of foxes and bouts of the myxomatosis virus has seen them done for. It's a far cry from medieval days, when they were farmed for their meat and fur in pillow mounds – man-made, flat-topped warrens, usually surrounded by a fence.

I walk across the plane of detritus, saddened to think that, unless it is removed, some of this will still be sitting here in 2500 AD and beyond.

Over the coming months and years I will hear many stories from old-timers about the balmy summer evenings when they played here on the tip, and with each telling their faces will darken as they recall a darker and more tragic side to the Scout Rock story.

SOUNDS OF THE outside world permeate this deep green space – distant traffic, the wail of a siren, the sonorous clang of a factory door – but visually I am enclosed on all sides by rock and root and bramble. Archaic refuse underfoot. Birdsong on the breeze.

I have discovered a new realm on my doorstep. A personal Eden.

There are no paths in here, no maps to guide the way, so I pick a deer track to raise me up from the ocean of stinging green. Nettle-sting welts and horse-fly bites already mark my bare arms.

The deer track rises towards The Rock at a diagonal that is uneasy underfoot, but it is dry and as the slope steepens there are snags of heather to use as handholds. I am soon sweating, breathless and moving up through trees that are anchored in the hillside, signposts to the sky.

I reach a point of no return: I can either slip dangerously back the way I came, or push on up ahead, ducking branches, pulling myself up through the ladder of heather and not stopping to look down as the canopy of the trees falls far away below me. A perilous passage deep with bracken opens up ahead between two sections of imposing vertical rock.

In my eyeline I see birds' nests trailing daubs of runny white guano below them, and great cracks in the stone from which trees have somehow taken root.

I stoop and scramble, using fingers, hands, thighs, feet and little dignity, stopping only when I find a sure footing. Here I turn and the woods are laid out beneath me, the crowns of the tall trees 100 feet below, a lake of kindling atop a shaded netherworld of poisonous plants and rubbish. Passing from one world to the next – inner to outer, lower to upper – I feel capable of flight.

In the far distance, squinting through the summer's haze, are a field of buttercups and goal posts and a single tree with a rope swing swaying from its bough, and beside it the old six-house hamlet, and our cottage.

Beyond the woods, the town, the valley, the county.

England, Europe, Earth.

There's a jutting crag just above me and I reach it, touching its stone, warm in the afternoon sun. Ten more yards up through a tilted trough of deer prints and more bracken and I reach the summit of The Rock, finding myself in a different terrain entirely.

TED HUGHES'S GRANDMOTHER, Annie Farrar, grew up here at Hathershelf, on one of the many farmsteads.

In 1927 her daughter Edith and husband Billie moved down to Aspinall Street, Mytholmroyd, just visible from the top of Scout Rock. It was in this house that Ted Hughes spent his earliest years in awe of the mass before him.

I walk through the fields that form a plateau above the swooping cliff. Here above the tree line, away from the confusion of refuse and rampant wildness, I can get a true measure of Scout Rock. It is not a big landmark at all, less than a mile from one side to the other, and perhaps only 300 steep, sloping wooded yards from top to bottom through the dense and disorientating centre. A little over ten acres in total.

A small place, then.

An insignificant space.

Laid on a flat cam stone near an old wall's sheep creep (also called a 'hogg hole' in other parts of the North) I find the fleshy remains of something laid as if in sacrificial offering. I move closer. It's a degloved rabbit, always so much slighter when relinquished of its coat. Entirely skinned, it looks like a wet, pink, blind kitten. It is already busy with bluebottles whose eggs will fill its orifices, and it gives me the fear, though the only creatures to be feared in Britain are humans. I'm reminded of J. A. Baker writing in *The Peregrine*: 'We are the killers. We stink of death. We carry it with us. It sticks to us like frost. We cannot tear it away.'

I hear a screech then and look up.

Above, a dark shape is circling. It is a raptor, a bird of prey, a hawk or a falcon perhaps, with long leather jesses trailing from its ankles like the tail of a kite. In time I will learn that kestrels, Harris hawks, merlins and peregrines stalk these skies.

I walk on.

I do not return to The Rock for two years.

Chapter Three

It is a dark November night and a gale is blowing in across the South Pennines, bending trees and sending wheelie bins sliding down back ginnels slick with the perilous algae that clings to the old stone.

The wind rattles the panes of the farmhouse kitchen a mile across the moor from Haworth, and as our car headlights pick out the five-bar gate of the farm it feels as if little has changed since those days when the Brontë siblings holed up nearby, scratching their pens across stiff paper by candlelight.

In the farmhouse kitchen seven female puppies paw at the sides of the box that they have shared since their birth six weeks ago, next to the old soot-marked range that is kicking out some heat. They reel and skitter and try to hoist themselves out of the box to freedom.

Their mother mopes past, exhausted, her elongated teats like chapel hat pegs. Dogs do not make for sentimental parents; hearing the commotion being made by her litter, she leaves.

The puppies are Patterdale terriers, with a fraction of Jack Russell stirred in a generation or two back. Patterjacks. One dog sits aside from the pack, already out of the box and patiently resting on his haunches. He is the only male, a tiny quivering thing attempting patience. If he owned a suitcase, it would be packed and ready by his side.

The puppy is the size and colouring of a pint of freshly poured Guinness – all black save for a lightning bolt of white running down the matting of his chest, through which pink skin is visible.

I bend and scoop him up. His face has not yet formed into the extended snout and ragged maw of today. Instead it is fuzzy and convex, almost cartoon-like; a drawing of a dog.

He lets out a squeak and then nips my finger.

I pass him to Della.

'Is that the one, then?' asks the farmer's wife.

We look at each other.

'Yes,' we agree. 'This is the one.'

'Any idea what you might call him?'

A gust of wind rattles the windows even harder and the little dog's sisters cower in their box for a moment. In the range a burning log collapses in on itself. There is a puff of rising embers. Outside, a toothless whistle through the dead heather.

There is only one name for this small, dark stranger from the moorlands.

'Heathcliff,' I say. 'We thought we might call him Heathcliff.'

THE DAYS AND weeks that follow are spent becoming quickly smitten with this furball of limitless piss and energy. Mostly he ignores the indoor pen I have made for him, ignores the blanket-lined den inside it and the array of toys arranged there, and runs straight for the curtains where he squats and urinates and then, straining with a disconcerted look on his face, moves onto the other thing that all creatures great and mercifully small do. Right there on the rented beige carpet. He looks at us with brows raised quizzically upwards.

A dog is an explorer's best friend. He or she is every rural lurker's alibi, their gateway and guide. A perfect excuse for tramping and trespass.

Though small, Patterdales are as sturdy as the gullies and rocky scree of Cumbrian fells demand, as tenacious and playful and persistent as you might expect of a dog bred for digging, rooting, flushing, haranguing and thrashing. Foxes mainly, but rats too.

Their necks and jaws are strong, their heads powerful, their limbs lean. They have exceptional hearing and enough stamina to easily cover twenty-five miles a day. Also Patterdales are working dogs particularly adept at flattening themselves, legs spread like a spatchcocked chicken in order to squeeze into tight spaces beneath boulders or into rabbit warrens. They are diggers rather than chasers, and historically would often be used by poachers in tandem with a sprinting breed such as a lurcher.

As I soon come to discover, Patterdales are also loyal, playful, stubborn, emotionally manipulative and have an utterly inflated sense of physical self. They are a game dog, which means they never give up on their prey, yet also obey their master's orders.

For the next year Cliff is a tumbling, darting streak of chaos. Several hours of every day are devoted to attempting to exhaust him. I watch as his world widens from pen to cottage, garden to meadow, meadow to moor to valley length.

We soon become inseparable, and scale every hill together, share every torrential downpour, every sandwich. This place that is new to both of us opens up as he learns to clear stiles, squeeze beneath fences, never bother sheep. I spend a week rebuilding the last stony remains of Stubb Dam after it is washed away by a sudden rush of water one night, backfilling it by hand with scavenged rocks, tree trunks, discarded tyres, reeds and pond silt. Cliff busies himself pretending to assist.

His shoulders broaden, foot-pads harden and his coat becomes coarser – broken is the correct term – and on our daily walks people I don't know call out, 'Hi, Cliff!' from across the road (they never know my name), and as they do he curls back his top lip to give a fleeting glimpse of the pink marbling of his mouth and a flash of his small top teeth. A canine smile.

And through this dog I too begin to appreciate the small things often lost in the mad scramble of modern life: how to exist in the moment, or enjoy food after a long, breathless walk. See the sea, as if for the first time. Stand ankle-deep, sunken in an ancient wood. The soporific effect of lying on a rug in front of a banked fire.

Naturally he tests patience and boundaries which, to him, are at best elastic, and his appetite is vulgar. I make a list of everything he consumes in the first few months.

* A frozen soiled nappy.
* A plastic bottle of drinking yoghurt.
* Coal (lots of).
* Kindling (lots of).
* Tennis balls (many).
* An electrified speaker cable.
* A washing-up glove.
* Aluminium foil.
* A poetry collection.
* Excrement (cow, sheep, fox, horse, goose, dog, human, misc. unidentifiable).
* A full bottle of maple syrup, upended.
* A deer leg.
* A badger paw.
* A condom (used), found in a car park in Skipton.

One day in a nearby field, several weeks after a neighbourhood cat has been reported missing, I see Cliff rolling in a patch of a matted mess of something vile in the long grass. I call him but he ignores me. After several more attempts he eventually bounds over. There is an object in his mouth. Only when I bend down do I see what it is: a decomposed cat's head, its liquefied eyes staring back at me as if it is emerging from within him like a monstrous two-headed hydra of myth, a diabolical cat-dog hybrid.

Yet still, most nights, sniffing his head as he falls asleep on my chest, I often remember a line from Christopher Isherwood's novel *A Single Man*, whose melancholic narrator George recalls the scent of the ears of his fox terrier, killed in a car accident alongside his partner Jim, as having the 'smell of buttered toast'.

Mainly Cliff becomes the key to unlock my new surroundings.

I go where the beast goes.

THE SEASONS TURN like rusted wheels and the stars reel. Seeds take root and sprout, and then reach for a sky busy with transport and cross-hatched with softening vapour trails. Life expands and retracts and I slowly begin to gain a better understanding of my surroundings.

I learn that the Upper Calder Valley is only so green in the summer months because it rains almost all the time. I realise too that its dramatic topography of cloughs and royds – narrow ravines, gorges and clearings – and jutting rock formations was carved by ice and water, and that this is an ongoing process. I become accustomed to changing wet trousers two or three times a day. Mud, mould and moths that eat my best woollen garments become unavoidable.

The first winter back in the North is the coldest I have

known. In mid-December snowstorms roll across Britain and on Christmas Day visiting family get stuck as car wheels spin in snow banks. Rime coats the old flags and everyone in the hamlet comes out with spades to hack at the ice impacted down the lane, and perhaps for the first time in my life I feel part of a continuity of the centuries.

On these snow-dense walks, Cliff becomes reduced to a black smudge ear-deep in blue drifts, or disappears from view entirely. Often I have to dig him up and clear his paws of snow that is jammed in there.

Our old stone cottage becomes an icebox and my meagre log store is soon depleted. From this treacherously cold winter grows an obsession with scavenging, sawing, splitting, stacking and seasoning wood that continues today.

Temperatures plunge further in January. We collect cones that first winter, pickings from the pine plantation up top, then burn these fragrant Fibonacci spirals of smoke between the stiff stone walls on those nights dragged corpse-deep below zero. It feels like some sort of arrival.

Satellite images show Britain as entirely white; roads are closed, cars abandoned. There are power cuts. In total twenty-one people die as a result of the month-long cold spat.

I see the valley anew. Early one morning I pile on the layers and walk into the fields, where everything is motionless and silent. All things containing water or sap are frozen. Each blade of grass, each branch. Nothing moves.

The roads are empty, the railway track unused, and the sky a foreboding wash of monochrome static. A wan sun tries to push through the armour of the day, but can only offer a meek pinkening light. The thermometer says it is 16° below.

A car tyre hangs by a rope from the lone tree in the field; here a fortnight earlier Cliff lost his puppy teeth after locking onto the old black rubber. The rest came out when he bit into my wellington while I walked home.

Nearby a through-line of prints veers off across the crust of the morning, and along the valley the great wooded quarry of Scout Rock resembles the Russian Taiga in miniature, a netherworld of ice and rock, a frosted fantasyland. A palace of bone and needles. An ice basin. Morose in the damp months, today the woods and rising rock appear as if thrust from the earth and dusted in icing sugar. I think of Superman's Fortress of Solitude and The White Witch of Narnia enchanting children with cubes of Turkish delight. Increasingly I find myself standing looking at the distant quarried theatre of Scout Rock, drawn to it for reasons I do not understand.

Winter over, the seasons creak onwards, the dog grows and I walk a pair of wellingtons to tatters once a year.

After an arid summer and another dramatic winter, Della sees a tall, narrow terraced house for sale at the base of The Rock. It has a roof that leaks when it rains heavily, and a garden forever under threat of being consumed by the out-of-bounds acres behind it, where decaying dampness seems to eat through the marrow of everything. It has been on the market for months without an offer. We buy it.

From my new office window I can see out across the valley, to the same flanks that Ted Hughes climbed as a boy, his young thighs aching as he strode up the humped hillock in search of weasels to smoke out from drystone walls, or where, as he wrote in 'Sacrifice', he and his Uncle Albert 'lammed our holly billets across Banksfields – / A five-inch propeller climbing the skylines / For two, three seconds – to the drop'. (Albert later committed suicide: 'When he tripped / The chair from beneath him, in his attic'.)

At the top of the valley I see Heights Road and Midgley Moor with its many quarries, and traces of Neolithic stones in the copper-coloured sod.

Downstairs in our front room there hangs a large oil painting of the corner of Aspinall Street, just yards away from Hughes's place of birth, positioned as if offering another window onto Calderdale – one that has been frozen for ever, flattened into base colours. It was done by our postman, Alan, a Marxist and misanthrope with a PhD in horror films – he is officially a Doctor of Horror – and a love of contemporary Norwegian jazz. Alan lives frugally in a house with his partner within the twenty acres of woodland surrounding Lumb Bank, the handsome but half-derelict eighteenth-century former mill owner's house that Ted Hughes bought in 1969, the year of his second *annus horribilis*, in which his estranged partner Assia Wevill killed both herself and their four-year-old daughter Alexandra, and during which his mother died. Hughes's first wife, the brilliant American poet Sylvia Plath, who killed herself in Primrose Hill in 1963, lies buried up beyond Lumb Bank in the cemetery at Heptonstall, an incongruous East Coast / Ivy League presence in a graveyard of old-time West Yorkshire family names (Sutcliffes and Crabtrees, Greenwoods and Crossleys), eternally trapped in the soil beneath the stricken Yorkshire skies of a valley in which she never wanted to live.

In 1975 Lumb Bank was leased from Hughes by the Arvon Foundation, its fifteen bedrooms adapted to house the visiting writers who still attend its weekly residential courses. It was purchased from the Hughes estate in 1989.

Alan the Postman, who slightly resembles both Jeremy Corbyn and Van Gogh, tolerates the passing poets who stop to admire his garden and chicken coops as best he can. He has no television, internet or mobile phone and his water comes from a storage tank. In the big winter freezes, when temperatures fell to sixteen below, his supply froze completely, so for weeks he took to breaking the ice to bathe in the river that runs past his window. Once he cycled to Walnut Farm, the Elizabethan house belonging to the writer and cold-water swimmer Roger Deakin in Suffolk, and pitched his tent nearby. Alan enjoys reading a lot of critical and political theory, and will destroy any argument that you may care to present to him within seconds.

As a postman Alan has been walking the wet cobbles and claggy tracks for years now and he always knows exactly how many days it is until retirement.

'How's it going, Alan?' I ask whenever I see him.

'Only one thousand four hundred and thirty-one days until retirement. I'm not sure I can stand it.'

Or: 'What's new, Alan?'

'Only one thousand one hundred and seventeen days and—'

Here he checks his wristwatch.

'—three hours until retirement. I'm surrounded by idiots.'

Or: 'Winter's coming in cold.'

'Yes. And only eight hundred and forty-one days until retirement. This job is killing me.'

Recently Alan's interests have turned away from painting landscapes and he has instead been preoccupied with attempting to capture 'the spirit of jazz' on canvas.

I saw him the other day.

'What have you been up to, Alan?'

'Only four hundred and forty days until I retire. Only just over a year of this fucker left.'

FROM OUR NEW home I begin to weave a wider web of walking, radiating centrifugally from the mysterious escarpment, and wandering further out across the valley to explore the woods, moors and hidden corners and Mytholmroyd itself, whose construction is a time-map of human habitation, from the oldest ruins of dwellings dating back 500 years through to post-war prefabs and more recent canal-side flats, with balconies and satellite dishes.

I learn that many of the local landmarks are named from a recurring set of stock words, most of which are monosyllabic. You can roll them like boiled sweets and suck on them for a while before spitting them out: *shelf, stake, carr, royd, lumb, stall.*

Stubb, slack, holme, broad, crag.

Some words – *royd, clough, ings, naze* – sound more like ailments or bodily functions. Coughs and sneezes. A clearing-out of the pipes and passageways. They are phlegmy words. *Delph.* Bless you. Others meanwhile read like the running order for a Saturday-night bill of club singers or the roll-call for the local darts team: *dean, cliff, lee, dell.* All are terms that have existed for centuries and have grown out of the landscape to describe areas such as low marshlands, wooded vales or grazing paddocks, around which life has slowly congregated.

Born from the soil, they have evolved into various configurations, or are often used as suffixes. Unlike in the suburbs, they are not names that have been decided upon by planners or selected by committee, but simply sounds that have been repeated enough times down the centuries to one day be chiselled into stone, carved into wood or written on a record, a deed, a map, an app.

There exists no better anthology of the poetry of a place than an Ordnance Survey map. Unfolding my most-used map (OL 21: South Pennines) and holding it up now, I see that a hole has worn right through the section that marks a stretch of the valley directly in front of my house. It is a shabby gap that stretches up above Wadsworth Banks, the steepening fields in which Ted Hughes roamed freely as a child, from Throstle Bower Farm up to Cock Hill. As I press it to the window over the exact area that it marks, the first sunlight in weeks shines through the hole.

And that sunshine is a form of poetry too.

DELLA'S ATTIC OFFICE is windowless save for a skylight that, when pushed open, is like a transom directly into Scout Rock. To stand on a chair and peer your head out feels as if you are an extension of The Rock, part of it. At night the woods loom dark and amorphous, a black wall from which there come wild screams and terrific howls.

Ted Hughes's biographer Jonathan Bate writes of the poet having a similar experience: 'Ted shared an attic room with [brother] Gerald. When he stood on the bed and peered out through the little skylight, the dark woods of Scout Rock gave the impression of being immediately outside the glass, pressing in upon him.'

The sun moving across The Rock's frowning brow is the only clock we have up here on the third floor, Scout Rock acting as both time-keeper, barometer and something altogether more ethereal. Stalker of dreams. Shadow presence. Nemesis.

Perhaps it is the poet's privilege to rose-tint retrospection or backdate memories with meaning, keenly applying adult understanding to childhood experience, but Scout Rock became an eminent and defining memory in Ted Hughes's creative career. Literally, a touchstone. Across his work, its mute and lofty presence becomes more broadly representative of the power and mythology of the English topography. It is most directly addressed in one of his more obscure pieces, 'The Rock' (1963).

This essay serves as the perfect primer to Hughes's poetry, encapsulating as it does his prevailing themes within just a few short pages: the violence of landscape, haunted memory, myth, the animal kingdom, a changing England, the inner self and the close proximity of death.

Hughes came of age facing the stone of Scout Rock, as it too has quietly ushered me into middle age. His formative years in which the self is indelibly shaped were spent bookended by stone and rock older and greater than any living thing. Even closer to home at the end of his street was the looming stone church of Mount Zion, which he alluded to in his early poem 'Crag Jack's Apostasy', where 'all the dark churches / Stooped over my cradle once'.

The influence of this landmark runs through his work like gritstone does through Yorkshire itself. In his essay Hughes describes Scout Rock first as a sublime structure possessing almost mystical power in his young eyes, a monolithic mystery towering over his entire short existence, and then on closer inspection as a place of danger and death.

He recalled hearing of a tramp who was napping in the bracken above The Rock being mistaken by a farmer for a fox, and shot dead when he reared his sleepy head. Here a relative of the poet accidentally 'took the plunge that the whole valley dreams about' while out shooting rabbits along the fields that fringe the cliff edge, the sudden sheer drops obscured from view behind gorse and more bracken. There still is scattered a wrecked wall there today, whose only purpose is symbolic. One or two older locals have told me in hushed tones that in more recent years Scout Rock has been used as a springboard for more than one swan dive into the great abyss of eternity.

The essay was written in 1963 for a BBC Home Services wireless broadcast series called *Writers on Themselves*, and subsequently appeared in the weekly magazine *The Listener* on 19 September 1963, one of half a dozen pieces that Hughes contributed to the publication. A slightly revised version appeared in the hardback collection *Writers on Themselves* the following year, alongside contributors such as David Storey, Richard Murphy – and Sylvia Plath. Her essay 'Ocean 1212-W', first broadcast on 19 August 1963, recalled the summer of 1938, when the great New England hurricane struck: 'The sulfurous afternoon went black unnaturally early, as if what was to come could not be star-lit, torch-lit, looked at. The rain set in, one huge Noah douche. Then the wind. The world had become a drum. Beaten, it shrieked and shook. Pale and elated in our beds, my brother and I sipped our nightly hot drink. We would, of course, not sleep.'

Every bit as rich and evocative as Hughes's autobiographical piece, Plath's essay was, sadly, both broadcast and published posthumously. The poet had committed suicide six months earlier, on 11 February 1963, at the age of thirty.

Death, death, and more death.

Was, I wonder, 'The Rock' written during those darkest days following his wife's suicide? Certainly 'The Rock' seems a weighted piece of writing, pressed down upon by shadows, prose that is rooted in a more innocent past of childhood, but branches out into a present defined by the cold strike of mortality and grieves towards a future that appears uncertain. Responding to Plath's death in a letter to a friend at the time, Hughes wrote: 'That's the end of my life. The rest is posthumous.'

('But it wasn't though, was it?', critics of Hughes might counter. '*You* got to live.')

The writing and publication of 'The Rock' coincided with the next stage of Hughes's life and saw him seeking solace in prose that revisits those first carefree six or seven years here in the Upper Calder Valley, a time defined by wanderlust and adventure against the 'curtain and back-drop to existence' of Scout Rock: 'If a man's death is held in place by a stone, my birth was fastened into place by that rock, and for my first seven years it pressed its shape and various moods into my brain.'

Jonathan Bate notes that William Wordsworth, a writer whose presence is felt in Hughes's work, also 'remembered a towering, shadowed rock as a force that supervised and admonished his childhood'. He is referring to the cliff face that a young Wordsworth recalls looming at him in the darkness while rowing a stolen boat on Ullswater in one of his most renowned works, the epic 'spiritual autobiography', 'The Prelude':

> When, from behind that craggy Steep till then
> The horizon's bound, a huge peak, black and huge,
> As if with voluntary power instinct,
> Upreared its head. – I struck and struck again,
> And growing still in stature the grim Shape
> Towered up between me and the stars, and still,
> For so it seemed, with purpose of its own
> And measured motion like a living Thing.

Shaken by his nocturnal experience, the young Wordsworth immediately returns home and falls into a state of despondency, his brain working with 'a dim and undetermined sense / Of unknown modes of being', and where for days afterwards 'There hung a darkness, call it solitude / Or blank desertion.'

For Bate, Wordsworth's rock – most likely a crag on the western shore, somewhere between Glenridding and Patterdale

– 'cast a shadow of guilt and fear over his filial bond with nature. For Hughes, too, to speak of living in the shadows of the rock was a way of externalising a darkness in his own heart.'

Ted Hughes describes Scout Rock as something that imposes its personality on the local area, but, growing up here in the 1930s, he was also aware that Mytholmroyd was imbued with a sense of residual melancholy from the First World War. Many men from the town had joined the Lancashire Fusiliers, including Hughes's father, William 'Billie' Hughes, who was one of only seventeen men from the regiment to return from the Dardanelles Campaign. He survived after a bullet lodged in a pay book in his breast pocket – the book literally saved his life.

The economic circumstances of an overwhelmingly working-class area in recession must also have defined the mood of inter-war Mytholmroyd in the 1930s, yet writing in those weeks after Plath's death, it was Scout Rock that came to symbolise the dank lassitude of the place in Hughes's memory: 'It should have inured me to living in valleys, or gulleys, or under walls, but all it did was cause me to hate them. The slightest declivity now makes me uneasy and restless, and I slip into the shadow of the mood of that valley – a foreboding heaviness, such as precedes downpour thunderstorms on Sunday afternoons.'

When I first moved to the area I heard of something called 'valley-bottom fever', a colloquial term used to describe the psychological effects of being starved of sunshine, or not leaving

Calderdale often enough. It is what the removal men alluded to and with each passing year I believe it to be more apparent.

Hebden Bridge in particular has gained a slightly erroneous reputation as 'suicide central' after the local film-maker Jez Lewis released *Shed Your Tears and Walk Away* in 2009, a moving documentary made in response to many premature deaths amongst his contemporaries. Lewis had the idea for the film when he returned to the valley to attend the funeral of a friend who had died from an overdose; it was the fifteenth associate from childhood who had died prematurely, through drug misuse or suicide. At different points in its history the town has certainly seen such spates of suicides, which have pushed its rate to far greater than the national average. Though complex sets of problems unique to each individual are the cause, it leads me to wonder whether the landscape itself is a contributing factor.

Moving to the dark side of the valley, we soon discover that from late September to March our house receives little or no natural sunlight due to Scout Rock blocking the sky behind us. As the sun moves east to west, unseen behind the outcrop, it is like living beneath the wing of a great raven, or perhaps in the folds of the grim reaper's robe.

In the depths of winter the valley becomes a shrinking corridor and by January a hunger for light – real light, and visual space too – becomes so insatiable that we find ourselves fleeing, to Manchester or Mexico, or anywhere away from the bottom of this blackened trough. Valley fever is real. I feel it as a damp ache, a slow deflation of the psyche like a month-old party balloon. We move to the foot of Scout Rock in the week that we attend the funeral of a young friend who also committed suicide. The move provides necessary distraction and catharsis. The short relocation is an act of letting go, and while I heft crates of books and records up three flights of narrow Victorian stairs, Della cleans the old cottage from top to bottom in a daze of shock and grief.

The move finally complete, we paint the entire house white, the colour of light, of life, of purity and goodness. Of everything that death is not. An act of defiance against the long October shadows.

And then we open our small rectangular skylight onto the black stone, toast our absent friend and let the future in.

MY INFATUATION WITH the dense woods on my doorstep grows as I spend more and more time in this private paradise. Despite its reputation it is a place of calm and daily escape and I begin to tramp new paths through the undergrowth.

I fall over perhaps once a week in Scout Rock, often more in the wet months. I slip rather than trip. In the greasy soil, or from rocks whose gleaming surfaces are as slick as engine oil. Down holes unseen. I crash through dead bracken. Fall onto moss mattresses. Slide through shit of unknown origin. There I go, snatching at tussocks and roots, slipping then standing to see the brown streaks that coat me from toe to head, the dog looking on quizzically.

Once I fall sideways down a bank for eight, nine, ten feet, twisting into a reverse standing position, then give myself a full row of tens and take a bow for the imaginary crowd. They offer a standing ovation. I walk on, garlanded with imaginary bouquets.

Despite the pitfalls Scout Rock becomes a place of familiarity and safety beyond the grasp of modernity. Time crumbles here. Years pass. In *The Hill of Summer* J. A. Baker writes of experiencing a similar 'primitive feeling of security, as though one were out of reach of the suddenly-flung spear, of the stunning leap from darkness'.

THERE EXISTS A photo of Scout Rock taken by Fay Godwin that appears in *Remains of Elmet*, her 1979 collaboration with Ted Hughes, in which the pair offered poetic and visual responses to the Calder Valley and its surrounds. (In 1994 the book was updated and published as *Elmet*, Hughes declaring this as his definitive collection of writing on the area.)

Elmet was the ancient Brittonic kingdom of the native Celts that covered much of the West Riding between the fifth and early seventh centuries, and part of the larger *Yr Hen Ogledd* – the Old North – region that incorporated numerous minor kingdoms from southern Scotland down through the Borders,

Cumbria and Yorkshire. The Upper Calder Valley was one of the last remote outposts of the kingdom of Elmet, a near-wilderness of moorlands and poor agricultural soil, poky valleys and flooded marshes, and therefore difficult to inhabit. Those that did live here must have been of a particularly strong mettle. As Hughes noted in his introduction, Elmet was 'the last British Celtic kingdom to fall to the Angles'.

A recent genetic study entitled 'People of the British Isles', whose findings were published in the journal *Nature* in March 2015, revealed a localised 'genetic cluster' for Calderdale that is distinct not only from the rest of England but from the rest of Yorkshire, and in fact corresponds with the kingdom of Elmet. From this it can be concluded that many Calder Valley residents are direct descendants of the Celtic *Elmetsaete*, and clearly haven't strayed too far in the 1,300 years since the end of the kingdom that inspired Hughes to name a collection in its honour.

The majority of Godwin's photograph is dominated by the trees and the familiar black gritstone of Scout Rock; it offers only a detail of Scout Rock, a small portion of its curved elliptical breadth, but it is enough to convey its commanding presence.

For years this picture confused me. I knew it was taken close to my house, but could never quite get a purchase on the exact point from which it was shot. I walked up and down the street and amongst the row of birch trees that create a corridor between the railway sidings and the scrubland out front, checking the angles, comparing the shot, trying to match the houses. It took a long time for me to realise that all but the grandest dwellings in the photograph have been knocked down. The whole terrace is gone.

I walk past that one remaining house almost every day and in fact know the owners, the Santa-Claus-like eccentric Jerry, publisher and proprietor of a business selling the largest range of bee-keeping books in the English-speaking world, and his wife, Ruth, an expert recorder player and respected academic on the subject of early music. Jerry and Ruth own an orchard, gardens and a wood, where the local primary school keeps a beehive or two for after-school apiary lessons, and generously let members of the public cut through land that sits at the foot of The Rock, leading right past their kitchen window into a meadow, all overlooked by a coterie of Jerry's feral peacocks. These exotic birds are plagued by the fox that periodically slinks down from the woods to snatch the peahens, just as those in the area are plagued by the birds' determined honking as they strut their stuff several thousand miles from their natural habitats.

The peacocks of Mytholmroyd are, on occasion, *daft*.

When not roosting up on Jerry's roof or decorating the branches of the trees around, languidly flouting their assets like Parisian prostitutes in a 1920s bordello, the peacocks are prone to wandering along the lane into the local primary school or running amok down our street. On several occasions I have awoken to their brazen, kazoo-like calls outside our window, their indolent faces at the window, iridescent necks shining in the morning sun.

Occasionally, as I pass them, a male will flush his feathers into full plumage in a dramatic display akin to the opening of a large elaborately embroidered parasol in a small, drab room, a wall of eyes staring back at me in one of the most stunning sights of the natural world. Many of their discarded tail feathers decorate our mantelpiece.

'They're a bloody nuisance, but I do like them about the place,' Jerry tells me in a clear-cut, educated English voice whose booming timbre seems in danger of causing landslides from The Rock above.

Once I asked this apicultural aficionado just how much of the surrounding land and Scout Rock he actually owns.

'How much?' he bellows, turning around with the permanent appearance of someone who is slightly affronted, and pointing up the cliff face. 'To the skyline, dear boy. *To the skyline!*'

WHEN I AM not working or walking I begin to spend the dankest days in the local library amongst the *Emmerdale* scriptwriters, local historians or revising students, learning more about The Rock.

I discover that quarrying took place there in the 1800s, before it fell into disuse, and that the woodland – which I initially assumed was ancient – was established later, most likely in the late-Victorian period. Maps from 1907/08 and 1933/4 show some variation in the extent of the spread of trees, while the 1964 map illustrates that clearance has occurred across the site.

This fascination extends beyond the cragged confines of what lies beyond my doorstop to any surrounding landmark, stone, scarp, outcrop, crag, cairn, rock, ruin or marking that I happen to come across. Within them I find a mixture of history, mythology and etymology. I catch glimpses of past lives, but more than anything I unearth the poetry of the place; poetry that stretches way back to the pre-times. I make lists. Endless lists.

Stones, Ruins, Cairns, Boulders and Geological Curios of the Upper Calder Valley

The Devil's Rock
Rudstoop Monolith
Robin Hood's Penny Stone
Robin Hood Rocks.

Churn Milk Joan
Miller's Grave
Great Rock
Midgley Moor Standing Stone *or* Greenwood B.

Two Lads
Roms Hill Stone
New Edge Chalybeate
Scout Rock

Bridestones
Slack Bottom Stone
Turley Hole Stones
Turvin Stone.

Stones Farm
Standing Stone Hill
King Common Rough
Rocking Stone

Internos

The soil is rich with stories to pique the interest of the curious. It is the Yorkshire way to mythologise, and the only thing that spoils a good story is the truth.

One of the better-known local anecdotes about Scout Rock concerns a hoard of 597 silver coins dating to the third century that was found in 1952 by two men, Harry Bentley and Frank Sutcliffe, while out rabbitting one day above the town tip. In the library I sift through further drawers of laminated maps, and sure enough find the location of the hoard marked on a map dated 1964, a cross signifying the inaccessible spot at the foot of The Rock, which also happens to be one of the very few places where I occasionally see a solitary rabbit. A verification of sorts.

Local folklore has it that the coins belonged to a Roman soldier, or an associate of the occupying Romans, who cached his stash for safekeeping, intending to return to reclaim it. But for reasons unknown he never did, and here they lay undiscovered for 1,600 years, as further regimes rose and fell. And still the coins sat there, stowed in the soil, a buried strand of the valley narrative.

It's a story confirmed by Barry, whom I bump into in Redacre, a strip of old woodland across the valley from The Rock, above the canal and sewage works.

It's early September, a warm, damp and uncharacteristically humid day, and the smell of processed effluence from the processing plant, stale and greasy like an old oven glove, is strong on the breeze. Here in Redacre, Ted and Gerald Hughes once tried to raise the spirit of an ancient Briton who in local folklore was said to have lain buried beneath a giant stone.

Barry is fifty and has lived in Mytholmroyd all his life. He is a builder's foreman and never in too much of hurry to share a story or two, usually with a tone of incredulousness or amazement, whenever our paths cross while he is out walking his Collie. He and his wife Jane like classic rock music, so in return are always happy to hear about my past encounters with the likes of Mötley Crüe, AC/DC and Guns N' Roses.

Barry was the first person Cliff met after six weeks of housebound quarantine as a puppy. As such, he has a special fondness for him, and Barry responds by stooping down to let the dog lick him all over. Knowing where Cliff has been and what he's eaten, it's something which I resolutely refuse to encourage.

'Hey, it's good for you, is that,' proclaims Barry as the dog frantically cleans his grinning phiz. 'It builds your immune system up.'

Sometimes Cliff is so excited to see him, he rolls onto his back and emits a submissive sprinkling of golden urine into the air or up Barry's leg. He doesn't seem to mind.

'It's only a bit of piss.'

BARRY'S FAMILY ROOTS run deep, and his knowledge of Mytholmroyd is as good as anyone's. His understanding of the place is through its people. The friendships, the feuds, the farces.

Jane is also the current holder of the World Dock Pudding Championship title. Held in Mytholmroyd annually since 1971 when it first appeared as prelude to a local arts festival, the contest is open to anyone (hence the 'world' part) who wishes to compete in a culinary contest to cook the tastiest example of the local seasonal delicacy, dock pudding. It is a dish born out of necessity.

During the Second World War the notorious Lord Haw-Haw, the German radio propagandist and Nazi collaborator, reported that people in England were so poor they were eating grass. He wasn't entirely wrong; what he neglected to mention was that, in the Upper Calder Valley at least, it was by choice and had been that way for centuries.

Dock pudding recipes differ and are often closely kept secrets, but all are based upon a fried mixture of oatmeal, onion, butter and seasoning – some participants add an egg – to which are added the core ingredients of locally picked nettles and a sweeter variety of dock leaf known as *Persicaria bistorta* or common bistort (also known as Snakeroot or Easter-Ledges), picked from river banks and railway sidings.

Cooked down, the docks closely resemble spinach. In times of plenty the dock pudding mixture was often fried in bacon fat to create something once described as 'looking like a cowflap', and traditionally eaten at breakfast time. In flavour and consistency dock pudding is remarkably similar to the Caribbean/ West African side dish of callaloo, whose recipe also varies, but which in Jamaica is made from the amaranth plant, with only salt, onions and scallions added to it. Despite the obvious cultural and geographical differences between a Pennine moor town whose indigenous ethnic population is overwhelmingly white, and a Caribbean island whose population is largely black (though Yorkshire and Jamaica have almost the exact same square mileage), the culinary link is a reminder that people the world over are not leading vastly dissimilar lives.

'I entered this year with a carrier bag, and got nowhere,' says Barry ruefully as we stop for a woodland chat. 'But Jane went and won it.'

'A carrier bag?' I ask.

'Aye. Of docks. I followed the exact same recipe – same amount of nettles, same measurement of oats – but the thing is my bag were half the size of Jane's, so I only had half as many leaves in there. The judges said hers was the best they had ever tasted. She did well, considering.'

'Considering what?'

'Well,' Barry continues. 'She had lupus three months back. I didn't think it were serious until I Googled it. I thought: she's in hospital, she'll be reet. Then the doctor told me a seventeen-year-old lad had died from it in 'Royd last year, and that it were touch and go for forty-eight hours. Mind, I swear she's allergic to fresh air, is Janey.'

Talk soon turns to Scout Rock, and sure enough Barry reveals himself to be a mine of information as he shares stories about playing in those woods, and how, a generation before him, his mother picked bilberries up there as a child, or the times when he would excavate old drink cans from another era and old pop bottles with stoppers intact.

'I expect you know about the hoard of coins found up there,' he says. 'Roman, they were. Oh, aye. A mate of my Mam's ex-partner found them. What was his name? Cracking fella, he was. Ex-military. Mad as anything. He loved guns. Guns and animals. Proper nuts, but a lovely guy. Christ, what were his name now?'

Cliff continues to lap at Barry's face.

'Anyway. When he were a kid him and his mate used to go into Scout Rock Woods to watch the Spitfires do their training flights overhead. Apparently there's something about the shape of this valley that made it perfect for their manoeuvres, so they used to go and sit beneath a certain tree because the planes would fly so low that they'd clip the tree tops and it would rain leaves down on them. This was the 1950s, not so long after the war.'

Barry pauses to let Cliff give him one last big lick and then stands.

'Anyway. They were up there one day plane-watching when they found this bag of coins. Roman. And not just coins either – they reckoned there was a note in there too from this Roman fella. It said how he had been working on a road here and he had decided to defect. He'd had enough. I mean, imagine what it was like in the valley then.'

'Grim.'

'Grim? *Grim*? I'll say. There'll have been nowt here. If it wasn't the rain that got him then it'll have been the wet it carried with it. Any road, he said he was burying his coins and buggering off to start a new life for himself somewhere else in the North of England and that he'd back for his bag in a bit. But he never returned.'

'The note must have weathered well?' I say. 'The Roman Empire ended over sixteen hundred years ago.'

Barry shrugs.

'Hey, I'm only going on what I was told. Of course this bloke and his mate reckoned they were quids in – well, you would, wouldn't you, finding treasure like that as a lad – but when they took them to the police station the coppers said that they belonged to the state, and took the coins off them. They were gutted. They're in Bankfield Museum at Halifax now. But what was that fella's name? Lovely bloke. Right mad, but lovely. See that porch on me Mam's house over there?'

I follow Barry's finger across the valley to the old stone house in which his mother lives near The Rock.

'He were fixing the roof on that one day, and he fell off. Cracked his head on one of the flags. He got up, but he wasn't right. They said he'd got an edema. Swelling on the brain. He died two days later. Terrible, it was. Terrible. He loved Scout Rock, he did. Loved it.'

I look down and Cliff is on his back, pissing up Barry's leg like a cherubic fountain.

Chapter Four

Despite the reputation of the typical Yorkshireman or woman as being dour or curmudgeonly, folk around the area, I find, are forthcoming in their opinions – so long as you approach them in the right manner. The Upper Calder Valley is accepting of outsiders.

The old-timers of Mytholmroyd prove to be a valuable source of stories.

'You'll know about Devil's Hump, I expect?' says a neighbour, a sometime folk singer who used to write a column for the *Yorkshire Post* on his life as a street sweeper, when I mention my interest in The Rock.

I shake my head.

'Oh aye. The first time we visited 'Royd was in '83, and we came in over Sowerby way, the back way like, and when we drove down along the bottom of Scout Rock, near where the gates to the old tip are, above the bottom tree line in the shadows, we came across a pentacle sprayed on the road and next to in big writing it said "Devils' Hump", because there was this right big hump in the road that you had to navigate on the way down. It were right Satanic like, you know. *Well*, we thought.

What a place. We bought a house that day and have stayed ever since. The hump's gone now, mind. Council flattened it. The devil stood no chance.'

More often than not, though, the mere mention of Scout Rock draws a darkened look and furrowing of brow from locals of a certain age, for the woods were once host to a much more tangible problem than low-level devil-worshipping: that of the controversial dumping of asbestos, and a multitude of deaths caused by it.

The asbestos came from Acre Mill, a large mill near Old Town high above Hebden Bridge that provided jobs for generations of local workers. Built there in 1859 due to a plentiful supply of water straight off the moors, it began as a woollen mill before switching to cotton. In the 1920s it was briefly owned by the Dunlop Rubber Company Ltd but was then abandoned.

As the Second World War approached, Acre Mill was repurposed when a company called Cape Asbestos was given the government contract for the mass-production of gas-mask filter pads from blue asbestos in 1939. The material was the new thing, a non-burning mineral mined in Canada, Australia and several African countries and which came in three forms – white, brown and, the most toxic, blue – and acted as a highly effective insulator of heat, electricity and sound (its name is derived from Greek, meaning 'inextinguishable').

Asbestos is highly carcinogenic. When inhaled, asbestos fibres cause lung cancer, asbestosis and various other illnesses, all of them fatal. The first related death was recorded as early as 1906, but with business good and profits booming, the war years saw 100 million such filters produced at Acre Mill by 600 conscripted workers.

When the war ended, interest in asbestos did not. In fact trade flourished as Cape Asbestos diversified with a range of alternative products, including textiles, pipe lagging, tiles and rope. Workers were attracted to the area due to the dramatic landscape, cheap housing and guaranteed employment.

Several people have told me of memories of snowball fights in the asbestos fibres and relatives coming home 'looking like snowmen'. Others have described the inside of Acre Mill as being like the eye of a sandstorm, where the fibres fell inches deep. Footprints laid in it would disappear under new layers within a half-hour.

DEATH BY ASBESTOSIS is cruel and mercilessly slow, and could make even the most devout person of faith question a God that allows such a death.

Asbestosis and its sibling illnesses cause the membrane of the lung walls to thicken due to scarring. Lungs are resilient and have a natural reserve capacity, but asbestosis challenges them. Defeats them. It takes over healthy lung tissue and turns it to stone. Worse, it can exist undetected and symptomless for years. Decades, even. So by the time of diagnosis it is usually too late. By then there will be pain, breathlessness, coughing – so much coughing – and a complete debilitation of the body.

Breathing becomes increasingly short to the point of impossibility and sufferers endure chest pains so terrible a vocabulary does not yet exist to describe them. The damaged lungs will struggle against the disease, and this will put pressure on the heart, which will not be able to take the strain indefinitely.

The first links to cancer were medically reported in 1955 and letters were despatched to Cape warning about the safety of their workers here in Hebden Bridge. The claims were rubbished, the warnings discarded and Cape Asbestos stayed in the valley until the early 1970s, relocating just before the screening of a moving 1972 *World in Action* documentary, 'The Dust at Acre Mill'. In 1976 the building was razed by fire, its charred remnants sealed off and finally demolished in 1979. With it went the roll of honour to the twenty-six mill workers who served during the First World War: men with old valley names like Jesse Raggett and Percy Rushworth, Willie Winearls, Fred Sporle and Irwin Topham.

Asbestos was finally banned in the 1980s, but due to its after-effects remains the largest killer in the British workplace today. A report in the *Daily Telegraph* in 2007 noted that approximately the same amount of people die from asbestos-related illnesses as are killed on the roads – between 3,000 and 4,000 per annum. Deaths are predicted to peak in 2020.

The damage was already done. By 1979 over one in ten workers from the valley were diagnosed with crippling strains of cancer such as mesothelioma and asbestosis, and 750 employees are now believed to have died from asbestos-related illnesses while others – partners of former employers – developed other conditions, often simply from washing their overalls.

Alice Jefferson lived in Mytholmroyd and worked at Acre Mill for only nine months as a teenager in the 1950s. Described by her doctor in 1982 as a 'typical West Yorkshire lass: she's tough and realistic and you can't kid this lady', the forty-seven-year-old became the best-known victim of asbestosis in the area when she was the subject of another documentary, the award-winning, film-length *Alice: A Fight For Life*, made by Yorkshire Television. This moving piece documented her slow and painful demise and her attempts to seek recompense. Initially offered £13,000 by Cape Asbestos, she declined and, in great pain, attended a court hearing while heavily dosed on morphine and barely capable of mobility. She was instead offered £36,000, and remarked at the time that it was not much, and what she 'really needed was a new body'.

It was revealed soon afterwards that a compensation arrangement of a mere £1 per week paid to the widows of workers who had contracted asbestosis had remained unchanged since the 1930s.

A month after filming ended, Alice died. *Alice: A Fight For Life* did, however, introduce the true horror of asbestosis to the nation, and was indirectly effective in changing legislation about its use, handling and disposal.

THE CALDERDALE ASBESTOS scandal is now widely recognised as the worst ever industrial accident in Britain – worse than any explosion, landslide, building collapse or mining disaster – yet because it was not a single, time-specific event it is less newsworthy.

Mentally it casts a long, dark shadow across a beautiful green valley. The story lives on in those elder residents around Mytholmroyd today, who recall dusting asbestos off the wild fruit that they picked and ate, before invariably naming the parents, aunts, uncles or siblings they lost to the disease. The repercussions continue.

There is no sign of Acre Mill today. The area has since been landscaped, and though a memorial tree was planted alongside a plaque in 1999, it was soon vandalised and then removed.

Looking along the valley from the old site up near Old Town, following the quadrumvirate of parallel arterial byways of road, river, railway track and canal, the eye is drawn past other factories and beyond the housing estates of Mytholmroyd to the wooded quarry that watches over it all. Scout Rock.

The disposal of such a hazardous material must be carefully and sensitively managed. When in the 1950s the owners of Acre Mill found they had an asbestos surplus that they needed rid of, they did not manage its removal carefully or sensitively at all. Instead they took the piles of killer fibres and loaded them into trucks and then dumped them within a mile or two, close to homes at Heptonstall, at Carr Head landfill site, at Pecket Well, Mount Skip and at Scout Rock. Especially at Scout Rock, where the town tip already existed. Like the laziest of charladies, they didn't even bother to sweep it under the carpet. They merely brushed it away from their own doorstep; out of sight, out of mind – just. In the case of Scout Rock they literally drove it as far as the eye could see and then thought: this'll do. They were back to the depot in time for a mid-morning snout and cuppa.

There the asbestos sat for years, just beneath the topsoil of this place made sacred in my mind, where rabbits breed and foxes play and deer nibble on bark and leaves.

Reporting in an article in the *Daily Telegraph* in 2007, Mark Piggott wrote of a local lad, John Pinder, who had 'laiked' (played/scavenged) on the tip at Scout Road, Mytholmroyd, in the 1950s. 'Scout Road was like an Aladdin's cave,' said Pinder. 'You could find bogie [go-kart] wheels, and inner tubes to float on the canal. But there was a lot of asbestos about: when the lorries came down from the mill carrying bales, people took in their washing.' Pinder, sixty-three when the article was written, was diagnosed with mesothelioma and was undergoing chemotherapy.

He had recently lost a case against Cape for exposing him to asbestos fibres at a young age; their legal argument was that they could not be responsible for the security of council-owned tips. It was just one case in hundreds, a small footnote to an ongoing narrative of accelerating ecocide.

In 1978 it was briefly considered by the local council whether the asbestos tip in the heart of Scout Rock might make a good picnic site.

Cape Asbestos has long since left the valley and is now a multinational company employing over 16,000 people in twenty-three countries. It ceased the manufacture of asbestos products in 1981 and as Cape PLC specialises in insulation, scaffolding and fire protection, with various offshoots in the chemical, gas and oil industries. It has many major industrial clients in the energy sector.

In 2005 the company created a £40-million fund to cover any future asbestos-related claims made by former employees. It is expected that such cases could continue until 2050, when illnesses or deaths in Calderdale may still be occurring. In 2016 Cape PLC's revenue was £863.5 million, up over 21 per cent on the previous year. It is registered as a business in Jersey.

Years of campaigning and press coverage ensured that action was at least taken to secure the asbestos graveyard at Scout Rock during the 1990s. After all, a primary school sits just 100 yards down the hill on Scout Road, as do the houses in which I and my neighbours live.

Societies were formed, articles written, local TV news stories run to coincide with various anniversaries, feasibility studies commissioned, motions raised in Parliament, inquiries launched, legal action undertaken and the corporate culprits never allowed to forget their actions.

Buried asbestos is not actually a major threat unless it is uncovered (in the event of something such as a landslide) and then dries out and becomes airborne. When wet it is harmless. A major clean-up operation was undertaken in 1993 and over the following years £1 million was spent on improving the former tip that I walk through daily. A decade later government funds were given to carry out further tests to ensure that no asbestos dust was being released into the air.

One local dog-walking friend recalls seeing dozens of men 'dressed like spacemen' up in the woods for months at a stretch as they carefully dug up and removed the hazardous material. 'All the leaves on trees in Scout Rock Woods turned grey,' she tells me. 'But then as soon as they left, they grew green again. And now look at it.'

We turn our heads along the valley to where the woods are thick with swaying boughs and branches and a lush canopy in fine fettle. It is a tainted Eden. A paradise lapsed.

CHARLES DICKENS WAS especially drawn to the valley's old homesteads and stone halls, which were long since abandoned even then. He devoted a considerable section of his travelogue 'The Calder Valley' to the 'scores or hundreds' of old hall-houses

from the Elizabethan and Jacobean eras that dot the hills around
The Rock today, whose multitude testified to the wealth of the
area in the seventeenth century, where 'houses, or the remains
of them, tell us that knight or yeoman, cavalier or Puritan, has
fixed his abode'.

Poking about during his visit here in 1858 Dickens discovered in the dilapidated chambers of these many residences
'chairs, chests, tables, bedsteads, relics of the original occupants
of the place'.

The houses clearly ignited his imagination, for his descriptions of these homes, built by Royalists in lofty or isolated
positions, read like passages from his own classic ghost stories:

> The tenant will often tell how the 'Romans' [i.e. the
> Catholics] once dwelt there, and will point out secret
> hiding-places in the thickness of walls where the proscribed
> were secreted. And the old gentry are not quite departed
> either, for yet they haunt the place, and if you go at the
> right time you may hear the clank of a sword in the hall, or
> the foot of a cavalier in the chamber overhead, or the rustle
> of a silken farthingale. In some of these houses, too, they
> tell of deeds of violence wrought long ago within the wall,
> but yet expiated, and uneasy ghosts drag chains at midnight
> in the staircases. It may be safely said that there is scarcely
> one of these edifices which has not something curious in
> itself or its traditions well worth investigating . . .

And even if you don't believe in ghosts as the spectral floating
forms of childhood horror stories, hearing the tales still told

today by those who survived their time in the mill, or walking alone through the wooded slopes of The Rock, where the asbestos sat for decades, it's hard not believe in the concept of places being haunted.

That is why whenever I mention Scout Rock to locals of a certain age or background, another shadow appears, this time across the eyes of those who have never once entered the leafy interior of this *terra incognita*. No matter that it has been cleared, secured and is subjected to regular readings for asbestos. No matter that the woods are alive with plants and mammals and birdsong. To many The Rock is a beast, a ghost, the elephant in the room. It is a killer, cast to the edge of the community. A long-doomed place buried in the soil of memory. It is as if it, the landscape itself, rather than the actions of greedy men, is somehow to blame for the tragedies that have seeped into the collective consciousness of all those who live in close proximity.

THOUGH THE VALLEY is a moody mistress and laden with these tragic undercurrents, when experienced at the right time it is also the most beautiful, bountiful, abundantly green place in the world. It is not all gloom. Far from it.

On certain days, when the sun is softly sinking behind Heptonstall church up on its hill, which appears in the pinking light like a ladder to another dimension, or a sugary mist whorls down from the moor to cast the valley in a focus so soft it borders on the mystical and a séance-like mood of communion with the dead pervades, or feeling June-drunk on the abundance of plant life and visually dizzy from the chlorophyll overload, my past life in the city – indeed the concept of *all* cities – seems like nothing but a story that I once read, in a book that I gave away to a stranger.

In these moments of quiet revelation, when the landscape and elements collude to create small pockets of perfection, the rain and the mud and the shadow of The Rock suddenly seem not only bearable but necessary, for nothing good grows without rain, and a shadow cannot be cast without a burning, raging silver sun behind it.

It is full of surprises too.

One spring night a mighty crack splits my sleep like thunder just beyond the bedroom, like a symphony of dynamite lit in the deep centre of The Rock, and I am awake immediately. Bolt upright, fumbling for the bedside light.

There follows a deep silence, like that which follows a cata-clysmic incident – a shooting or a car bomb, perhaps – and it leaves me wondering if the great crashing sound was summoned in a darkened dream state, yet Cliff barking in his bed downstairs tells me otherwise. The atmosphere is changed, as if the shifting of nearby space, by force, has impacted on the energy of the room. The air feels stretched tight. High-tensile.

The reverberations of something unseen have pulled me from my duvet and have me standing barefoot on the cold bedroom floor, rubbing my eyes. One loose floorboard creaks underfoot.

At first light I'm up to see snowfall and am soon striding up the road to pull aside the secret metal railing that is my entry point to the woods before scrambling up the coated slopes to Scout Rock.

After the incoming spring's false promise of radial sunshine, with coagulating bouquets of frogspawn gathering in every pond, puddle and old stone roadside trough, and hopeful hosts of golden daffodils tilting in the clear late-March mornings, there has been a sudden late snowfall, as deep as it is unexpected.

Here on the dark side of the valley, in the shadowed corners that see no sun, there are drifts that have buried stone walls and rendered them invisible, while up top on the moors at Blackstone Edge the wind has whipped the fresh fall into a wall that will make the road over to Manchester impassable. Later I will read reports of cars abandoned as the temperature drops, turning the great drifts of snow that sit nine or ten feet deep into icy blocks. When the first advancing diggers arrive up there they disappear into the blizzard to carve a single-lane corridor through a sinuous passage of mute nothingness. What was a road becomes for the next week or two a beautiful tunnel whose pure white walls reflect the blue of dawn and the pink of sundown before inevitably becoming mottled with flecks of dirt and mud and oil, the snow regressing into an ugly state that suggests decomposition and the soiling of something unsullied, as it always does, for a snowfall that lies and lingers is always a drama unfolding all the way from innocence and virginal purity to deflowering and the slow-melting inevitability of death.

There are few things quite as moving as a snowman disappearing from view.

But here in the woods the snow is draped over the rolling tangles of brambles. It bends timber and reshapes my private hallowed space into a sculptural terrain whose angles and edges have been smothered away, leaving only sensuous curves, and here and there I see the occasional fist-sized lump of balanced snow fall, gone in a magical dust-puff of powder flung from a lightly sprung branch like digital glitter flashing momentarily in the magnesium sun. Everything is muffled. The birds are dismayed.

I head directly to the very centre of the woods. I feel the pull of the place because I am in tune with it now. A note plucked up here vibrates down into my bedroom 200 yards away and the resonance is different this morning. The pitch has shifted. The melody of stone is askance.

I see the old tip, whose normal bounty of peeking plastic and half-buried bottles is now entirely covered by a white surface embroidered with a pattern stitched by the tiny two-point markings of sparrow's feet.

And there, on the flat plateau above: a hunk of rock the size of a Transit van.

It has fallen and come to rest lodged against a tree whose trunk has snapped and whose roots have been yanked from the soil, yet are still just managing to cling to it like fingertips on a window ledge. The huge boulder must weigh several hundred tonnes.

Behind it is a trail of destruction where it has bounced 100 yards or more down the steep banks, leaving in its wake more snapped trees, a dotted series of craters dug in an instant and a stream of rocks, pebbles, rubble and slag cast as ballast along the way.

And way up high in the overhang of the cliff is an ominous black gap like a tooth extraction, a gaping hole in the face of Scout Rock's face. At either side and above it, other slabs and miniature escarpments jut out like pieces of a Jenga puzzle, perilously positioned overhead, waiting their turn to freefall like skydivers. Time and gravity will make it so.

The freezing of the water that runs down through the rock from delphs and fields above, and the springs that bubble up through the millstone grit to slake the thirst of the cows that graze in their summer-sky palace, have caused the cliff to contract. Great sections of it have cleaved away in the night. The crashing, cracking sound that I heard must have echoed from one side of the valley to the other, causing me to wake in fright.

Near the great boulder are smaller ones of different sizes, each trailing deep divots and shattered silver-birch limbs snarled and snagged and dragged down behind them.

The land above is crumbling away, and in just a few moments in the night this place that I wander daily – which I have made, in my imagination at least, my own – has changed, so that I now need to pick a new way through the fallen trees and the loose morass of stones.

Tree roots long buried now reach upwards, and with their unearthing comes more of man's rubbish lifted from a secondary layer of the tip that is tangled within them. More plastic, more glass. More crap.

Scout Rock is reshaping itself, though of course I have to remind myself that this is nothing new. The land simply runs to a different clock, where a single tick-tock might represent a century, a millennium, or the blink of a watching raven.

FIELD NOTES I

My pockets contain all sorts.

While I seem incapable of leaving the house without a variety of items (apple, oatcakes, phone, keys and dog-shit bags), which are then usually added to by other objects that I acquire along the way (acorns, feathers, leaves, moss, stones, bones, skulls, owl regurgitations), the truly essential items are a notebook and pen, wedged into my inside pocket, right over my heart.

What follows are some of those field notes scribbled in a variety of books, in situ.

A. E. Housman wrote: 'I could no more define poetry than a terrier can define a rat', and these may not necessarily be poems, but rather lines and lists lifted from the landscape, narrative screen-grabs of a microcosmic world that are correspondent to places or themes explored elsewhere, or fleeting flash-thoughts divined through the process of movement.

They are missives from the mulch, if you will. Postcards from the hedge.

This is what I see at the other end of the telescope.

※ ※

Unearthed

Unearthed:
a leg bone
over two hand
spans in length,

knurled
black hip
as big as a
pugilist's fist.

The scaffold of a life
draped in moss.

Scout Rock Woods in Early Summer

Twilight, and two deer
navigate the chicane of
towering hogweed stems,
alert to the universe.

At the snap of a twig
they take to the slopes,
rising like a miasma,
lost in all that rot.

My eyes are left uncertain.

Upwind and out-flanked
by them once again,
I feel the earth's camber
in my hips, knees, ankles.

The shifting terrain leaves its mark within.

Tonight my frame
will feel the ache,
and recall the flared nostrils,
the steaming pelts.

Their every sinew poised for silent flight.

Scout Rock from the Scarp

Heather-sprouting dead weight
crag at my back,
I survey the ghost of a glacier's
sculptural remnants.

Time is everything down there
but meaningless up here,
as something wet drips down,
soiling the impermanence of this page.

Scout Rock from Hoo Hole

Beneath the soil
    the skull of the earth.

Beneath the loam
    the shadows of bones.

Beneath The Rock
    the index of history.

A King Is Dead

An old soul goes
and with him the last
trace of Elmet too.

The church bells
chime differently
this time;

one sonorous note,
bent around metal as
the new bridge trembles

and the coffin crawls over
and the choir look out
across the rushing Calder.

Place Names of the Calder Valley and Surrounds

Mount Zion
Mount Tabor
Mankinholes.

Kebroyd
Dobroyd
Triangle.

Burnt Stubb
Barkisland
Bogden (submerged).

Slack Bottom
Scout Bottom
Shackleton.

Bedlam Hill.

Old Chamber
Jerusalem
Callis.

New Delight
Lumbutts
Warland.

Jumble Hole
Hoo Hole
Horodiddle.

Mammal

The dog's snout, damp
as it yawps half buried
in a den of chambered dirt.

Embedded, a creature gazes back
into a pink marbled portal;
finds a gateway to deliverance.

Brontë Falls

A stretch of stone
bridges one world
to another and
another and
another.

A greenfly journeys
a universe in
the black
lens of my
sunglasses,

a passing man
scales the bracken
to take a picture
containing
no rain

and the bubbling stream
is steady
as it
raises a
gritstone throne.

Plant Yourself

Imagine a cathedral made from deadwood
then occupy it.

Turn your body into a museum and
never dust it.

Make a mountain out of a molehill
then climb it.

Plant yourself.

The Sparrowhawk

The sky-thump of the sparrowhawk's descent.
Its target, a startled pigeon taste-testing spring.
The downward death-spiral of a shadow enfolded.
The bigger bird dead before it hits the ground.
Grey feathers falling, light, like crematorium ash.

Scout Rock from Stoney Royd

The croak of the raven
is full-throated –
digital, almost;
a warning shot:
watch out! imposter
in our midst, lads.

A Rare Hare

A hare
the size of a dog
is put up
in the old plantation
by the
bone-snap of dry pine.

We both
are startled for a moment –
frozen there, framed
by the setting sun,
as underfoot an island
writhes with worms.

Shadows Across the Stream

Seeing the stream in summer again –
the way the water has peeled back
the laminated rock like the pages of
an old book dropped in the bath,

I am reminded of the power
of time, and the way it is
measured not by clocks
or photographs or funerals

but by
sand and stone and soil and silt and
shadows stretching and shortening.
Shadows stretching and shortening.

Scout Rock as seen from Banksfield, above Mytholmroyd, date unknown. The old town tip occupies the plateau in the centre of the wooded area. Today it is much more densely wooded and overgrown.

Left: Giant hogweed in Scout Rock during winter.
Right: Cliff the terrier above Scout Rock, looking across the Upper Calder Valley. Hebden Bridge sits beyond the trees in the distance.

Left: The Bridestones above Todmorden.
Right: Rain-mottled marks in millstone grit, which runs through the South Pennines of West Yorkshire and Lancashire.

The old tip in the heart of Scout Rock, Mytholmroyd, where decades-old discarded items slowly rise from the soil.

PART II

Earth

Chapter Five

S ince I was young I have always wanted to be in the landscape. Not passing through, skirting over or observing it from a distance, but *in it*. A part of it. Immersed so totally that it scratches the skin and stains the pores. Fills the lungs, the veins, the bowels.

Once, at the age of seven, inspired perhaps by *Fantastic Mr Fox* or Jean George's *My Side of the Mountain*, I asked my dad if I could dig a big hole in the back garden of our semi-detached house. When he wondered why, I couldn't provide an answer because I knew what I intended to say would sound ridiculous: I had a strong urge to be in a cool, damp place with the soil and the worms and the turf for a roof.

I never did dig my hole, but I like to poke and prod and explore, and this desire to climb into the landscape – to touch and smell and consume and burrow – remains as strong.

THE DARK CENTRE of the vast, diamond-shaped expanse of moorland that is marked on the map at its four distant corners by the towns of Haworth, Hebden Bridge, Burnley and Colne is the very definition of Yorkshire uplands.

At first glance the moors offer little but miles of heather and grasslands which, in those brief, bright moments between rain showers, might make you think fleetingly of the oceanic prairies of Idaho or Oklahoma. Here the moors are punctuated by a series of reservoirs, each with its own mood and personality. Their near-onomatopoeic names offer a kind of chiselled-down poetry of wind and water:

> Walshaw Dean
> Watersheddles
> Widdop.
>
> Ponden
> Lower Laithe
> Cant Clough.
>
> Gorple.

Each body of water has its creation story, and each represents triumphant feats of engineering and human ingenuity over geographical adversity.

By the Widdop waters the wind whispers through the swaying grass and an occasional shriek might ring out. Time stumbles and then slips away; the clock melts into a gloop and for a moment life in the crowded cities seems like an unfathomable fever dream of the future, a Bosch painting brought to life in luminescent technicolour in contrast to the dun, muted tones and disorientating perspective afforded by all this space.

Of Widdop, Ted Hughes wrote in the poem of the same name: 'Where there was nothing / Somebody put a frightened lake', describing it as a place where 'heath-grass crept close, in fear'.

Viewed from a bird's eye, or the human modern-equivalent wonder of Google Earth, however, the moor is a time-map of markings, a place of plotted old paddocks trodden out by the hooves of horses, and fire-blackened heather patches; of walls built stone by stone, each hoisted by hardened hands with fingers as fat as sausages, only to tumble down and then be built up again by the sons of sons of sons of the original wallers. It is a terrain of scars and quarries and land-wounds, of multigenerational deer runs and sheep-cropped planes, of dug ditches, dikes and drains, and hidden corners that never see sunlight, of gulleys gouged ('by the sufferings of water', wrote Hughes in 'West Laithe Cobbles'), and lone, low-skulking farms policed by the throaty bark of caged dogs, of quad-bike carvings, of belching bogs and farting quags and sodden sumps that bubble up from sulphurous subterranean waterways.

Here from the eye in the sky the moor is a series of lines marking much movement and displacement, and advancing man's endless sculpting, shaping, colonising, divining, drifting, digging, mining, building, taming, quarrying and grazing, all in an attempt to make the landscape work for him, for *us*, rather than remaining subservient to these merciless and unforgiving uplands.

The moors remain largely uninhabitable.

There are few trees up here. Those that do exist grow short and hunched like purblind crones. Their roots run deep, though, and they grip like ticks; a storm might strip away their bark, but rarely could it upend them. Proud, they stand stiff, symbolic middle fingers raised to the elements.

From the comfort of this satellite view beamed down into our hand-held devices we can instead see the moor shot through with a network of curious capillaries carved by the insistent rock-drill of rain. Water has the whip hand here; neither fire nor rock nor man can contain it indefinitely. It can be corralled and drained or redirected, but it still keeps coming. Always. Nothing stands in its way.

And what begins in stagnant bogs or trickling rhylls eventually turns into the pools, streams, rivers and reservoirs that define this terrain of seasoned wonder. These are the places in which I come closest to being in the heart of it all. These are the places in which I choose to swim.

CRIMSWORTH DEAN IS a long, narrow valley through which a beautiful beck flows down from the moors. It was adopted as a spiritual home of sorts by Ted Hughes and his older brother Gerald, who claimed that visualising this secretive valley had helped him through his years as an RAF flight mechanic in the Second World War.

Today the valley is home to a scattering of farmsteads, too widely spaced to form a village. The buildings endure because they are made from the same gritstone on which they sit, sturdy and true. These houses belong here because they are *of* here.

In the past, to live in Crimsworth Dean was to opt out. It was – and is – neither hamlet nor village, but an idea. Hebden Bridge is only two miles downhill across the moor and through grazing fields and woodlands, but in a rain squall those are two of the longest miles a man or women might care to walk. From up here the town is secreted around corners, and might as well be a continent away.

The Dean was the subject of a study by Martin Parr, the great photographer of a nation at work and play. Before he achieved international acclaim, he lived in Hebden in the late 1970s and extensively photographed the area. His black and white shots of this remote, scattered community offer some of his finest early work: here was an inward world still in thrall to Methodism, where familial ties were tightly knotted. Life was seasonal and determined by the calendar. Ritual was important, as was worship. People knew their place and their place was here, between rock and cloud, God and the devil. Many of the images were collated in his 2013 collection *The Non-Conformists*, whose title referred both to the numerous Non-Conformist Methodist and Baptist chapels to be found around Calderdale, and to the fiercely independent nature of the townsfolk.

Looking at Parr's photographs of the smoky backrooms, the tweed jackets, the communal buffets eaten on austere wooden benches that scrape across stone chapel floors, one feels adrift in time and perhaps even faintly nostalgic for a simpler age, even though common sense tells us that, despite terror, recession, conflict and right-wing Twitter trolls, we've never had it so good.

In Parr's pictures we see the late 1970s but could be looking at the 1870s, or perhaps any time in the preceding centuries. People still farm the land up here but this is a world away from the rural depictions of furtive romps in the hay-ricks of L. P. Hartley or the lush picnics enjoyed in H. E. Bates's 'perfick' English summer days. It's not even the fecund landscapes of longing of D. H. Lawrence. This is hard-scratch upland farming of unforgiving soil, stubborn rocks beneath the coulter blade and sheep found fallen down crags, their eyes pecked clean by dawn. It's not a place for growing, only grazing. Co-existing rather than conquering.

Writing in the 1970s, the local poet Glyn Hughes noted that many of the Upper Calder Valley farms lacked 'that air of abundant, teeming life; of the centuries of manure, producing abundance; of the movements of animals and the carting of hay and of crops deciding the ways over the hills'.

Sheep still fill the fields as they have for centuries, and in March cows bounce gleefully across the paddocks following their winter's barn-bound incarceration, but now the Methodist chapel has been converted to a private residence and trampolines sit saggy in gardens beneath slow-rusting satellite dishes. Organised religion is losing the battle, though on a clear day, while cricking one's neck to take in the rushing banks of over-head clouds, or staring deep into the black, unblinking eye of a heron disturbed by the thud of oncoming footfall, the idea of a God or gods still seems almost believable.

Along the top of Crimsworth Dean runs Haworth Old Road, once the favoured route of traders, tinkers, labourers and land workers making the slow walk between Hebden Bridge and Haworth, and it is this narrow road that I drive down now to reach my preferred swim spot.

CRIMSWORTH BECK WINDS down the Dean via low-flowing levels and shallow pools that compose their own chiming music, before reaching a packhorse bridge built in the early 1700s. Sitting above the natural pool of Lumb Falls, the bridge is one of the earliest remaining signs of habitation here where the markers of modernity are scant.

Back then the bridge served the Limer's Gate ('gate' meaning 'way'), an old trail that ran limestone deposits across the bor-der from Rochdale and Wycoller through the Calder Valley to Halifax, crossing the unforgiving Wadsworth Moor at 1,400 feet above sea level.

Lime was a key component for countering the high acidity level of the soil, which makes diverse crop cultivation so dif-ficult. When built, such packhorse bridges had low parapets or none at all, so that those horses heavily laden with panniers full of lime or transporting other goods such as coal, wool, cotton, calico, finished cloth and salt could cross the water unencumbered. Today an iron-rod rail provides a spot for visitors to lean against while they take their selfies above the waterfall and the beautiful pool below, and in so doing get to share a view with the world that was once seldom seen by all but the hardiest trailmen.

The ghost of a White Lady is said to haunt this bridge, but then a White Lady is always stalking one rural spot or another, including a dull copse close by me in the suburbs of my childhood – Witch's Wood – in which I only ever saw older boys sniff so much lighter fluid that they went cross-eyed. The copse is now a golf course feature.

Formed by the collapse of a hard gritstone cap, here the waterfall presents itself. The steady flow of the beck rising and rushing with the rainfall has scraped away the earth's carapace to uncover and erode the softer shale beneath it. Once this dean held a glacier the size of 10,000 cathedrals, a solid mass squeaking and groaning under the weight of itself, but today it has been reduced to a liquid memory, a minor waterway carrying messages from the past to be filtered through the present, and sent on into infinite futures.

A mile or so downstream from here the beck joins Hebden Water down at Midgehole, which will in turn feed into the Calder. But trapped in here, suspended in time, is a perfect circular pool lined by rocks alive with rare lichens and mosses.

THE LURE OF swimming in cold water is strong, the after-effects as powerful and addictive as any narcotic or extreme sport. Once experienced, the adrenaline high is difficult to match.

I have loved to swim all my life. In London I swam most days in an outdoor pool, and like many people my interest was reinvigorated following a reading of *Waterlog*, Roger Deakin's talismanic 1999 account of his wild swimming adventures, in which, in this age of health and safety and borders and boundaries, the simple act of exploring a river or tarn can become an act of dissent. For me swimming is not even always about the act itself, but rather the immersion in landscape, the subversion of form and the frog's-eye view that is gained. The visceral nature of cold water is incomparable. It makes you aware of your blood, your heart, your muscles, your *mortality*. There are deeper psychological implications too, which are not difficult to fathom. In *Haunts of the Black Masseur*, his study of the meaning of swimming, Charles Sprawson notes John Cowper Powys's thoughts on swimming: 'In a state of "loneliness" a human being feels himself drawn backward, down the long series of his avatars, into the earlier planetary life of animals, birds and reptiles and even into the cosmogonic life of rocks and stones . . . [the swimmer] transported back to that world of weird ritual and mythology.'

Sprawson also explains how the philosopher Ludwig Wittgenstein, who, while at Cambridge, followed in a tradition of other adventurers by swimming outdoors, including in a pool favoured by Byron, observed a link between philosophical thought and the corporeal act of cold-water immersion: 'Just as one's body has a natural tendency towards the surface and one has to make an exertion to get to the bottom – so it is with thinking.'

Or perhaps swimming is simply about glimpsing death and then turning away from it, yet returning again and again to face its dark allure, because up against the grim prospect of the limited life of the human body one never feels more alive.

Later, on a warm July day here, I will watch as two young men and a woman tip an urn of ashes into the water below, the fine motes of something once human drifting across the surface and then settling there, before they jump in to join their absent loved one.

Cold-water swimming is also a proven antidote to anxiety and depression, its healing properties only recently beginning to be recognised in the broader field of medicine.

Close to the waterfall at Lumb Falls there is a small plaque bolted to a boulder to mark the spot where a photograph of six young local men was taken shortly before they were despatched to fight in foreign fields during the First World War. None were to return. This picture, faded from a century's sunlight, but now made immortal on the internet, shows half a dozen men in their finest – perhaps *only* – woollen suits, complete with matching waistcoats, shirts and ties, and sporting boaters worn askance. One or two clutch canes, while one boy in front and centre offers a sheepish smile.

Though holding themselves still for the camera, the men appear relaxed, at ease, unaware of the horrors that awaited them. Through modern eyes they appear of indistinguishable class; they could be passing characters in an Evelyn Waugh novel or the barely literate sons of weavers. This does not matter; what is of importance is that we know that death does not discriminate and that war will be upon them soon. It will wear them, then discard them.

They sit on a bank where bilberries that are as sweet and fizzy in the mouth as home-made lemonade still grow today and where, as Ted Hughes wrote in the poem 'Six Young Men', 'You hear the water of seven streams fall / To the roarer at the bottom, and through all / The leafy valley a rumouring of air go.'

Mortality rates amongst the young in the Upper Calder Valley remain much higher than the national average today. Buried close to Sylvia Plath in Heptonstall Cemetery are young victims of heroin. Last month someone else in Mytholmroyd suffered a fatal overdose. The month before that a teenager was killed on his motorbike.

Cold-water swimming solves few problems, but it does help.

In *Haunts of the Black Masseur*, Sprawson delves through several centuries' worth of writing on the subject to draw a clear link between the addict and the swimmer, illuminating along the way certain common attributes shared between the most ardent practitioners. 'Both the opium addicts and the swimmers tended to be solitary, remote figures, who felt themselves superior to dull, conventional minds,' he writes. 'The descriptions of their experiences are like those of a man who has just explored an unknown territory, and returns to astonish us with his discoveries. On the whole they reject the material world, the industrial system and contemporary society. They were generally out of harmony with their age, idealists who felt deeply the futility of life, the contrast between what life is and what it ought to be. It was as though water, like opium, provided the swimmers with a heightened existence, a refuge from the everyday life they loathed.'

The shock of cold water is a brutish panacea to gnawing anxiety, creeping depression. For some it brings them into being, in a way that drugs may once have taken them away from themselves. Swimming is also the antidote and antithesis to the virtual world and all its attendant nebulous threats.

Nevertheless, just as each season's turning offers a continuum of signs and signifiers to prepare the natural world for the death-time of autumn, so too my mind and body conspire to put me into an altered state, and it is not always one I welcome. The older I get the more I appear to react to the seasons, feeling great surges of energy during spring and summer that can produce much activity and pay creative dividends, but which are then followed by crushing slumps and prolonged bouts of ennui and self-loathing that at the worst of times make simple day-to-day activities such as partaking in a coherent conversation, deciding what clothes to wear or going to the shop for groceries feel like near-impossible tasks.

I have learned to seek the signs, gathering like locusts in a place beyond the horizon. There they slowly crawl through the crops of my imagination, gorging themselves before taking flight and swarming my mind. When the plague comes I am overwhelmed, sucked dry, drained, left a spent husk prone on the sofa.

I have come to understand that what I experience is perhaps a sense of mourning for a passing summer, tied in with the anxiety I would feel throughout childhood at the prospect of being incarcerated in a classroom and tied to the trauma of routine, noise and confinement for another academic year.

Though I like the headiness of the season – its perfumes, the fruit that it offers, the sense of renewal, where puffball spores sing their potential; in each song a rumour of a thousand more – often the very thought of autumn seems to evoke a sense of doom and death. The first leaf withering to gamboge and then burnt orange, curling and then falling to start the carpet of winter; the scent of bonfires on the breeze; that morning you awake and breathe in air that has an edge. The clouds pressing down. All have their effect on me. I think of 'Hill' by the poet Helen Mort: 'Autumn, the Calder Valley chimneys breathing light / the beech trees mimicking a corner of night – black trunks / the spans between them tiny measures of the sky.'

Then my body rebels as if I were part-animal, my energy waning as if controlled by a dimmer switch to put me into a power-save mode of part-hibernation. The doom becomes a black obelisk of the imagination, blocking all natural light, scratching at visions, it prods, probes, cajoles, whispers my worthlessness, niggles and needles, casts a hoar-frost across everything. No club or cudgel or spell can shatter it, but a bolt of cold juddering through these stupid bones of mine seems to help.

Sometimes such an act of doing requires a certain level of unthinking. Sometimes you just have to jump in and let the endorphins have their way.

Because swimming is poetry too.

This simple act, undertaken for thousands of years, offers perhaps the ultimate communion with landscape and is responsible for some of the best pieces of writing from those Romantic poets who drew on the sublime experience including Byron and Coleridge, Swinburne, Southey and Shelley, who could not swim and in fact drowned when his boat capsized off the coast of Italy, but nevertheless enjoyed outdoor bathing, and once turned up at a dinner party naked and with seaweed in his hair. 'Poets make the best topographers' wrote W. G. Hoskins, author of *The Making of the English Landscape*.

I read the following words, taken from Coleridge's notebooks circa 1800, before taking a dip in Lumb Falls, and in doing so feel part of an unbroken continuity where men and women are linked together across eras by water and rock alone: 'The white rose of Eddy-foam, where the stream ran into a scooped or scolloped hollow of the Rock in its channel – this Shape, an

exact white rose, was for ever overpowered by the Stream rushing down in upon it, and still obstinate in resurrection it spread
up into the Scollop, by fits and starts, blossoming in a moment
into a full Flower.'

I HAVE BEEN coming to this pool for several years, always in
the morning, before the groups of teenagers make the hike up
from the town. On this September day dead leaves are already
circling the pool, which is the colour of long-stewed tea. The
blade of autumn is carving fine slices of chilled air.

I swim towards the main flow beneath the falls where the
water is like a rolling boil, an unrelenting and hypnotic squall of
foam and fret. It is the only danger spot: beneath it after several
days of rain one could conceivably be pushed under and held
there, but if I manoeuvre round it there is a shelf of rock on
which I can sit, carefully positioning myself so that the water
thuds at my neck, back and shoulders. Here the noise is thunderous, the massage intense, the best I've experienced.

As I brace myself and grip the shelf beneath me I find that
the stone peels away in plate-sized pieces, my palms lifting the
pages of this great stone book. Thousands of years of constant
flow have loosened the laminations, so the softened sheets of
stone lift off with ease.

I hold up a piece that has the shape and appearance of a naan
bread, its surface pocked with divots created by the cold drip of

the decades, and then I launch back into the water (the slab of waterfall rock sits on my desk beside me now).

Around me the first leaves continue to fall. I drink a mouthful of the pool and let the flow take me, pushing me away to the shallows, a piece of fleshy jetsam reclining on his back and clumsily expelling a small fountain of this cold, dark tea up into the perfect autumn morning. An exile on my own imaginary Elba.

The wall of stone that surrounds the pool is thick with plants, grasses and mosses. I take the smallest clump of grass in case the mosses are rare and exotic, and use it to scrub myself all over, the rough stems that secure it to the stone acting as a course sponge over my already glowing skin. I barely feel it scratching at me, the coldness an anaesthetic of sorts for my outer layer.

At the age of twelve I had a kidney removed. In the days before keyhole surgery the procedure was significant and for twenty years afterwards I lost all feeling around the right side of my torso and hip; as the scar tissue and severed nerves slowly began to heal, feeling gradually returned. The effect of the cold water now is comparable. When I crack my ankle on a submerged rock, the cold masks any pain. The rough moss barely registers. I am benumbed, one step removed from discomfort. In fact, I would say I am closer to a quiet sense of euphoria.

As I dry off afterwards, I pour out my own invention, 'The Yorkshire Espresso' or *Yespresso* ©: twice-brewed tea with the bag left in to mash for an hour or two in advance, then drunk black and sugarless in short, flask-cup shots. Each bitter dose is like a normal cup of tea condensed. Ultra-tea. As dark as the water that drips from my shivering body.

Below the waterfall flows onwards, a comforting crash and boom of spray and spume, just ferocious enough to instil fear and admiration, an open vein of the valley whose purpose is gushing wonder.

I RETURN AND keep returning, often alone.

I keep breaking from my work to drive up to the moor and down the dale, even though the weather is turning as rotten as the worm-chewed apples that bob in the valley's silted mill ponds.

With each day the tone and hue of the waterfall alters. In mid-September, after another prolonged downpour, it is roaring, and from a distance the central flow of fluted water appears as solid as a gleaming marble Ionic column, the spiralling, spitting aquatic scrolls of its capital flowering out over the circling pool below. Yet when experienced close up is in fact a shower of deep amber jewels, thunderously strewn.

I am careful as I push out off the rock and swim towards the centre of the pool alone, passing through a swirl of twigs and leaves and into the turbid froth at the foot of the falls.

I position myself on the usual stone shelf for a shoulder massage but the heavy water has other ideas and dispenses me quickly with a flurry of smacks about the head, throwing me back into the pool, punch-drunk and reeling, and laughing too.

Like a journeyman pugilist that won't be put down, though, I come back at it, but this time box-clever as I circle around the waterfall and take the side entrance, slotting into the small space behind the main unbroken gush of pure water and the concave of the back-rock that has been hollowed away.

Here I crouch like a troll behind the falling veil, once again between stone and water, concealed from the world. Only as I catch my breath back from the stun-gun immediacy of the cold do I notice a strange and foreboding sound, a drone, deep, wide and sonorous. It is a dank hum, a stone-chant, a hypnotic bombination. It is a deep bass vibration that I find myself sitting within.

This drone can only have been created by a specific amount of water falling at a certain amount of litres per second, and created in this very cavity, at this very moment. Caught between waterfall and crag, I feel the sound run through me. I am its instrument, its conduit. The drone is in my bones as it emits a note quite unlike any other. I have discovered a new note. A new sound.

The boom in my blood and organs now, I do not move. There is a sense of dramatic foreboding to its timbre but it is compelling too, and reaches back to something embedded in a subconscious past when our forefathers might have cowered naked and afraid in such caves or hollows, hiding from the peals of thunder as they churned over the moors, the taut air around them crackling, malevolent and prognostic.

I stay in this space and am lost in the drone for some time. Its pitch does not falter, but when my skin is dimpled and I am beginning to shake beyond control I push out into the pool again, straight into the churning centre, tumbling in the barrage of its chorus of detonation.

Another baptism, full immersion.

THE DRONE IS too intriguing to keep secret, and I tell my friend Kev about it.

A music fan, sound man (he has just returned from a tour of South America mixing the live sound for Public Image Ltd) and expert in all things auditory, Kev is keen to hear what I have described to him, perhaps a little too excitedly, as 'the missing note, the new sound'.

As we walk down the stone steps Kev tells me about the recent show in Argentina when he looked out from his sound desk and saw a vortex appear in the crowd before John Lydon, an empty space defined by the swirl of bodies around it, with the occasional flailing body making a break across the kinetic whirlpool of the circle-pit. Standing over the water now, we watch as leaves and twigs similarly spin out across the swirling circle, pulled into the centre by the rumbling undercurrents of the falling water.

We slip into the water like toads off a rock, down into the depths and emerge gasping.

'How do you like the temperature, Kev?'

'I feel . . . *discombobulated*,' he says, his voice booming around this shrunken theatre of stone and dripping moss.

Today the flow has eased a little, and the waterfall has retreated slightly. I pass through the drumming drapes of peat-bog water and into my stone echo chamber.

I sit and wait beneath the torrent in the crouch-space but there is no missing note today, no new sound, only the usual *thrap* and roar of the rapids hitting the rock.

What I experienced the other day was created and performed solely in the moment, and existed only in the moment: a vibrating drone in whose composition I was inadvertently complicit. I was both player and played, and feel an idiot now to even think that the hypnotic drone-note could have been maintained for days when all the parts that created it – rainfall, air temperature, humidity, angle of trajectory – are subject to continued change.

Like a live improvisational jazz score – 'The Lost Drone of Lumb Falls' – it was concerned only with the then and now, a fleeting exploration never to be repeated, and I feel privileged to have been its sole recipient.

MY OTHER FAVOURED swimming spot is quite different to the Romantic, moss–draped hollow of Lumb Falls.

Gaddings Dam is a large, man-made reservoir measuring 200 yards in length and 100 yards across, up on a patch of moor known as Langfield Common, high above Todmorden, overlooking the nearby hillside villages of Lumbutts and Mankinholes. It is most notable for hosting England's highest beach, a small, triangular patch of sand pressed into one corner, sixty miles from salt water.

The first owner of this stretch of open moorland was one Sir Stephen Hamerton, who rebelled against King Henry VIII's Church of England, for which he was pardoned, but then took part in a greater Tudor rebellion dubbed the Pilgrimage of Grace. He was one of many wealthy landowners who was executed by either hanging or beheading – or, in the unfortunate Hamerton's case, *both* – at Tyburn in 1536 (the North Yorkshire villages of Green Hammerton and Kirk Hammerton bear his name today).

As one of the many rewards for its suppression of this uprising, the Crown generously awarded ownership of Langfield Common to itself. In time, these exposed grasslands were sold as pasturing 'gates' – areas divided up according to the number of cattle.

The reservoir came much later, in 1833, when the Industrial Age was working at full coal-fuelled, water-driven, steam-powered capacity, and the Calder Valley was run by people like the four Fielden brothers, mill owners and empire builders, who instructed its construction to power their triple waterwheeled mill at nearby Lumbutts.

This stone-lined body of water known as Gaddings Dam is rumoured to have been built by convict labour, most likely sourced from Salford House of Correction in Manchester. Though no written evidence has been found to support this theory, rocks were mined from a nearby location dubbed Jail Hole Quarry, and some of the stones still bear the marking of a government arrow. So a man who robbed a ham from a butcher's in Wythenshawe might have inadvertently found himself breaking rocks in this godforsaken backwater.

The water of Gaddings holds its own stories: there have been drownings here. Three boys in one night, pulled from the water one summer's morning in 1889. The following year an epic thirty-six-round prize fight between two men from the small Pennine town of Whitworth took place by the reservoir, far away from any figures of authority who might have tried to stop it.

At any time of the year Gaddings is dramatic and beautiful, a sublime spectacle. It is reached following a brisk walk straight up the valley side's slopes from the Shepherd's Rest pub – fifteen minutes for a fit person walking alone, or twice that when burdened with beer coolers, boom-boxes and inflatables, as many day-trippers are during the hottest summer days, when scores congregate on this elevated anomaly of a beach that I like to call the Rochdale Riviera.

Anyone turning back to see the way they came is rewarded with a valley-wide view over Todmorden. (One theory as to the origins of the town's name suggests it is derived from two different old words for death – *tod* and *mort* / *mor* – and a third, *den*, meaning wood. Therefore: death-death-wood. Todmorden. And always pronounced with the second and third syllables blurring and flattening: Tod*mudden*.) Then, as one turns to take the final crooked stone steps up to the water, the rest of the world disappears from view. Here at an altitude of 1,200 feet there is only the water, the rocks that line it, and the moor dotted with gently bowing tussocks, black-eyed sheep in coats as tough as wire wool and the call of curlews.

The impossibly small beach appears surprised to find itself up here, and on summer days has a golden tone, yet in the winter months takes on the appearance of fine glass. In fact the sand is made from gritstone that has rubbed itself down to rough grains by a breeze that blows in across the water, sweeping it away into the corner.

Often in winter, when the breeze becomes a cruel and relentless wind that shrieks like an embittered harpy, the sand is whipped over the wall and thrown out across the moor. In time, though, more sand is heralded in by the wind, shaped and slung, the beach continually being refreshed for those that use it.

Past the beach, visible through a haze, sits the stone digit of Stoodley Pike in one direction, and in the other a series of silently spinning turbines that harness the power of the sky. Often the clouds appear frenzied here, hungry as they scarf up air space.

A foreboding hollow in the moor, the reservoir has the feel of a flooded volcano, a place to evoke feelings of wonder, fear, delight and reticence.

I have swum Gaddings in all seasons, and the water temperature varies greatly, from highs of around 18°C in July or August to a notch above zero in winter. At its deepest point it is four yards, so on a pleasant day the water's surface can hold the sunlight's warmth, though rarely maintains it overnight. Most of my swims here are in temperatures below 10°C: bracing, no matter how enthusiastic or experienced one might be.

And even after all these years I still barely consider myself a 'swimmer'. I am someone who simply puts on some cheap shorts (and neoprene gloves in the winter) to do a simple breast stroke without style or grace, in any direction that takes me. I have yet to master the front crawl; I leave that to the male try-hard splashers – and it is always men – who monopolise our municipal pools on their lunch breaks, chopping all comers out of their way, swimming especially aggressively at the appearance of a woman in a bathing costume.

I've never owned a wetsuit; without one experiencing the sensation of the water's cold is like rebooting one's memory bank. It is what the writer and English eccentric Frederick Rolfe – better known as Baron Corvo – called 'the grand sensation of enquiry, of experiment, of daring discovery'. The key to entering Gaddings Dam on a cold day is to exhale slowly. Ease into it, and expect the shock. Resist the urge to gulp in air. It *will* be cold, but in this moment there is revelation too. Where once you thought you were awake, now you really are.

And if the water proves to be unbearable you can always climb out, let the body accept the surprise that the mind has already anticipated, and then get back in again. Blood is powerful.

Machismo should be avoided at all costs. A cold-water swim should only be done for enjoyment, and never to prove a point.

SOMETIME BEFORE THE Second World War the valve mechanism beneath Gaddings Dam was disabled in the open position, and the reservoir slowly drained away to leave a huge stone-lined crater in the moor.

Over time, though, rainwater gathered again, but left via an outflow until the 1960s, when a local engineer finally blocked it off so that Gaddings might be fully replenished. It was privately purchased in the 1970s, but in the 1990s an inspection declared that, in accordance with the Reservoirs Act, an extensive programme of repairs was required, which its owner was not in a position to do. The draining and abandonment of the reservoir was one of the suggested courses of action, so in 2001 the Kinks-sounding Gaddings Dam Preservation Company Ltd was formed by a group of volunteers to preserve this magnificent body of water, which they continue to do today, steadily replacing the 2,000 stones that have been dislodged or hefted into the water, maintaining paths and controlling the outflow.

I learn a lot about the history of Gaddings from Keith, a volunteer and unofficial custodian of the water, who I sometimes swim with. He is up at the reservoir most days, working for a few hours, then stripping off his overalls and swimming naked. Afterwards he likes to let the sun or wind dry him off.

'The last heatwave, a thousand people must have walked past me laid out, starkers like,' he says. 'But I don't give a fuck.'

Before he got into swimming Keith was a spelunker. He travelled widely, exploring some of the world's deepest cave systems, often for days at a time. 'When Chris Bonington was conquering Everest,' he tells me, 'we were nearly as deep below.'

He also explains how in the particularly harsh winter of 2010, he and two female friends dug through a foot of ice in air temperatures of −15°C to create a narrow channel in order to enjoy a bit of private lane swimming.

'It's the best time for a swim, is winter,' he says. 'The only problem was, when I got home I couldn't feel my hands. For three months. Another time I was up here in the winter, just as it was getting dark, and I emerged from the ice water, naked, clutching my clawhammer, right as this woman was walking by. I think she saw the funny side.'

Gaddings is that type of place: a magnet for the hardy eccentrics of the North, and addictive too. The reservoir has a pull. It has charisma. Once conquered it becomes friend rather than foe, though perhaps a friend never to be fully trusted.

Today the water is good. It feels slick on the skin and fine to the taste. On some days you can see for three yards through the murk, and dunking my head in the early spring makes my skull feel as if it were made of diamonds.

Keith tells me it was a late one last night. He was out on call as a volunteer for the Mountain Rescue. It was, he says, a relatively easy job. A suicide down in the woods at the bottom of the valley. 'Clean' is the word he uses. No need for wandering knee-deep through bogs in pre-dawn darkness. No abseiling down wet gritstone crags. No need to hurry.

'A hanging. It was near your place, actually. I reckon the midges must have got to him.'

I glance sideways at Keith. He shrugs.

'It's the only way to handle the job,' he says of the gallows humour.

He goes on to explain that yesterday was very similar to another suicide he was called out to eighteen months ago, below Scout Rock tip. 'It was just off the path where the kids go by,' he says, matter of factly. 'Had to cut him down.'

Keith removes his clothes and stands naked with his hands on hips, squinting out across the nipping water and ignoring the stares of a passing party of wide-eyed walkers.

OFTEN WHEN I am over the deepest reach, supported only by the dark mystery of what lies beneath, I like to float onto my back and remain as still as possible so that the reservoir's surface settles. On a warm, still day it becomes a mirror to the sky, capturing the sun, collecting clouds and reflecting them back on themselves. I see no one, hear no one. There are no buildings or engines or sirens. There are no signs restricting movement. No cameras watching on.

Occasionally a vapour trail drawn like a chalk line across the sugar paper of summer may be spotted dispersing far overhead, but otherwise everything is elemental.

Water.

Rock.

Grass.

For a few minutes I am weightless once more in perhaps the quietest place on this chaotic island of ours.

One day I watch as a tiny curlicue-shaped feather falls from an unseen bird, a piece of down that settles beside me on the meniscus, complicated in construction yet somehow simple and of great efficacy; timeless yet present in the here and now, finely balanced on the narrowest point of its concave back, perfect as it gently drifts away from me.

In autumn I often find moths fluttering as they drown, so I scoop them out and put them in my hair until I am back on dry land, then shake them out onto the rocks where they dry off, and then take flight on new moon-seeking missions.

Chapter Six

One of the most magical aspects of this area is its illusionary power to alter perception. Things far away suddenly appear close, insignificant landmarks grow tall or vertiginous crags are shrunk down to size upon the turn of a corner, none more so than Scout Rock, whose mood, tone and colouration, and its stature too, are wholly dependent upon whether it is viewed from the bottom of the valley or high up on the correspondent moor.

Perspective cannot always be relied upon to be true and the way in which the clouds, rain and sun conspire to play visual tricks is especially apparent here. The land distorts, flattens, elongates, and sometimes the ghost-gaps left by the absence of ice mountains disappear entirely.

Interviewed on Melvyn Bragg's Radio 4 documentary *The Matter of the North*, the poet Simon Armitage, who lives in Marsden, fourteen miles away in the Colne Valley, spoke about the impact of Scout Rock upon Ted Hughes's thinking.

'That rock barred his view to the south and he talked about it as a great impediment to his vision,' said Armitage. 'I have a theory that all his poems are an attempt to escape those valleys. The Calder Valley is that bit steeper, it's that bit deeper, it's that bit darker. Ted, in his ricocheting imagination, would go from valley to pit to trench to underworld, and that rock came to symbolise something that was cutting out the light that he needed.'

In the same programme Bragg finds Scout Rock somewhere deep in Hughes's *Prometheus* poems, dedicated to the fire-stealing Greek deity and creator of humanity:

> Pestered by birds roosting and defecating
> The chattering static of the wind-honed summit
> The clusterers to heaven, the sun darkeners –
> Shouted a world's end shout.

It's all about the push-and-pull between light and dark then, and perspective too. I have a neighbour, a woman of maturing years with hennaed hair, a *Load*-era Metallica T-shirt and fibromyalgia. Her name is Jeannette, but, as she proudly tells me, her family call her the Dragon.

The Dragon grew up on the edge of Erringden Moor in a strange stretch of valley side above Charlestown and Horsehold, a barren, farm-flecked place pitched high between Hebden Bridge and Todmorden.

Close by to the lone house where she grew up is the monument Stoodley Pike. The original pike collapsed four decades after it was erected when it was struck by lightning in 1854, on, as a lichen-mottled engraving on its façade notes, '*the day the Russian ambassador left London before the declaration of war with Russia in 1854*'. It was rebuilt two years later.

The Dragon tells me several tales of growing up on the edge of Erringden Moor. The moor, she explains as we walk our dogs in the park, is 'where strange things happen, and have done for centuries'. She speaks of childhood visions of moor-top creatures, half-human, half-animal, dancing in her bedroom. 'I rushed to tell my parents, but they said I was just dreaming,' she says. 'They didn't believe me, but I swear they were real. Yes. They were real alright.'

She tells me of elongated white dogs that stalk the uplands, and men who have gone missing up there. She tells me that her own dog Mungo, a Lhasa Apso/terrier cross whose claws she likes to paint with vivid nail varnish, once spent a full week wandering the barren, heathered plains after disappearing.

'He came back a knotted mess of fur and tagnuts,' the Dragon says. 'He's not been the same since. I think he saw some things up there.'

She also swears that Stoodley Pike itself moves. For many, this 120-foot-tall obelisk, erected in 1814 after the Battle of Waterloo to mark the defeat of Napoleon and the surrender of Paris, is the definitive landmark of the valley. It can be viewed from an infinite number of points for many miles in all directions. Perfectly positioned, it rarely disappears from view.

'It follows you about, does that,' says Jeannette. 'I've seen it. It moves when your back is turned. Folk don't believe me, but it does. Oh, it does. You'll see.'

Inwardly I scoff at the idea that a monument nearly forty yards tall and several thousand tonnes in weight could move, but I understand the topographical illusion. I have experienced it many times myself.

Guy de Maupassant wrote that Paris's most famous landmark followed him everywhere in the city: 'To escape the Eiffel Tower,' he said, 'you have to go inside it.' (He took to dining each day in the restaurant at the base of the tower, claiming it was the only place where he couldn't see what he called the 'iron enemy'.) Through our own movements, The Pike, like The Rock, changes from being the static, solid entity that it is up close, to something fluid and movable, its stature partially dependent upon the eyes that view it. But I favour Stoodley from afar, for wherever you go it is always there, mooring one's movements, drawing the lost back from their strayed paths. It is the valley's compass needle.

The Rock too seems capable of movement – all the way across the moors and into a Manchester art gallery on a damp Tuesday morning. I turn a corner and there it is again, insidiously lurking in the far distance of a photograph, framed and hanging on the austere white wall.

I'm here to escape the long valley shadows and the cold glare of the computer screen after several weeks of writing, but even here, far away from the valley, The Rock will not let me go. It has me. Is following me. Dominating all thoughts.

The picture is by the Dutch photographer Hans van der Meer and is part of an exhibition entitled *Strange and Familiar: Britain As Revealed by International Photographers*, curated, by coincidence, by Martin Parr.

Once more it feels as if The Rock is silently sitting at the centre of things, a spindle around which various merging strands spin. Increasingly, in my mind at least, The Rock is the link in the rusted chain of events, stories, people, places, poems and photographs that form a collective narrative of a place.

I move in closer. Passing visitors might not immediately be drawn to The Rock in van der Meer's photograph, as it is a background presence only – apparitional and miasmic, insignificant – their eyes perhaps instead focusing on two footballers shown in the foreground. I recognise it as Stubb Field, right next door to our old cottage. It was here, by the corner flag, that I first gazed across to The Rock long before I mentally adopted it as my own.

Behind them, The Rock has been reduced to inconsequence by distance. There is implicit humour here too, for the pitch is quite clearly sloping; before it has even begun, the game is weighted in one team's favour. It is the literal opposite of the level playing field of cliché.

I move in closer, my nose nearly pressed to the print.

Two women wander over and peer at the picture. One is of middle age, and the other her mother.

'Ooh,' says the younger. '*Mith*umroyd.'

'You can see my house,' I say with a level of volume that surprises even myself.

'What?' she says, a little caught off guard.

'My house is on there.'

'Is it really?'

'Well, nearly.'

'And that's where you live, is it? *Mith*umroyd?'

'Mytholmroyd,' I say. 'Yes. That's Scout Rock.'

I trace my finger around the route of one of my favoured wandering spots.

'I walk up there most days.'

The women stay for a length of time that they judge to be polite before moving on, and wait until they're out of earshot to remark upon the odd man who is standing by the one photo-graph and remarking on it to passers-by.

My gaze held by the wooded quarry, I wonder why exactly it is that I have been obsessing over this place. Why here?

Eventually I move on, walking through the gallery and the gift shop and out into the street, where a tram pulls up and shoppers pass by, heads down, each lost to the noise of their own internal soundtracks, and a light rain steadily falls across the North.

THREE MONTHS LATER, or perhaps four years earlier, I am shambling along in the dripping shade of The Rock, lost in thought, when the dog runs off ahead, barking. He has many distinct calls dependent upon the circumstances, and this is an insistent rasp of warning. Urgent and on guard. Stranger alert.

Cliff is in peak terrier mode, baying insistently as if he has cornered a fox. I call him away, but he is deaf to my demands.

Recoiled and poised in readiness, he is instead directing his full-throated ire at a large boulder. Once it was a part of The Rock itself, but now it sits alone, shed-sized and surrounded by the shattered glass of bottles shot by an airgun years ago.

Only as I move closer do a I see a foot protruding from beneath the sarcophagus-like space beneath one edge.

I freeze.

I see a shoe, a sock, an inch of dirty ankle. The foot is unmoving. The leg inanimate. The dog still barking.

Stepping lightly, I circle round and find myself face-to-feet with a man who is tucked beneath the stone, staring directly at me over the end of his toes.

'Sorry about him,' I say as I crouch to clip the lead onto the dog's collar.

The man's hands are clasped behind his raised head. His face is blank, eyes glassy. I am unnerved by his silence and the way he is looking right through me.

'Are you alright there?' I ask.

The man has the appearance of one who has used the soil for his pillow and the stone for his blanket, a bottle clasped tightly to his chest, perhaps, with the stars and howls of the animals as his only company.

Again he says nothing. He just stares without expression through eyes of polished blue glass.

I flip the scene and see it from his perspective, observing a stout man, swarthy, over-bearded, moss stains on his ripped coat, battered hat worn askance, muttering to himself, possibly photographing objects poking through the soil or chewing on a leaf and spitting it out in disgust and slipping and cursing as he descends a wooded outcrop where no path leads. He is accompanied by a dog as black, scraggy and cartoon-like as Dennis the Menace's Gnasher, pink gums and sharp teeth showing.

Fair enough, I think. I wouldn't approach me either.

So I step away slowly, and then turn and leave the man, horizontal in the languid afternoon beneath his piece of rock.

HE HAUNTS MY mind that night though. The prone man – probably pissed – is the first I have seen in the wooded base of The Rock, and I wonder if he is up there now, alone in the dark, gin-leathered, hiding from his life. Whatever the reason, he is part of a long tradition of rural wanderers, a throwback to the days when tramps and vagrants walked the lanes, and were accepted as a thread of the fabric of rural life as surely as the lark, the woodpecker or the robin.

The next day I repeat my circuit of the woods and come upon the boulder again. I make even more noise as I approach so as not to appear as if I am ambushing him, and this time the dog stays tethered.

But he is not there. I crouch and see his hollowed-out spot, just the correct length and width in which to squash in tight between soil and stone. Instead in his place beneath the stone is a large human turd, standing in the shaded hollow like a monolith.

Either dark, malevolent forces capable of shrinking a sleeping man down into a solidifying piece of excrement are at work in this hollow deep in these trees, or I have been sent a symbolic message – a dire warning of sorts – or I have an overactive imagination. I beat a retreat. I never see him again.

ONCE THIS WAS a land of outlaws, and the woods often provided shelter for those who led peripatetic lives or simply did not want to be found. It wasn't hard for a person to vanish. Turn a corner, crest a brow, and they could be gone. Find a hollow and bed in. Seek a cave and go to ground. Lose yourself.

Now cameras and phones track movements, and even the sky is dotted with eyes. An image snapped in the street outside my house is beamed to a satellite and back to a website that I log onto. I zoom into my office window and I can nearly see my desk. My clutter. My left elbow.

Zoom out to the top of The Rock, and I can just make out the location where a spring bubbles up from the ground at the bottom of the grazed field on Scout Rock Trail. To the untrained eye it is barely a puddle that the Jersey Shorthorns and Belgian Blues lap at with their muscular sandpaper tongues, but I know it is just one exit point of a vast and intricate network of waterways that bore through clay and gritstone.

William Blake saw the world in a grain of sand; now with advancements in technology we will soon be able to see a grain of sand anywhere in the world.

But in past times the Calder Valley readily harboured those who wished to slip from view.

One local legend is that of Tom Bell, who lived in a cave in Hardcastle Crags, leaving it only to rob nearby villages of their farm animals. His companions 'were crows, rats, weasels and stoats'. He wore a chain-mail suit and avoided capture by wearing boots with the toes and heels reversed, so that his footprints led in the wrong direction. The story has it that Tom Bell died in his cave when his stomach exploded after gorging himself on his ill-gotten gains and was found by two children, his decomposing body pecked away and gnawed at by birds and vermin.

A natural fissure 140 feet in length known as Tom Bell's Cave still exists deep in the woods. In it a skull was found in

1899, believed to be that of the legendary outlaw himself. It was sent first to a doctor in Todmorden and then a professor in Manchester, who dated it as Neolithic or early Bronze Age. A photograph of it exists today, and he resembles Hamlet's deceased court jester – that 'fellow of infinite jest, of most excellent fancy', Yorick. But then, don't they all.

Such mythical stories like that of Tom Bell are often born out of real events, though, and this particular legend may have its source in an incident dating to September 1779 when a man walking by Hathershelf Scout – the Scout Rock of today – saw his dog run into a narrow cave after what he assumed was a fox. Though the cliff face has crumbled over the years and been quarried in the interim, it is still possible to see what may once have been the deepest part of caves or grottos, slowly erased with the peeling away of layers of rockfall.

A 2014 article by Jean Griffiths in *The Yorkshire Journal* takes up the story: 'Thinking that the dog was chasing a fox, he followed it into the aperture which expanded into a small cavern. Instead of finding a fox he came face to face with a ragged outlaw hiding out and defending his cave with his pistol. Eventually the outlaw was overcome by force. This outlaw was Joseph Bailey, a journeyman blacksmith, and the cave was found to contain stolen goods from Rochdale Parish Church. It was also well stocked with cured meats to satisfy the needs of a long concealment. Joseph Bailey was convicted and transported for his crime.'

Griffiths also observes that it's only a small leap from 'Bailey' to 'Bell', and that with each retelling perhaps the name has changed and the location nudged a mile or two along the valley.

THERE IS SOMETHING about this ten-mile or so stretch of upper valley that continues to attract creative and unconventional thinkers. We already know that Ted Hughes kept mentally returning to The Rock and its surrounds throughout his life, perpetually trying to recapture the wonder of childhood.

The Upper Calder Valley attracts many whose lives and work are inextricably linked to the landscape of the area, with an abundance of artists, poets, writers and performers dotted around the place. It is a destination that offers a chance to recalibrate the senses, or perhaps the terrible weather means it is a place where you can simply *get stuff done*.

There is a woodcut by the Vorticist artist Edward Wadsworth entitled 'Mytholmroyd' that for me sums up an aspect of the creative mentality of this area. Conceived in 1914, it is one in a series of works inspired by the North of England – others include 'Cleckheaton', 'Newcastle' and 'Slack Bottom' (in the village of Slack, above Heptonstall).

Born ten miles or so away in Cleckheaton, Wadsworth had trained as an engineer and it was with an engineer's eye that he reconstructed the landscape of Mytholmroyd for the new machine age. Here is a town exploded into industrial abstraction, its monochrome and proto-Brutalist geometric shapes owing some stylistic debt to the Italian Futurists, who rose in tandem with their British-based upstart counterparts.

But mainly 'Mytholmroyd' is a bold vision for a new movement intent on nothing less than an art and design revolution led from the front by the artist Wyndham Lewis. It is a work that captures the feel of this place with its steep valley slopes, hunkered-down dwellings, secreted stone stairways, rising chimneys and cathedral-like mills consecrated only for the worship of production, as it surely was a century ago. Starkly comprised largely of triangles and four-sided shapes – squares, rectangles, rhomboids, parallelograms – and devoid of colour, it would almost certainly have baffled residents of the town.

Wadsworth's 'Mytholmroyd' is an energetic and provocative piece, delivered with violent intent. Here past and present collide during uncertain times, just as the great death machine of war was threshing and shredding young bodies across the farmed fields of Europe; yet Wadsworth achieved a sense of post-Impressionistic vigour and imbued it with the spirit of place. He saw Mytholmroyd for what it was, and might be.

The writer and artist Paul Buck moved here 'by pot luck' in the 1970s with his partner Glenda and one-year-old son to the hillside hamlet of Foster Clough, directly across from Scout Rock, just below the edge of Midgley Moor on the light side of the valley. Once ensconced in their stone eyrie, Paul forged a place in the avant-garde literary/art world with his seminal and often controversial magazine *Curtains*, 'to explore the area between poetry and prose', and which published writings by such influential French figures as Georges Bataille, Maurice Blanchot and Jacques Derrida.

Foster Clough is a fairly remote spot, accessible only by Heights Road, an elevated stretch that runs the length of the valley's northern side which on clear days offers fantastic views in all directions, especially of Scout Rock, which appears on some days like a giant obsidian iceberg rising majestically from its surroundings, but on others a drab, tree-lined basin good for nothing but sluicing out the surplus water that drains and drips through its dreary stone via slow-running rindles.

On the many days when the heavy mist settles down in the trough of the valley, Foster Clough and its surrounding old farmsteads and hamlets can feel like islands adrift in an ocean of slate-grey sky.

'At the beginning I couldn't not wake each day and be influenced by the view over the Calder Valley,' Paul Buck recalls. 'The only area that we could really explore was around us on the Heights Road and the moors behind us, where we walked.'

Here on the hillside Paul and Glenda also entertained a steady stream of writers and artists from Britain and abroad, including such figures as Throbbing Gristle founder member Genesis P-Orridge and his Psychic TV band mate, the industrial music pioneer Monte Cazazza. Both had built careers on provocative work deemed shocking to the art world: while still a student at the California College of Arts and Crafts Cazazza famously laid a huge cement waterfall down the main staircase of the university building, and was also known to build oversized metal swastikas on occasion. P-Orridge – real name Neil Megson – was a cult figure with messianic tendencies, already long established as the de facto leader of the Hull-based art collective COUM Transmissions and, later, Throbbing Gristle.

'They did not come for the view, though they admired it,' says Paul of the pair's sojourn in Mytholmroyd. 'They actually came to see a book I had, a huge encyclopedic work on dead bodies, a pathologist's reference work. This book was unusual, and a number of people wanted to see it.'

Members of Throbbing Gristle returned to the area in 1982, when Cosey Fanni Tutti and Chris Carter worked with the visual artist and former COUM Transmissions member John Lacey, who was living along the road in Todmorden. Near to Lacey's house was Robinwood Mill, a five-storey-high disused mill that once employed over 300 workers, many of them children. The musicians broke into it and used its cavernous spaces to film a video for their eleven-minute proto-acid-house track 'Dancing Ghosts', released in 1984.

Writing in her 2017 memoir *Art Sex Music*, Cosey Fanni Tutti recalls the atmosphere of Robinwood Mill:

The dusty, worn wooden floorboards were solid underfoot and light streamed in from the windows that lined the walls. There was an underlying feeling of some lurking presence, giving it a creepy atmosphere that was magnified tenfold when we returned to film in the evening . . . When we finished, the atmosphere had changed. It felt as if our actions had disturbed the equilibrium of whatever energies were present – that we were not welcome. Behind the lights was a blanket of blackness that none of us wanted to look into. The hair stood up on the backs of our necks and it was fast approaching midnight.

The musician Colin Robinson is perhaps typical of the type of person – though he too is *not* a typical person – that this stretch of the valley attracts today. Like many of the contemporary free-thinkers before him who helped save Hebden Bridge's old industrial buildings and houses by squatting them in the 1960s and 1970s, and in so doing prevented a motorway being built through Calderdale, he moved his way up from the South of England, living in both Leeds and Manchester and then in 2011 finally edging his way in.

He first moved across the valley from Scout Rock into an old house once inhabited by one of the notorious gang of eighteenth-century counterfeiters and murderers, the Cragg Vale Coiners, but now lives in an old cottage in the woods near Hebden Bridge in sight of Foster's Stone, also known as The Sacrificial Stone, where he records, releases and performs avant-garde music at a prolific rate – much of it an instinctive reaction to his immediate surroundings. 'There's something inspirational about the whole place,' he tells me:

> The nature of the landscape, the stone buildings, the slightly unkempt and untidy feel of the area – attractive but not twee. What I particularly like are the industrial remains: the old mills and mill ponds, the buried pieces of machinery, forgotten things half hidden beneath the undergrowth. I like looking at old photographs and maps too, and comparing them to the present day; industrial archaeology has always been a hobby of mine. When I'm recording in my studio, I can look out of the window onto fields and farms that haven't changed much in the last two hundred years. The railway runs nearby, but even that's been there since 1840.

Colin's more recent projects are more closely aligned with the landscape around Mytholmroyd. Under the name Churn Milk Joan, he works in collaboration with an American friend, Richard Knutson. They take their unusual name from the standing stone that has marked the boundaries of Wadsworth, Hebden Royd and Sowerby high on the edge of Midgley Moor directly opposite Scout Rock since the Middle Ages.

Perhaps Colin's most productive outpouring comes via his solo project Jumble Hole Clough, named in honour of the beautiful wooded slack, or side valley, in the Charlestown area just beyond Hebden Bridge. Here alongside a babbling stream and the occasional sighting of deer there is to be found an abundance of industrial ruins that he and I are both fascinated by: the scattered foundations of several long-abandoned mills, silted-up ponds and ghostly farmsteads including Beverley End, an elaborately terraced area of hillside that contains squat stone niches which once held skeps – primitive portable beehives made from rope or wicker. As well as harvesting honey up in this obscure valley, it has also been suggested that medieval wine was produced here too, though it's hard to imagine grape vines ever taking root.

At the top of this narrowing intake was Staups Mill, built in the eighteenth century as a cottage, factory and barn next to a waterfall. *Staup hoyles* are a local term for stepping stones or indentations made by feet on soft ground (and have also been recorded at various times as stoaps, steps and stalps), suggesting that Staups Mills is just one more valley curiosity whose name has been shaped by the land from which it grew. It is also a reminder that language is not fixed, and that the names of all our landmarks of today – whether village or valley, mountain or major city – will not remain as we know them now; their names will change with the altering terrain, gradually chiselled and chipped away by time and even re-sculpted in the changing shapes of our mouths, teeth and tongues.

Who knows what Jumble Hole Clough will be called in 500 or 1,000 years' time, but for now it is logged in the annals of both local history and Britain's rich esoteric musical underground.

THERE SOON COMES a hunter's moon – the first full one after the harvest moon that shows itself closest to the autumn equinox.

Tonight it is a perfect circle in the black, bituminous sky above The Rock, a wax-white adolescent face trapped between the railings of night, as bright as the sun, a pewter plate polished to perfection and placed there. It changes the air. It changes everything, as if emitting a charge. Animals become alert, and all is illuminated by a woozy light. A narcotic night of possibility and potential.

It is a time for wandering through the trees, where the woody thud of conkers sounds like the footsteps of a following foe in a fireside ghost story.

After walking for many miles down railway sidings along the valley floor I still feel a restless energy coursing within. My limbs harbour snakes, and though the fire is lit and fizzing with the sap from some birch logs, their papery bark retracting and curling as the heat licks its way around them, the desire to be outside is still strong.

Because on a night like this the moon is intoxicating. It can make a person unsteady on their legs, and the blood fizz in the ears. Its creates a thirst, a hunger, an appetite. A need. The hunter's moon is so called because it was deemed the best time for hunting parties to pursue their quarry. In towns across the land nightclub bouncers and police always find their hands particularly full on such nights.

It makes me think of the eminent poets of the Tang dynasty during the seventh to ninth centuries, writers such as Li Bo or Tu Fu, in whose work the moon often features as friend and drinking companion, such as the former's 'Alone and Drinking Under the Moon':

> When I am drunk, I lose Heaven and Earth.
> Motionless – I cleave to my lonely bed.
> At last I forget that I exist at all,
> And at that moment my joy is great indeed.

WITHENS CLOUGH IS one of the archipelago of reservoirs that sit in the most remote parts above the valley.

Not to be confused with Top Withens, the ruined house believed to have been the inspiration for the Earnshaw residence in *Wuthering Heights*, Withens Clough is the nearest reservoir to The Rock, over five miles up the longest unbroken incline in England, beyond the village of Cragg Vale, a place of raw beauty, secreted from the world in its own dank valley at the outer edge of Elmet.

Cragg Vale holds the remains and wreckage of centuries of industry: one-slab stone bridges, the foundations of mills with rotten waterwheels beside them and farms that sit like stone birds in nests made from abandoned cars, upended fridges and the non-biodegradable detritus of the consumerist age.

Man's mark is everywhere around these lands. Our crude autographs are indelible, written in rusted metal remains, things dumped down lanes, or leaking petrol that gathers in puddles on land where bison once roamed. Yet ugly can be captivating too. Beauty fades fast; time feeds on it like a revenant, but flawed is fascinating. Scars tells stories. Stories are all we will have when the buildings crumble.

Here deer have stalked the heathered slopes since medieval times, when the entire area was a deer park out of bounds to all but the handful of wealthy gentry who divvied up Yorkshire. Cragg Vale is also the valley that has the honour of being the last recorded place in the country where livestock suffered rinderpest, otherwise known as cattle plague.

There sit high on the moor above the lone reservoir of Withens Clough two ancient cairns called Two Lads that I am keen to find on a mild Sunday morning when I set out with a Pink Lady apple and a Tunnock's Tea Cake in my pocket, the dog skipping ahead as we cross the reservoir dam. The first sight: a hunting hawk like a child's kite untethered over the water, the flat sun as meek as a mouse behind it.

I follow the reservoir path then cut up an obscure clough called Deep Slade that is dense with leathery grass and hidden holes of water; all around me I can hear it running and pooling, yet it's rarely seen. The walking conditions are the stuff of turned ankles and twisted knees: low-level treacherous. I already have one knee strapped up after the 1,680 miles that an app tells me I've walked this year – almost exactly twice the length of Britain, while barely leaving the valley.

The dog hops on ahead, each leap like a fox cub practising at prey, until we come upon a few scattered gritstones that act as a ladder through all that grass into a bank of heather that appears to propel us upwards, bouncing like Spring-heeled Jack all the way to a further morass of gritstone boulders, one of which has been carved by the wind from all angles, as if turned on the lathe of time. In some towns or villages they might be considered major landmarks, yet here in West Yorkshire, where there is an embarrassment of geological riches, this cluster does not appear on the map that I have left at home along with my water bottle, though I discover later that it may be known as the Hattering Stones.

Far below me the reservoir is laid languid across the moor and the sun on the water looks briefly like boats, white triangles drifting a fleet of flapping sails, until a cloud crosses the sun to destroy the illusion.

Beyond the water, over the next brow, right on cue, the pointed tip of Stoodley Pike stands true like a sundial, its stone needle stitching clouds to the etheric tapestry.

Between here and there sits another marker known as the Te Deum Stone, which is engraved with a cross and the Latin inscription *Te Deum Laudamus*, meaning 'We Praise Thee, O Lord'. It was believed to have been erected in the 1680s by one Robert Sutcliffe, as both a sign of devotion and a marker for those crossing the vast, unforgiving moor on an old corpse road. Coffin bearers were said to rest their cargo on the stone and pray there.

I think too of bodies that are surely submerged in the sod, preserved in the bog for 2,000 or 3,000 years, their skin like hide stretched tight across bone frames. Eyes closed, mouths passive, everything retracting yet intact. Perhaps there are remnants of final meals in their stomachs too or the last words on their lips, skull holes staring. Bone fragments and beside them their effects: a twisted lanyard, a gourd, a charm. A spear sharpener. A flesh-stripping river stone.

I eat my squashed Tunnock's Tea Cake and have a drink of rainwater from a stone bowl cut by ice and wind, a dark face reflecting back at me, and I taste heaven and dirt.

The sugar drives me onwards another a mile or so over a flat moor plane of hag and heather, and the cold water trickles down through the core of my trunk. The landscape in me.

Two Lads is comprised of two sturdy boulders sitting about ten yards apart, each crowned with a cairn of stones built piece-meal by passing walkers over decades.

The communal and unspoken aspect of cairn-making is a perfect example of art and functionality working in symbiosis: an unspoken process of understanding without instruction, each visitor adds a rock until something is created communally by strangers who will never meet. A cairn can never be built in a hurry either; by its very definition it is something that takes months, perhaps years, of footfall.

These cairns do not display the looseness of the Cumbrian cairns of slate and shale that I grew up visiting, and instead appear to have solidified into two single entities, their stones drawn together into something more sculptural.

Here it is believed two boys were caught out in a blizzard while crossing the moor and took shelter behind the two rocks. As I touch one, lines appear in my mind fully formed. It may sound like mystical hokum but it's as if the rock has given me the poem and I have merely transcribed it, a ten-second effort summoned from the stone. Without thought for metre, scansion or rhyme, my fingers numb, I write them down:

> Boulders stacked as boys
> become men, each rock
> clinging close, the sum
> of their parts: two cairns.

Later, as the valley succumbs entirely to the dying season, a sudden low fog lingers at the foot of The Rock. It appears as if in a dream, a shape-shifting icing-sugar mist perhaps fifty yards in length, trapped between the trees and the factory, the terraced houses and the raised bank of the railway sidings.

Here the air feels several degrees cooler. It reaches no more than head height, the tresses of mist trailing as if taken by an unseen tide to leave a dusting of dampness in the dying minutes of a winter's day (a friend calls it 'rabbit fog', as you can only see their ears protruding from it; someone else I know calls it 'moor grime'). For a fleeting moment this ethereal vapour becomes first an oversized swan gliding through the fading light, then a wave curling and rising to break on an unseen shore.

The fog fills the moment and I walk towards it, into it, yet never quite reaching it. Elusive, it is always several steps beyond. I stop and taste a sweetness on my tongue and feel strangely light-headed yet unburdened by thought as I stand there watching it swirl and dance across the grass with silent balletic grace, as behind it The Rock shrinks back to a silhouette, a fortress that holds within it the forthcoming night, and at whose feet a hundred fires might be lit.

Chapter Seven

Walking is writing with your feet.

When we walk our footprints mark the soil like the crudest of hieroglyphics, and our minds take fanciful turns. Over long, solitary miles abstract or disconnected thoughts can often find purpose in words which then link to form cogent sentences. Writing and walking are co-dependent.

Walking this valley has taught me to write using all five senses, as well as activating that mysterious sixth sense that we might label intuition. Because writing and wandering are both intuitive: even without a destination in mind you trust your inner compass to guide you, and when you arrive somewhere agreeable you stop, look around and take it in.

Writing is a form of alchemy. It's a spell, and the writer is the magician.

But it is archaeological too, an act of digging and looking. Writing is an attempt to tap into narratives, and to look in either direction along the timeline. To the past and the future. It is an attempt to understand the tiniest fraction of everything that there is to know.

Stories are around us, and when we walk we stumble upon

them, and in these moments we might hear our ancestors speak to us. And we listen.

I SET OUT on a misty winter morning for Hardcastle Crags, a popular wooded valley past Hebden Bridge, to let the land tell me its stories.

The Crags has long been a renowned beauty spot and place of pilgrimage. Alfred Wainwright wrote of hearing about excursions here as a child before he ever saw the place, when it was 'better known than the Lake District . . . a Mecca and many were the pilgrims'.

It is one of those interminably damp days when there is a slickness to the rocks and the entire skin of the earth seems uncertain.

Instead of following the river upstream to Gibson Mill, now converted into an off-grid visitor centre and café, Cliff and I take a lesser-known path up through the woods where birch and pine, oak, sycamore and holly meet the sky, and the land slips away to my left.

Often I let the dog lead the way and when he picks up the anointed trail of a deer, or perhaps the low tunnel of a brock's run, I find myself taking routes shared only by animals. This way new perspectives are gained.

But this is National Trust territory and there are plenty of paths and wayfinding signs as I lean into the diagonal of the hill and hurl sticks for the dog, who is built for powering up and down rough ground, his tongue lolling, black, wide eyes wet with canine delight.

Now a place of conservation, Hardcastle Crags has served different purposes throughout the centuries. Farming and weaving took place here, and people burned charcoal in this valley too, solitary men stacking their solitary hearths with lengths of felled trees to create a more efficient and lasting fuel. Elsewhere there are the sunless remains of old quarries.

The woods are busy with fallen boulders, deep-set and green-coated; some call this area Little Switzerland, due to its similarity to Alpine terrain. In his poem 'Leaf Mould' Ted Hughes calls it 'an echoey museum'.

I seek out Slurring Rock, a jutting slab that sits above a scattering of such boulders which form a natural maze-like playground that I explore, walking through the spiked fronds of last summer's bracken, blunted and rotting now. Slurring's name derives from ancient dialect for 'sliding', acquired over years of children riding down the rock, the tacket soles of their clogs gliding like blades across ice. The best of the young slurrers might even have produced a flash of sparks.

I stop and touch Slurring Rock's smooth slope and hear the summer laughter of times gone; giggling ghost voices, each an untold life story echoing down through the layered eras of the wooded valley. Time here is measured by depth of stone, height of sky. Scuff marks.

The dog leads me out of the trees and across open fields to the tiny hilltop hamlet of Shackleton. Perched 1,000 feet above sea level, its name is believed to derive from *Shackletonstall*, first recorded in 1219 and meaning 'a farm on a narrow tongue of land' belonging to the Shackleton family – *tonstall* is an old word for an enclosure for cattle. A medieval vaccary – a clearing in the forest where the lord of the manor would breed and graze cattle – existed here. The walled remains of other vaccaries from nearly a thousand years ago can still be found in the region.

There are no trees up here now though, just cloying mist and ponderous sheep, and a cluster of cottages flanked by derelict stone barns and disused farm outbuildings.

I FIX CLIFF on his lead and he pulls me through the mud like an ox with a plough across the same fields that feature in the Ted Hughes poem 'The Horses', from his first published collection *The Hawk in the Rain*.

Here in the 'evil air, a frost making stillness', in that space between woodland streams and night sky, a seven-year-old Hughes comes upon ten horses at dawn, as motionless as 'grey silent fragments / of a grey silent world'. Only when the curlews call and the sun erupts do these creatures come into being, 'steaming and glistening under the flow of light'.

This solitary moment stayed with the poet down the years. It was inspired by a night's camping in 1937 or 1938 in a quarry in lower Crimsworth Dean with his brother Gerald. Rising early, Hughes had scrambled up out of the trees and into the field beyond Shackleton, and here he saw the horses that would feature twenty years later in the book that brought him to the attention of the world.

It was this night – or certainly one similar, in the same location around the same time – that proved to be the making of Hughes as a writer. As he explained in a letter to his old school friend in Mytholmroyd, Donald Crossley, the quarry is where 'I had the dream that later turned into all my writing – a sacred space for me.'

I cross the fields along an ancient packhorse route that leads towards Lumb Falls and the long hard miles past that across the moors to Haworth. Here I pass a semi-derelict, roofless farmhouse known as Abel Cote Farm, beside which is parked an inhabited and well-maintained static caravan – there is a vase of flowers in the window – with a breathtaking view, and then continue towards two stone monuments approximately the height of a man standing beside the old trail.

Below me is Outwood Farm, another once-derelict farmhouse. Seven or eight years ago, while pressing my face to the dusty glass windows of this fled place, I saw inside the remnants of lives once lived: gaudy 1960s wallpaper peeling off in strips, a broken chair with busted springs dangling, an old piano, warped from the damp climate and sagging beneath the burden of time's passing. I saw also a single curtain too, sun-perished, washed out and worn through. (This briefly glimpsed insight with its linger-ing presence of propriety, so evocative and sad and unknowable, inspired the writing of one of my novels.)

The building has been bought and renovated now, and is alive again, so instead I loop back on myself and take a track down into the trees towards the quarry in which Hughes camped eighty summers ago, and that he forever called his 'sacred place'.

Here I find a hollowed-out excavation about 100 feet across, right next to the track that leads down to the National Trust office. The location was recommended as a perfect camping ground to the young Ted by his Uncle Walter, who regularly camped there with his own brother Tom before the First World War. The quarry was used as a stone dump and for storing National Trust equipment. It was remembered by Hughes as a wild paradise.

Eight species of bat have been identified as living in the sur-rounding trees, including pipistrelle, whiskered, Natterer's and noctule, while the decaying wood of fallen or felled trees pro-vides an ecosystem for all manner of invertebrates such as moths, a variety of beetles and the Northern Hairy Wood ants, famed for their hillock nests that begin two feet underground and can rise to six feet in height, each labyrinthine mini-metropolis hosting half a million inhabitants. Studies have found 400 such colonies in and around Hardcastle Crags and it is at this time of year, early winter, that the ants emerge from hibernation to begin repairs on their nests, collective thought driving their industrious impulses.

But the quarry is empty as I scramble the steep declivity above it; a decade of exploring The Rock seems to have given me a goat-like ability to keep my footing on such slopes.

I am trying to locate an obscure stone that was the subject of a short ghost story that Hughes wrote on commission from his friend Michael Morpurgo for a 1994 anthology *Ghostly Haunts*, published to celebrate the National Trust's centenary. The story also appeared in the prose collection *Difficulties of a Bridegroom*, chosen by Hughes as 'the natural overture to the sequence', whose stories explore shape-shifting, ghosts, dream states, animalistic impulses and hallucinated half-worlds where reality and fantasy become interchangeable.

Written nearly sixty years after the event, 'The Deadfall' reaches back once again to that same – or similar, repeated – night's camping in the quarry with Gerald in the brothers' two-man Bukta Wanderlust tent that also inspired 'The Horses'.

As he relates in the story (as well as in numerous letters, poems and interviews across his career), it was here that Hughes had a dream, a nocturnal epiphany, that he credits with turning a curious boy into a man with the eye and soul of a poet.

Up on the slope, in a thin strip of a copse between the drystone-walled open fields and a steep drop to the quarry below, he and Gerald found a deadfall, a primitive natural trap in which a large stone is propped up using branches and then baited – in this instance most likely with a dead pigeon – in such a way that, as with a mousetrap, when triggered, drops to crush its prey. Deadfalls were first used by Native Americans, who taught arriving Europeans this simple method that requires only stone, wood and cunning.

In this unspoiled paradise tucked away from the eyes of any residences, and where the air was free from the blackening tresses of smoke streaming from the chimneys of Mytholmroyd and Hebden Bridge, the brothers found a fox, crushed beneath the might of the slab. To the seven-year-old Hughes death had entered the Garden of Eden.

Today the fox is no longer the portent of wildness it perhaps was. In fact, it represents the opposite: the tenacious metropolitan *Vulpes vulpes*' behavioural patterns have been recalibrated to ensure survival in our great sprawling concrete, asphalt and tarmac conurbations. They are behaving not as they should but as they *must*. Their continued survival depends upon co-dependence. In London I found myself living side by side with a fearless family of mean-eyed foxes who routinely climbed onto the corrugate roof of the shabby lean-to that joined our rented house. They could not be roused when sleeping on our picnic table. They were not wild. They were accepted tenants.

In Yorkshire I might see a fox every few months, and only ever as a fleeting carmine-coloured flash through the undergrowth, an arrow fired from the heart of England's history, or tenaciously scaling the near-vertical lower slopes of The Rock.

Mainly I smell the strong, dark musk in its aftermath, pungent, like burnt sesame oil. They are rarely seen.

Before carrying the stricken animal down to the quarry for burial, Gerald offered the flattened fox's bright tail to Ted, who declined, though later claimed to have found a small ivory fox, an effigy, in the soil that same day. For someone who would place great emphasis on signs, totems, shamanism and occultist interpretations, the effect was profound.

That night beneath canvas, the fresh memory of the fox stalked his sleep. As Gerald remembered in his memoir *Ted and I*, it was 'a vivid dream about an old lady and a fox cub that had been orphaned by the trap'. Real events switched to a fictional rendering decades later in 'The Deadfall', where fact and fantasy merge to create a memory-map whose only consistency is the certainty of the landscape. In the introduction to his prose collection Hughes himself admits to 'a few adjustments' between what happened and his story.

In simple language clearly aimed at young readers, Hughes recounts following the voice of an old lady from his tent up to the trap where a fox is snagged by its hind leg and tail. The suggestion is that she wants him to save it and has not summoned Gerald who, armed on the camping trip with a treasured American rifle with which the brothers sometimes shot rats, would most likely kill the creature. The fictional Ted then uses all his strength to lift the slab just enough to free it, fearful and hissing.

He returns in the morning with Gerald to find a big fox trapped again, the bait in its mouth. This time it is dead. It is then that he unearths the inch-and-a-half-long effigy, and the brothers realise that the old lady was the ghost of the dead fox.

His biographer, Jonathan Bate, writes that 'the dream of the freed fox and the ivory figure that symbolically transformed his lead animal toys into tokens of art came together as his retrospective narrative of creative beginning', though when asked, neither Gerald or their sister Olwyn could actually remember the ivory fox.

Readers and scholars of Hughes will be aware that his poem 'The Thought-Fox', through which the animal stalks the subconscious of a lone poet at night, and 'with a sudden sharp hot stink of fox / It enters the dark hole of my head', is now recognised as one of his most powerful and definitive works.

As I scramble to find the stone I stop periodically to consult a small chapbook called *The Ted Hughes Trail in Crimsworth Dean*, published by the Elmet Trust in 2008 and borrowed from the local library, where someone has had the good sense to laminate it against Hughesian weathering. The book is a guide based upon research done by Hughes's friend the late Donald Crossley, whose literary detective work in gleaning information and pinpointing locations from key poems in the area has been vital in joining the dots between work and landscape. A photograph of the deadfall stone taken by Crossley in this thin book was sent to Australia and verified by Gerald seventy years after the event and is the only published picture of it that I have been able to locate. The chances of finding a flat, graphite-grey slab in a valley of flat, graphite-grey slabs is unlikely.

Instead I stumble across the domain of a badger. First I find a familiar dug hole in which there sits a swirl of dull, tar-like faecal matter, then, a few feet further along, a rotten trunk, partly shredded, splinters and spelks scratched and cast aside, and claw marks in the soil. I can also detect the scent of life close by, as a hermetic matted hump sleeps off a night's adventure deep in its cool, dark chamber, the thump of my steps muted by wet, wintered soil.

And then I see it, set close to a tree, a stone so rectangular as to be almost the work of a mason's hammer and chisel. Its surface is mottled green and dusted with dead grass and leaves. I consult Donald Crossley's photograph and find the correct angle so that I can line up image against reality, and though the stone has become submerged in the decade or so since the picture was taken, and may not have been visited by another human in the interim, it is unmistakably *it*. I feel unduly exhilarated.

I sit down on the stone and share a cheese sandwich and bag of crisps with Cliff, our satisfied mastication the only sound, then I stand and, with a short stick, begin to scrape away the mud that has submerged it to a depth of six inches or so.

As I dig, my fingerless gloves become wet and soil clogs my chewed fingernails, staining them black, but with a little encouragement the dog digs too. Bred for flushing out rats and rabbits, he is far more efficient than I am. A minute or two's frantic scraping and I have cleared a channel around the deadfall stone, and with a foot placed either side of it and my fingers curled around its lip, back straight, I heave at it.

Nothing happens.

I take a breath, feel my back and biceps take the strain and then try again. It gives a little. This time I jimmy it and it rises from the dirt, an inch and then two inches. Here I can hold it for no more than a few seconds before placing it down.

Something is compelling me to look under the rock. What I am expecting to find beneath it I am not sure – the smashed bones of a fox perhaps? Or the essence of poetry itself?

I lift it again and try to push a small rock beneath to prop it up, but I need an extra limb to do so. Even just moving my feet means I can't sustain the weight of the stone that has sat for centuries here in this strip of trees high in the dean of mist and ghostly horses, shamanic fox dreams and badgers tucked away in their setts, as Hughes wrote, 'like a loaf in the oven'. All I can do is hold it there, frozen in the moment as mortal muscle does battle with eternal rock, and rock wins, and another myth lies dormant.

I slowly place the stone back into place and walk on, whistling an improvised meandering melody for a brooding winter's morning.

And then comes the rain.

FIELD NOTES II

Autumn Coming

The first tree to turn
is a flinted spark in
the tinder of the valley,

a burst of flame in the
outer dark; a lit wick
in the tallow to tarry.

Ribston Pippins

Gaudy baubles hang from the Calcarian frame;
conceived in spring, made plump by summer,
they are ripe for plucking now from this rusty ladder.

The wasps have been at them, nibbling bullet holes
already browning with rot. The worms have burrowed,
and woven webs dust the lustre as I reach and twist

and pull, and for every apple picked a second one
thunks to the nettle patch below, and deep in the
orchard earth a sleeping rabbit stirs to the vibration.

Favoured Swimming Spots

Black Moss Pot. Janet's Foss.
Grisedale Beck.
A lake in Kent.

A rockpool by Watendlath.
Snow melt over Marsden.
Sparth.

Caribbean. Aegean.
Mediterranean.
North.

An oxbow near Manesty.
Gaddings Dam. Lumb Falls.
Keld.

Storm Walk

Teeth jammed with blackberry seeds
we walk the corridor of flagging weeds
as September clouds
spill their ancient suitcases
trailing knots of dirty sheets.

On Lighting the First Fire

Autumn burns
the sky
the woods
the valley

death is everywhere

but beneath
its golden cloak
the seeds of
a summer's

dreaming still sing.

Towards Robin Hood Rocks
on a Damp Day in Mid-October

Mist wisps like the spun trails of kiting spiders
crown the bluebell woods, though down in the
dark mattress the bluebells are long gone, tilting
to time's strident march. A measured mourning.

Raining Acorns

A musket twig snapped
startles three deer
into my path.

The dog detects their presence
but sees nothing
as the forest

folds them into
its burning church
and it begins to rain acorns.

The Bat

Crawling and clinging
and clinging

it's wet snub-nosed snout
upturned to European darkness.

Ten thousand tiny histories
in each damp barb,

wings as lanterns to carry
a mastodon moon.

Bones folded in black leather
and arched angles.

Unruffled by the turn of events.
Thinking only of infinite blood.

A Late-October Monday Morning, the Week Before the Clocks Go Back

The
sky
is an
algorithm,

a series of
problems
that are solved
by rain.

Shoot Day

A limb of salmon motors
through impossible shallows
with muscular determination,
its dorsal fin cutting a V-shape
through gelid autumn waters
as the beaters arrive on the
hillside above to stamp the
startled grouse gunwards.
Here across the river their
flags sound like rocks rattled
in the stream bed, or guns
cocked, or cold death's biding.

Salmon Spawn

The last salmon leaps the ladder;
it has fought the flow
for centuries.

Patiently, it has waited until there
are no more poems left
to write.

A silver suspension, trapped by time,
thin belly-tickled by bed weed into
a trance

and back-ended by the song of the tide
until the final sun of autumn bridges
the run,

it explodes through the beats,
one last Olympic dash for glory, timed
to perfection.

Plaque above Lumb Falls in Crimsworth Dean, marking the location of the 'Six Young Men' photograph that inspired the Ted Hughes poem of the same name.

Horses grazing at a farm above Robin Hood Rocks, near Cragg Vale. Stoodley Pike is visible on the horizon.

View of Mytholmroyd from the middle of Scout Rock woods. Banksfield
Estate, built on the hill on which a young Ted Hughes played, and Calder High,
one of the first comprehensive schools in the country, are visible.

Left: Foreboding trees in Crow Nest Woods. Half of Calderdale's woods are
considered ancient (in existence since 1600 or earlier).
Right: A beast surveying his kingdom.

PART III

Water

Chapter Eight

In early November it begins to rain and it doesn't stop. Occasionally it eases or abates, or sometimes shifts in tone or mood to evince a false sense of optimism, before returning with renewed vigour.

There is more rain than there are adjectives to possibly describe it.

Rain becomes the daily reality, a transaction between sky and land over which we have no influence. Nature rears up to pull us out of our internalised digital worlds and back into that of the elemental.

Furious falls the rain like a snappy tantrum, a fit thrown by the whims of time.

It is the force, the life source.

I watch it from my window, inching along the valley, a hodden-grey scrim drawn close. At other times it falls in tall columns like the old stone chimneys that rise, periscope-like, up above the trees, or it spits sideways, wet flecks flying like sparks from a farrier's furnace. I am out in it every day, exploring, exhausting the dog and observing the inflections, living in a permanent state of dampness.

It drills, it spears, it skewers. Niggles.

It touches, it caresses, it kisses.

Hisses.

The rain is hostile. Sometimes it is so ferocious it becomes comical – 'film-set rain', we call it – so insistent and pervasive as to be febrile. Sometimes it speaks, the sound of the rain becoming a shopping list: 'stamps wax pomegranate' it whispers in a dripping ear.

The showers sluice away the top layer of autumnal leaf loam of The Rock's floor, carving new ways through the routes of least resistance.

Winter groans on as flat as a school assembly Lord's Prayer and it feels as if it is raining in my mind, my subconscious soaked, and even in dreams I see deluges of cocoa-coloured water.

And the River Calder rises.

A LOCAL DOG goes missing. It is a tan-brown terrier cross, female, about the same age as Cliff, spooked by the fireworks that whip-crack down the stone barrel of the valley without warning for weeks on end, a little earlier each year, the luminous paroxysms reflected in the eyes of trembling fox cubs born last spring, and sending the deer of The Rock into bounding frenzies over crag and wire in search of escape.

The squirrels scarper to the canopy, and another distant unidentifiable animal screams a fearful alarm.

But even as they run or burrow, or scatter from their crag-edge eyries, the wild creatures still find themselves pursued by booms and whistles and blood-red flashes, the sound of these cheap Chinese pyrotechnics bouncing off The Rock below, the gritstone reflecting rather than absorbing, and echoing back a mindless mortar attack on the nerve centres of all animals.

The missing dog sparks a Facebook campaign, and I coax Cliff from his cellar dwelling to spend three days wandering Scout Rock Woods as I shout '*Pickle!*' in an attempt to draw out a dog whose picture I have only seen online, yet feel somehow compelled to help find, as I routinely follow the progress of the scores of similarly sentimental animal lovers. I know no one else will think to search these woods. I doubt anyone else would dare.

For several days the search becomes an all-consuming, ever-shifting narrative whose conclusion I must know. After several days of terrible rain Pickle is found, shaken and half starved, but otherwise well. One sighting suggests we came within 100 yards of each other, my calls and whistles perhaps muted by the roar of the rain, or the missing dog merely looking on from a warm corner as I stumble and slip past it through the endless fucking mud.

AND STILL THE rain falls. It puddles and pools. Sits.

New streams emerge and stay for weeks.

The sky becomes a long and boring story without an ending. It just goes on and on, dispersing its wares, filling every nook and fissure, every trench and gulch, every divot, cleft and hollow.

It scours old rock and finds whorls there – grainy geological fingerprints free of the gelatinous algae that coats everything during the shorter days. It runs beneath our street, as ancient subterranean waterways are flooded back to life, and the old stone-lined springs and troughs where inhabitants drew their supply, and at which thirsty, steaming horses once lapped, are first refreshed and then overflow.

The woods below The Rock become a dank and desolate church of persistent dripping and leafless branches stripped bare, and the washed-away mud banks send me slipping arse-about-tit with increased regularity, thudding onto my shoulder one day, landing on my wrist the next.

Reanimated by the rain, the old town tip further reveals another trove of grubby treasures, as more junked pieces of the past poke through, including a very large moss-covered bone, one scorched-looking end the size of my fist. Species unknown.

Feeling like a meddling academic protagonist in a M. R. James ghost story, I carefully prise the jaundice-coloured bone from the soil and clean it with some dead leaves, then place it next to a glove for scale – it is twice the length of the glove and as wide as my wrist.

Another day during the same unbroken downpour I come across an old stone marker inscribed 'PUBLIC FOOTPATH', with arrows pointing in either direction. The footpath has not been public for a long time, and season upon season of gorse and bramble and soil and leaves have grown over it, rotting down to the humus that is spread thick over the gritstone foundation. The rain has revealed this mid-twentieth-century marker to me, raising it up, another relic of The Rock's unending story told piecemeal through hints, teases and suggestions.

The rain grows oppressive and the valley shrinks to the narrowness of a birth canal. The sun is a foreign country, a nostalgic memory. The hills sigh. Everything folds in on itself like a sleeping dog.

And I find I am exhausted from too many writing projects, the worry of trying to exist on a four-figure annual income, never quite knowing what I will earn from week to week, and continually adjusting my lifestyle and diet accordingly. My muscles ache. My marrow feels damp.

The daily explorations of The Rock provide a distraction: 'I cannot stay in my chamber for a single day without acquiring some rust,' wrote America's hermetic crown prince of woodland wandering, Henry David Thoreau in his 1862 essay 'Walking'. Knowing that I rarely feel worse at the end of a perambulation, I keep trudging the undergrowth. 'Roads are made for horses and men of business,' Thoreau also noted. 'I do not travel in them much because I am not in a hurry.'

Salvation from valley fever comes by way of a timely opportunity: a writing residency on Hadrian's Wall in Northumberland. Days later I'm driving through the worst storms in years before finding myself stuck in mud, in a raging wood where yards before me I see a tree being torn from the soil with an almighty splintering sound. I see snapped fences and a rising river. Back roads disappearing. Abandoning my car, I complete the final stage of my journey by foot in total darkness and awake the next morning to acre upon acre of flooded fields shimmering in the metallic morning sun. From the back door I can make out in the far distance the line of the ancient Whin Sill banks, a natural tabular layer created by flows of lava 300 million years ago upon which Hadrian's Wall was built.

My stay continues in a similar fashion: short, drenched days exploring Hadrian's Wall, and long nights by the fire. I take a lot of field notes, drink a lot of Yespresso. I talk to no one but the wind and the ghosts of shivering, homesick Romans.

THE SHORTEST DAY is approaching, and when the flood levels drop I leave these wild lands of dark, brooding magic and drive south again.

It rains for three hours all the way back, so that by the time I reach the valley the River Calder is rising, and the flood sirens wailing. I park and watch through my windscreen as water laps at the town-centre car park, then breaches a wall and rushes in thin and gruel-grey flurries around dirty tyres and door-steps. There is similar surface flooding in the villages and towns along the valley. Walsden and Brighouse. Cornholme and Callis. Todmorden, Mytholmroyd and Sowerby Bridge.

I go straight to the Trades Club in Hebden Bridge, where I have tickets to see a raucous group of musical degenerates from my old neighbourhood in Peckham called Fat White Family.

Though trains are cancelled and roads blocked, and only half the sold-out crowd have made it through the rain, what the audience lacks in density they make up for in intoxicated, northern European, winter-solstice, Viking-like behaviour. As the band launch into their single 'Is It Raining In Your Mouth?' drinks are first spilled and then slung stagewards, and garments and inhibitions discarded. The shirtless singer is wearing pâté on his face, and a loaf of bread as a bracelet, his concave chest scrawled with lipstick. He is moving incredibly slowly, as if his motor neurone system has malfunctioned.

Beneath blood-red lights the music feels like an end-times celebration; heavy and apocalyptic, but hedonistic and celebratory too, as if band and crowd are locked in a collective attempt to turn back the flood waters. A winter ritual. A pagan spell. A fight breaks out in front of the stage. There are fists and further glasses flying, and later there will broken jaws and police statements, but for now the band plays on, as outside the rain falls harder and heavier across the pagan Pennine plains.

I awake half deaf and exhausted, in the shadow of The Rock.

My throat is dry and scratchy, my limbs aching.

Illness is on me and it is still raining.

At my local doctor's I have the stitches removed from a deep finger wound caused by an encounter with a sharp knife and a stale Bakewell tart and, seeing that they are offering flu jabs, request one.

'Have you had cold or flu symptoms recently?' he asks.

I shake my head.

'Not really,' I lie.

That night I enter a deep fever realm. One of rain and rock once again. A world of infinite stone and endless water. Soaked in sweat, I see a weak sun and shadows from the stone refract in the water, bend to the meniscus of the stagnant murk and then dissipate into the darkness down there, where only blind and spineless eyeball-white creatures older than anything that has ever slithered or swum hang like apparitions suspended in the cold, mute nothingness.

Where there is no rock there is water in these ancient imagined lands of my deep subconscious, and where there is no water there is rock, and in the rock are troughs of dreck and pools of mulch.

A breeze is brought into being around the extremities of stone stripped of its outer contours, and behind the shrieking whistle of the wilful wind I hear the malignant seep and ooze of water as it turns into a soupy trickle, then a thousand trickles, each drilling at the rock and the rock ceding to it, tired, slowly submitting to its insistence. Gravity the only truth.

I sleep beside Della curled and shivering, and I awake drowning in the deep, drenched and feverish, soaked through. I stand and stagger around the room, then shed my bed clothes and pull on a dressing gown and walk myself out of the reverie and up the stairs into the attic office and collapse onto the settee there, a coarse blanket pulled over me, and the moon high above The Rock, which is framed by the rectangular skylight above. A porthole promising eternity.

My bones ache like ice water. My head is a stone bowl for grinding and my blood alluvial loess dispersing on an undercurrent. The moon washes over me in tidal light. My eyes are magnets and the night has a timbre. My skeleton is a rusted scaffold over which the fabric of the fever is stretched.

The flu jab on top of the existing flu has sent me into a heightened state of pyrexia, an intense delirium where illness and medicine do battle in the no man's land of my deep subconscious.

The hallucination summons more blind and spineless creatures from the deep pool of memory. Millions of years pass in the blink of an itching eye. They are in the room now, but without the water to hold them they are like wet, deflated balloons, membranes seeking form, skin in search of a body.

And then I am pulled under again as the moon retracts to the faintest faraway dot above me, the black water and stone shadows closing in and over, and the drum of my heart pounds.

I flinch and start through a half-sleep, the moon waxing and waning, the white creatures slithering, the nightmare of stone and water seemingly unending until meek December light draws the silhouette of The Rock closer, its peak a serrated line like that on the monitor of a life-support machine, and I welcome the white, mizzled morning and a snatch of birdsong.

The fever breaks.

THE FLU LINGERS, leaving me spent for days, my head feeling like a gnawed orange, my skin thin.

It lifts, finally, but leaves behind a reminder in the form of a hacking chest infection that feels like a wet, weighted web strung in my lungs. When I cough I sound like a crashed car.

I stay indoors, and watch the full shadows of The Rock stretch and then retract across the valley, never quite retreating enough to allow us any sunlight.

And still it rains. In the valley, in my mind and in my mouth.

Christmas comes and the sky offers the gift of respite, gratefully received as we spend the day with family on the fringes of Manchester.

But the rain begins again as we sit slumped in a turkey-induced torpor, and is falling at full throttle as the M62 rises through Saddleworth Moor on our return journey.

The wind wallops in and the hardest rain yet pelts with a ferocity not felt for years.

Della's father is a North Yorkshire cow man. He has spent the best part of seven decades in meadows and milking parlours. He knows weather. He understands rain; he reads it like a favourite book. From the back seat he offers a running commentary.

'Well, have you ever?' he says.

'I've seen nowt like it,' he answers himself.

The road climbs looping into the rage of Christmas Night, and all of the West Riding is a carwash. It is a storm even worse than the one in Northumberland, a squall in the darkness of the moor, where there are no street lights or those of other cars, just the blinking line of the cat's eyes that bejewel the road like fallen stars navigating a lost sailor. (Cat's eyes were invented just five miles away by one Percy Shaw in the Halifax suburb of Boothtown in 1933. One of fourteen children, Shaw spent his whole life in the town and, even after the success of his invention, lived a Spartan existence. According to *Halifax Today*, he was 'none too keen on places far away – London was bad enough', and once told TV globetrotting interrogator Alan Whicker that the capital was 'all rush, rush, rush and tip, tip, tip, very boring'.)

At Blackstone Edge the water blows in sideways off the reservoir in shattering sheets that slap the car with violence.

'Would you believe it,' says Della's Dad again from the back seat. '*Would you believe it.*'

I nudge my way through the screens of rain, and the wail, and the December dark.

We are at the highest point for miles, the entry into Calderdale across the moors and The Rock, and all that sits beneath it, and we follow the road downwards, a ghost-train ride through the wind and rain.

Blackstone Edge was a line of communication during earlier times. A neatly constructed causeway in relatively pristine condition still crosses the moor today, and though originally believed to be Roman in origin, it was recently identified as another packhorse trail laid around 1735.

Nearby is the Aiggin Stone, a seven-foot-tall medieval boundary marker somewhere out there in the storm, symbolically keeping Lancashire from invading Yorkshire – or vice versa. Its curious name is derived from either *aiguille* (French for 'needle'), *agger* (a Latin word for 'a pile, heap or mound') or *aggerere* ('that which is gathered to form an elevation above a surface'). Or maybe it's a bastardisation of the word 'edge', or the slightly more romantical *aigle*, as in eagle. Like so many landmarks around this valley, where kingdom is piled upon kingdom, no one can ever really know.

In his epic topographical poem *Poly-Olbion*, published in two parts in 1612 and 1622, the poet Michael Drayton constructed thirty songs of several hundred lines each that collectively attempted to map the whole of England in hexameter couplets. It was an extraordinarily ambitious project, and his

Yorkshire section covered by far the greatest land mass of the country as it valiantly surveyed the three Ridings by way of their rivers and the muse who travels them.

It was here, at this storm-wracked high point on the moors above Cragg Vale and Mytholmroyd, where water percolates in the soil before forging a way through the whole of Yorkshire, that the work begins:

> The Muse from *Blackstoneedge*, no whit dismay'd at all,
> With sights of the large Shire, on which she was to fall
> (Whose Forests, Hills, and Floods, then long for her arrive,
> From *Lancashire*, that look'd her beauties to contrive.)

As far back as the early seventeenth century Drayton identified this strange land as being primarily ruled by rain, the significant factor in shaping the topography and mood to far beyond:

> And that which doth this Shire before the rest prefer
> Is of so many Floods, and great, that rise from her.

On a night like this, such words appear to echo up through the ages, though for now I can only hear Della's father remarking on the storm that buffets my little car as Cliff cowers beneath the bags of Christmas containing presents and tubs of leftover food.

'Look at that rain. 'Orrible, it is. *'Orrible.*'

A century later, Daniel Defoe, arguably the first English
novelist, travelled this very road, and documented it in great
detail in his non-fiction work *A Tour Thro' the Whole Island of
Great Britain*, published in three volumes between 1724 and 1727.

Defoe's account is one of the earliest and most comprehensive of this area. In descriptions written after a perilous
journey through changing sub-zero weather, he captures a feel
for the place that stands true today. Here, during the climb up
from Rochdale, crossing the border line from Lancashire to
the West Riding, he experienced what we now identify as the
rare phenomenon of thundersnow: 'It is not easy to express the
consternation we were in when we came up near the top of the
mountain; the wind blew exceeding hard, and blew the snow
so directly in our faces, and that so thick, that it was impossible
to keep our eyes open to see our way . . . In the middle of this
difficulty, and as we began to call to one another to turn back
again, not knowing what dangers might still be before us, came
a surprizing clap of thunder, the first that ever I heard in a storm
of snow, or, I believe, ever shall.'

Uncertain as to what might lie ahead due to poor visibility
and the potential for perilous falls over 'frightful precipices',
and their horses spooked, Defoe's party of three explorers and
their two servants consider turning back, but after some thought
decide to press on.

They enter a hollow carved by the running waters of Turvin
Clough, which in turn becomes Cragg Brook, which feeds into

the Calder six or so winding miles away down to Mytholmroyd at the 'meeting of the two waters' that gives the place its name: 'The main hill which we came down from, which is properly called Blackstone Edge, or, by the country people, the Edge, without any sirname or addition, ran along due north, crossing and shutting up those hollow gulls and vallies between, which were certainly originally formed by the rain and snow water running into them, and forcing its way down, washing the earth gradually along with it, till, by length of time, it wore down the surface to such a depth.'

Defoe continues, ominously:

'We found a few poor houses, but saw no people, no not one; till we call'd at a door, to get directions of our way, and then we found, that though there was no body to be seen without doors, they were very full of people within.'

Alfred Wainwright liked it up on Blackstone Edge, and wrote of it favourably in his 1985 book *Wainwright on the Pennine Way*: 'Here matters change for the better,' he said of this early section of the 267-mile route in different weather to that experienced by Defoe. 'Left behind now are the dark peat bog moorlands, the marshes and the groughs that have so hindered progress thus far . . . life comes good again on Blackstone Edge.'

Wainwright's reflections were drawn after walking a relatively flat section of the Pennine Way on a day in which he bears witness to 'green returning to add brightness to the scene', allowing extensive views in all directions. His enthusiasm doesn't last long, however. Only a few steady miles later he drops down into the Calder Valley below Stoodley Pike, and is plunged back into the modern world, his eyes 'assailed by industrial blight immediately ahead: a stagnant canal, a dirty river, a very busy road . . . the nose is assailed, too, the point of entry being between a pig farm and sewage works. Clearly this is no place to linger.'

IT CERTAINLY ISN'T.

Driving on into the lashing night, it becomes apparent that rain is impervious to changing politics and technology, religion and economics. It has no opinion on terrorism, the European Union or the latest passing cult-of-personality who may have clawed themselves into a position of power.

Whatever is happening, the rain comes Yorkshiring down and there is nothing but one dog, two beams of light, three people and four rubber tyres eating up the road.

'Heck, there'll be hell to pay tomorrow if this doesn't let up,' says Della's father.

We drop from The Edge into Cragg Vale down the five or so miles of continuous descent. Compared to the Alpine roads of France it is not a steep incline – the average gradient is 3 per cent – but it is what the many weekend cyclists who use it as part of a circular route call a classic long drag.

In 2014 Cragg Road featured as a key stretch on the Grand Départ, the opening weekend of the Tour de France that, since the 1950s, has often launched in different countries. For two days the peloton zipped through the dales and valleys, a blur of horns and klaxons beneath a rare unbroken burst of sunshine. And now the road becomes a conduit for hundreds of square miles of moorland water, as ghylls and streams and becks race to find the path of least resistance.

To either side, drystone walls spurt jets of water, and through the wash of rain I see the occasional cottage window framed by fairy lights.

As in so many of the hidden little nooks that run off the Calder Valley, income in Cragg Vale once came almost entirely from weaving, first by hand-loom and then in the larger mills. A half-century before the great cathedral-like mills devoted to toil and industry arrived, Daniel Defoe describes seeing scattered houses, each strategically built next to a rill of running water.

Outside of each dwelling Defoe reports seeing a tenter – a trellis on which lengths of cloths 'or kersie or shalloon' were hung to be dried or treated, and upon which the sun shone: 'and, as I may say, shining (the white reflecting its rays) to us, I thought it was the most agreeable sight that I ever saw, for the hills, as I say, rising and falling so thick, and the vallies opening sometimes one way, sometimes another, so that sometimes we could see two or three miles this way, sometimes as far another.'

Though it is unnamed, Defoe could be describing the wooded
vale leading down through Cragg Vale to Mytholmroyd, where
he finds an industrious community holed up like hibernating
creatures, everyone working the looms and, here and there,
an almshouse for those 'decrepid, and past labour', adding: 'it
is observable, that the people here, however laborious, generally live to a great age, a certain testimony to the goodness
and wholesomeness of the country, which is, without doubt, as
healthy as any part of England'.

The healthy, wholesome life that Defoe perceived would
not last. The hand-loom around which whole families would
work and live, their eyesight troubled by the poor light,
joints slowly succumbing to arthritis, was replaced in the late
eighteenth century by the great spinning mills powered by
waterwheels and steam drawn from the streams. Cragg Vale in
particular earned a dubious reputation for housing those mills
notorious for the very worst child labour in the country, and
whose exploitative owners worked pre-pubescent children in
an atmosphere of chaos and noise where many lost digits or
limbs to machinery, or simply dropped dead from exhaustion.
All to meet a demand for calico cloth across the burgeoning
British Empire.

It was here too above Cragg Vale that I once witnessed the
aftermath of a miniature tornado that twisted its way down the
tight gulley and through the foundations of these fallen dark
satanic mills. It was at the end of a calendar year in which the

old village of Cragg Vale had also endured moor fires, deep snowfall and the discovery of a missing woman, murdered by her partner, a fell runner and stonemason, and found in a shallow grave amongst the thick grass and snowmelt quag.

And water is all around us now as thousands of new rills and freshets form. It ejaculates with unrestrained ferocity from waterways that have lain dry and dormant for decades, flipping dense metal drain covers like coins to fountain upwards from drains dug by men who had never known bananas or electricity or flight.

Chapter Nine

A siren drills deep into my dream. It is not that of the emergency services or a car alarm, but the same familiar foreboding moan of an air-raid siren rising to a protracted wail that echoes down the valley, chilling, portentous, fearful.

It heralds only one thing: floods.

The rain is still rattling down and it is early, 7 a.m., on a bank holiday historically devoted to sloth and indulgence, Boxing Day.

Della prods me.

'It sounds really bad out there.'

(I respond the same way as I did early on the morning of 11 September 2001 when I was woken in a hotel room on Sunset Boulevard by a call from a friend telling me to turn the TV on *right now*: I roll over and go back to sleep. I've just never been a morning person.)

I hear Della rise and look out of the window.

'Oh my God.'

'We'll be fine,' I say into the pillow. 'It didn't get us last time.'

'Last time' was three years earlier when a sudden storm one June day sent the valley's waterways surging downhill to flood

Hebden Bridge and Mytholmroyd without warning. Roads became rivers and the Calder swelled to meet the canal, and two waterways became a spontaneous lake.

I had watched from the window as two shirtless boys swam whooping across the park which only that morning had held little but an inch-deep murky puddle. Later, down on the flood-plain fields at Brearley, I kicked my way through the ballast and trash dumped by the river: bottles with their necks twisted, panels from an old tree house, discarded porn mags wadded into a washed-out brick of flesh tones, a milk crate speared by an alder branch, a child's ball still spinning in a miniature whirlpool, a bloated sheep folded around the bridge's stony buttress.

It was the worst flooding in thirty years and over 500 homes and businesses were badly damaged. Three weeks later a month's worth of rain fell again in the space of three hours, and when the waters subsided once more 500 tonnes of shale, gravel and gritstone rubble were strewn around Hebden Bridge alone.

So we have seen this before, and the sirens have been deployed as a warning shot on several occasions since, only for the rising river to quickly drop down to its usual slow-shifting, shallow flow, and in the wake of the siren's wail there is nothing but Hiroshima silence, and relief.

So balls to the river, I think, and try to sleep as the rain drums like a regiment marching out onto a burning beach. I drift off.

'I think you really need to come and see this.'

Della is back and soaked to the skin, the dripping dog panting beside her. I climb out of bed and go to the window. Below me Mytholmroyd is submerged again. The entire valley bottom is a river, perhaps fifty times wider than usual. The park resembles a lake of chocolate, but contaminated like a Willy Wonka nightmare. The seven-foot-high knoll from which I throw sticks for the dog is nowhere to be seen. The trees on top of it hold metal beer barrels in their branches, a further twelve feet up.

And bobbing pontoon-like on the surface of all that water are more barrels and planks torn from pallets, and several litter bins spilling out their refuse of cans and sweet wrappers and dozens of bags of dog shit, and there are footballs and car tyres and old wooden beams and a picnic table, and plastic bottles and recycling crates, road signs, uprooted saplings, empty coal sacks, traffic cones, plant pots and drainpipes and deckchairs, logs and dustbins, a child's bike and an exhaust pipe. There are tree stumps and carrier bags, a workman's helmet and ribbons of plastic police tape strewn in the branches, and it is all bobbing in the rank water as the rain drives down and the water keeps rising, edging up the road closer to our house, which thankfully – mercifully – sits up a hill.

And then I notice that there are neither birds nor morning birdsong.

They have flown.

THE TEMPEST HAS a name. Storm Eva. The one that I experienced up on Hadrian's Wall was Storm Desmond.

The naming of storms and hurricanes is a curious phenomenon, as if in bestowing upon them a benign Christian name we are taming or normalising natural meteorological occurrences that have been happening across the planet for hundreds of thousands of years, and in doing so bringing them into the human realm by identifying in them the worst of our own traits – rage, destruction, violence.

The naming of storms in the UK is in fact a very recent development; the first was Abigail in November 2015, conceived by the Met Office to identify more easily specific storms in media reporting. Next came Barney, Clodagh, Desmond, and now his mean sibling, Eva. The idea was inspired by the tradition of naming hurricanes in the US, where a more complicated rotating system was introduced so that monikers could be recycled and reused, except in the cases of those hurricanes so violent that they got to keep the names for ever.

From 1979 each list of names was initially used for six years, then rotated. Each female. Before then, the deciding body of the World Meteorological Organization 'retired' hurricane names, bringing to mind images of them being presented with carriage clocks and gently eased into retirement homes for hurricanes in Palm Springs, where each morning they are wheeled into communal lounges, perpetually asking the orderlies, 'When is

Cousin Bill coming?' even though Cousin Bill died forty years
ago.

I once kept a list of retired hurricanes in a notebook, which
began:

1954: Carol, Hazel
1955: Connie, Diane, Ione, Janet
1956: no retirements

And then continued on through:

1967: Beulah
1968: Edna
1969: Camille

In time male names were introduced and then retired, often for
political considerations; the records show that Hurricane Adolph
was mothballed in 2001.

My own list continued:

1995: Luis, Marilyn, Opal, Roxanne
1996: Cesar, Fran, Hortense (*Hurricane Hortense!*)
1997: no retirements

It went all the way to '2005: Katrina', the meanest femme fatale
of the meteorological world to date, so deadly that to call future

hurricanes by the same name was deemed 'inappropriate for reasons of obvious sensitivity'.

DOWN THE ROAD in 'Royd the water is creeping over doorsteps, up to letterboxes. The river is in living rooms and kitchens and cellars and gardens and shops and pubs and the petrol station.

The water is knee-high.

Powerless, people stand around in silence.

The main road where the two waters meet is impassable and on the bridge the rushing surge that rumbles just inches below me is a roaring beast, near-rabid in its foam-mouthed fury. When it begins to breach the bridge and the whole struc-ture flexes, I hastily leave.

The water is thigh-high.

A choir of sirens and alarms overlap. I pass the sheltered housing estate and see that the power is off and each flat appears empty. The residents must have been evacuated. I know several people who live here – most are retired and we walk our dogs together, trading gossip in the park. I enjoy the stories they share, which are tinged with pitch-black fatalistic humour that is counter to the constant downpours. Sandpaper-dry, it is a dehumidifier against the cloying damp-ness that rots all things eventually, including the spirit if you let it. An armour.

Several of these women worked as seamstresses in the factories at the fag-end of Calderdale's textile trade. One friend, Maureen, has worked with animals all her life, does paintings of First World War soldiers in silhouette, and owns a vast collection of Hammer horror films. She lives here with her Bedlington terrier Alfie.

But the flats on the estate appear lifeless. The murmuring feeder stream that flows past their neatly tended communal gardens has risen to consume the communal paths and walkways between the blocks, and the swirling water is up to the downstairs door handles. It is siling it down, the rain sharp like the barbs of wire fences.

The water is waist-high.

At the bottom of Cragg Road it is jetting out of the drains in fountains taller than a man, the veins of Mytholmroyd growling with the high pressure of the underflow, and by the time I've looped round to the second bridge over the river at Caldene Avenue, cars are floating down the main road like ice floes and bashing against the old stone walls. Not all have been abandoned.

The water is chest-high. The raindrops are bullets.

And then the river breaches its banks entirely, and things get a whole lot worse.

I ONCE READ that all a river requires to achieve continuous flow is a minimum downwards trajectory of an eighth of an inch per mile. Whether the Mississippi or the Ganges, the Aire or the Calder, an eighth of an inch is all the water needs to be in perpetual motion. Without that it ceases to be a river and becomes something else – a stationary pool, a stagnant trough. A grough. It becomes a ditch, a dub, a puddle. Anything but 'a river'. By its very nature a river is an ever-moving entity from its beginnings in underground springs or peat bogs to its conclusion in the sea. Everything else – the spawning salmon, the kingfisher that is a brilliant-blue smudge across the retina, or the sentry heron that perches poised like a feathered sundial – are by-products. They are the offspring of the trajectory.

Without them the river would continue, but without that eighth of an inch it would be nothing but a still and fetid trench just waiting to return to clouds.

THE CALDER RAGES so violently now that it ceases to be a river and instead becomes an unstoppable catastrophe. That eighth of an inch is irrelevant.

The emergency services are nowhere in sight. All the surrounding roads have become rivers, the valley a sudden low-budget Venice.

At home I change my sopping clothes and a message comes through from a friend of Maureen's from outside of the valley: none of the pensioners in the sheltered housing have been evacuated, and are in fact trapped, and have been for hours.

I change clothes and return, and this time see the faces of residents pressed to the windows of upstairs flats, pale and harried. Below each dwelling is a mess of floating possessions: photo albums, kitchenware, clothing, make-up, books, electrical equipment, furniture and a lifetime's worth of keepsakes (*chattels* is the old word for such personal effects; *gewgaw* is another).

The Rock watches over it all, a lighthouse without a light.

Only when it is underwater do you become aware of how uneven seemingly flat ground is, and the December water is icy as I walk into it. It curdles over my wellies and fills them up past my knees, waist and up to my chest, which still rattles with the hacking cough. The water is perhaps 1 or 2°C.

Voices echo around the courtyards. They belong to other locals who have dashed down to help parents and grandparents.

I'm cupping my hands to Maureen's front door, the river at my sternum, when I hear a noise above. An upstairs window opens and she leans out.

'What the bloody hell are you doing here?'

'I've come to rescue you.'

'Well that's very nice of you, but I'm dry up here for now. Mind you, Alfie's dying for a tod.'

Another face appears beside Maureen. It is Alfie, her terrier. The water is shortening my breathing.

'Aren't you getting wet?'

'Yes,' I say. 'A bit.'

More booming echoes of men bounce around the estate.

'*Lads, there's someone in here.*'

'Don't worry,' says Maureen, waving me away. 'We're fine.'

I wade through the water to join the men.

'What can I do?' I ask.

'Bang on every door,' replies one. 'There's folk trapped.'

We batter doors and shoulder them open against the dirty flow of the river which runs right through their bedrooms, filling their toilets, plastering leaves to their walls and wedging branches in doorways.

We prise windows and heave floating furniture out of the way. We splash through kitchens afloat with carved turkey carcasses, sodden Christmas crackers and unopened presents that grandchildren will never receive. We climb sopping stairwells. Shout down passageways.

A voice from one of the search party calls out.

'Over here.'

Submerged garden gates, barriers, bins and other obstacles make swimming too risky, so I wade across the forecourt and into a flat where a large man is sitting in a wheelchair, almost entirely underwater. On the windowsill nearby he has managed to place his TV control, an old pay-as-you-go phone and glasses.

'Morning,' he says.

THE UPPER CALDER Valley has such a rich history of flooding that its continued habitation is testament to little other than

Yorkshire stubbornness. ('You can always tell a Yorkshireman,' the saying goes. 'But you can't tell him owt.')

The local archives are full of records of flood incidents – of Elland Bridge being washed away in 1615, just as it will be again this very evening; of the water being so high in Hebden Bridge in 1837 that it 'came within half an inch of reaching the surgery of Mr John Thomas' (try saying that sentence in a Kenneth Williams voice); of a child drowning in the flash floods of 1857; of residents in 1946 raising their furniture on bread-loaf tins, and those who called it an 'act of God' being given short shrift.

Down on the main road all the usual markers of Mytholmroyd have disappeared from view: the cemetery wall, the pedestrian crossing, street signs, gravestones, the war memorial. All is water.

A man in his seventies doggedly attempts to drive through the flood in his Land Rover, only to be swept away. Rescuers arrive with ropes and boats and swim out to him just in time to wrench open the sunroof that peers above the water by only an inch or two, and he is reluctantly pulled out and manhandled into a dinghy. It is an operation captured by a resident and then relayed to Sky News ('live from Mith-hum-rod'). Later anecdotal reports suggest that the driver was a grumpy farmer who refused to leave his vehicle as he would lose the sacks of animal feed that he had just bought.

In the sheltered flats the wheelchair-bound man is insisting that he doesn't need help and would prefer to stay. The river is at his chin.

'Oh, I'm alright, me. Just leave us here.'

The water is still rising, I explain. Mixed with the detritus of the valley, it is now full of all manner of toxins, pollutants and potential infections. Also it is very cold. If he stays, hypothermia is certain.

'No really. I'll be reet.'

The four or five of us that have crowded into the water-logged flat in the late-morning gloom look at each other in silent agreement.

'Come on,' someone says. 'We're getting you up.'

We lift the man and as we do so his tracksuit bottoms fall down. Arse out. He does not have his dentures in and all his possessions are ruined.

'Can you walk?'

'I'll give it a go.'

I grab his glasses and phone and we guide him across the flooded forecourt in the thrashing rain. He might well be the largest man in the town. It is a major operation.

The river smells like a huge, wet dog, and I can feel my core temperature dropping.

Someone waves from a top-floor flat across the way.

'Get him in here. We've dry rooms.'

Further voices echo around the flats and more men mobi-lise: a woman is trapped by a fallen freezer. Someone else has commandeered a kayak, loaded it with all the medication for the estate's elderly residents, and is steering it across the current. We free the woman. We help guide the boat to safety. We bang on more doors and windows.

There is a sense of organisation to the chaos, a delegation of duties: *you do that, I'll do this. No one's seen Barbara in No. 7.*

Across the valley other such rescue operations are taking place, and other stories are unfolding. Hundreds of them. Thousands of them. And across North Yorkshire, Lancashire and Cumbria too.

Forty-five minutes pass before I realise my breath is a hacking rasp and the uncontrollable shivers have taken over. It is long enough to be in icy waters in an English winter. With shaking hands I take some photos on my phone, which has somehow stayed dry wrapped in a dog-shit bag and wedged into my top pocket – and held between my teeth at one point – and then wade out of the estate to where the river is only thigh-deep.

I squelch home, peel off my dripping clothes and step into a bath. It is half an hour before I stop shivering.

Then for a second time in the coldest month of the year, the power is cut.

THAT NIGHT, SUPREME silence.

With sub-stations underwater, most of the electricity in the area has gone down, as have the phone lines. Our mobiles, over-used in replying to messages from friends and relatives and tweeting pictures of evacuees carrying baskets of cats on their heads, both go dead.

The sun sets in the afternoon over a long, brown lake with a series of towns protruding from it that recall the drowned Cumbrian village of Mardale Green, submerged in the 1930s to create Haweswater Reservoir, whose ruins are still said to poke through during dry spells.

It is cold and the silence is eerie. No trains, no cars. Even the sirens have stopped. It is a place of sodden ghosts.

Looking out of the window I see only torch beams and candlelight in the windows half a mile away on the opposite slopes.

We are grateful to be dry, though along the Calder Valley nearly 3,000 homes are in the process of being evacuated or attempting to cope with severe flood damage, while 4,500 businesses have also been seriously affected. Some will never reopen. The premises of others – the local post office and travel agents, a house or two – will later be demolished. They are not worth saving.

We walk around Mytholmroyd and survey the damage. We see wrecked cars, wrecked houses, a few people wet and dazed. We try to reach friends with children in Hebden Bridge whose houses will have been ruined to offer beds or space or clothes but communication is impossible, and routes through still underwater.

How quickly we can be pushed back through the ages when robbed of all that we take for granted.

Back home, after a fourth change of clothes, I light a fire and heat some baked beans on the flat top of the wood burner. A huge chocolate panettone, given as a Christmas present, will form the bulk of our diet for the next couple of days.

The silent stillness plunges us back in time to the days before power, when Pennine families would sit around the fire, oil lamps flickering in alcoves, new myths being made and old stories being told. And it is raining.

And it is raining.

And it is raining.

WE AWAKE ON an island. The park is still twelve feet under, and workmen at the lorry depot next to it are using a generator to pump out flood water heavy with petrol and diesel straight into the neighbourhood's communal beds of fruit and vegetables. It reeks of industry.

The bottom of our street is flooded. To drive through it would send waves splashing into the old cottages that sit below the road level, as behind us The Rock leaks water from the moor like a colander. It streams down the wet, wooded slopes in dozens of underground springs and new streams to further flood our street, whose drains are plugged with the top crust of the wild, wet West Riding.

The water springs and surges. Sprays and spritzes.

Only when we walk uphill to get a better view over the valley do we see it: a massive landslide blocking the road forty yards from our front door.

Half the bloody hillside beneath The Rock and the old tip that sits below it has collapsed, and the topsoil has slipped like custard skin from a bowl tipped by the tremulous hand of a dinner lady.

It has brought down with it full trees from 100 yards further up the hill, and a great heap of soil. Trapped beneath both is a car belonging to my neighbours, Sheila and Brian.

One tree has slid in a perfectly vertical position, its tangled mass of roots, which are capable of drawing up to 2,000 litres of water per day, moving en masse, finally falling across the road, where it has crashed into the corner brickwork of a bungalow opposite.

Where once there was a hill, there is now a great streak of slick brown gravy the size of a dry ski slope, and the road is barricaded.

We are cut off on all sides: a flood downhill and a landslide uphill. Out front, a mucky lake. Behind us, The Rock. Trapped.

THE LANDSLIDE HAPPENED while we were out surveying the damage last night, the roar of the sliding soil 100 paces from our pillows drowned out by din of wind and the splash of torrential rain on pooling flood water.

I see Sheila, who greets me in the same sleep-starved and saturated state of mild excitation that I will see in many over the coming days.

'I was standing in the street looking up at Scout Rock, because the rain was coming down so heavily like,' she tells me of the previous night's events. 'And all of a sudden I could hear the entire hillside cracking. It sounded like the whole lot was going to come down. That's when we thought, God, we better evacuate. Then I remembered our neighbours Graham and Olive, who are ninety, and both a bit deaf. So I went to wake them, but it took a long time to get them up and dressed. Brian went outside to his car, which was parked here, right at the bottom of Scout Rock. Graham's son came down to get him from a couple of miles away up the road. He said to them "Have you got your pyjamas?", and of course he didn't so then so they went back inside to get them and this all took a while because, as I said, they're both ninety, like. Then it happened. Just like that: the whole hill slid.'

'I just got to the car when I heard a loud *swoosh*,' Brian will later tell an ITV news crew. 'I looked up and saw this massive tree stump coming towards me at a great rate of knots so I had no option but to drop down on the floor at the side of the car, and the tree hit it and spun round, with the roots facing in the opposite direction. Obviously I was shaken and scared and just lay there until it went.'

'I didn't know where he was,' Sheila tells me. 'It was dark, there was soil everywhere, and Brian had disappeared. But then I saw him down round the back of the car, from when he had flung himself. His little legs sticking out. I've seen nowt like it.'

She shakes her head.

'Nowt like it.'

The police call. They are advising a complete evacuation of the fifteen or so of our houses that sit at the top of the road, on either side of the great new blockade of soil and timber. Apparently a far greater crack has appeared in the earth across the entire hillside of The Rock directly behind our house. I know the area they mean: a sodden broad bog that could slip at any minute.

Having donned my boots and coat I climb up there, over new mounds of cloying soil, through which hundreds of tiny streams are trickling down. Soon I'm on all fours, clawing at clay and shale and rubble, the landscape reconfigured. Trees I take as markers have fallen; not storm-snapped, but entirely uprooted this time, the soil that held them washed away.

I climb to the peak of the landslip, and it feels like standing at the top of a great slick slide. I'm reminded of that moment when an old seaside rollercoaster cab creaks around the final corner and the grinding gears are silenced and you teeter on the brink of that first plunge, where even the breeze drops and everything is still for elongated seconds, and though it is expected there is still a fearful suddenness about the surroundings.

The slip is comprised of wet mud, in which I can see globs of unearthed matter and even more remnants from the tip.

Further on in the woods, sumps of flood water have gathered where normally the sponge of the earth would absorb them.

There are no deer. There are no foxes.

There are no rabbits or squirrels or birds.

But there is a crack 100 feet long; a dropped shelf of mud where the hill has slumped beneath the weight of all that water. Through the trees I can see our row of Victorian houses below. My woodpile. The office skylight.

All of it appears vulnerable. In the face of the elements suddenly everything that has been constructed in the valley seems like the fleeting folly of daft man.

IN HIS 1980 essay 'The Making of a Marginal Farm', the farmer, conservationist and writer Wendell Berry describes a situation that almost exactly parallels ours here at the foot of The Rock, albeit four decades and 4,000 miles away in Henry County, Kentucky.

Intending to utilise a stretch of wooded hillside for pasturing his cows, in 1974 Berry felled some trees and used a bulldozer to dig in a pond as a water source for his animals. Grass and clover were sowed to heal the exposed ground around it. Yet Berry underestimated the influence on the underground watershed, which, like that of Scout Rock, had already been affected by digging, draining and industrial and urban development in the valley's past: 'This means not only that floods are higher and more frequent than they would be if the watershed were healthy, but that the floods subside too quickly, the watershed being far less a sponge, now, than it is a roof. The flood water drops suddenly out of the river, leaving the steep banks soggy, heavy, and soft. As a result great strips and blocks of land crack loose and slump, or they give way entirely and disappear.'

After a particularly wet autumn and winter, and a period of big freezes and rapid thaws in quick succession, Berry's earthwork did indeed slump as 'a large slice of the woods floor on the upper side slipped', and three buildings were undermined.

Working in the traditions of literary ancestors such as Walt Whitman, Henry David Thoreau and John Muir, Wendell Berry's words, written as part of a lifetime's close study of the land on which he lives and works, resonate as I look upon the similar heap of sludge that has arrived on our doorstep.

As with Scout Rock, Berry's landslide was hardly a major disaster, but it represented a microcosmic shift that he saw as being a direct result of a consumptive economy, a theme he continually returns to. The ruining of watersheds is just one aspect of our 'taxing' of the land, and the erosion that inevitably follows – on a hill in Kentucky in the 1970s or a hill in Yorkshire today – is no natural act, but one hastened by industrialisation's short-term thinking.

'The trouble was the familiar one,' he writes in another essay, 'Damage'. 'Too much power, too little knowledge.'

DOWN IN MYTHOLMROYD devastation reigns.

The power is still down and all the local amenities – the cash-point, the doctor's surgery, the pubs, the churches, the Co-op supermarket that was once Mytholmroyd's one and only nightclub – have been beneath seven feet of water, which is slowly receding at a pace that seems spitefully leisurely.

The main road through the valley is blocked with silt, abandoned cars, all the rubbish that the river has dragged down with it. We can't get to Hebden Bridge a mile or so away, where the situation is just as dire. Only the Town Hall and music venue the Trades Club initially open to offer food and shelter for those whose homes have been destroyed. The water recedes and in amongst the ashen faces of those returning from Christmas Days spent away to find their homes empty shells, the smell of fetid river water all pervasive, are those of people we don't recognise.

First on the scene is the Sikh charity Khalsa Aid, whose volunteers mobilised at the very first news reports of the floods yesterday morning. They arrive in mini-buses with shovels and buckets, and great vats of curry and dahl, and foil parcels of chapattis that they warm and serve around the clock for days. Hundreds more, they tell us, are on their way up from London and the South-east.

Next come Muslim families bearing food parcels and blankets and a willingness to help in any way they can, and a group of young, strong men from the hilltops around Sowerby Bridge – mechanics, farmers, all members of a Sunday league football team perhaps – and Syrian refugees from Manchester, who very recently fled a war zone, yet who still arrive not in 'waves' or 'cockroach-like', as the tabloid hate-speak would have it, but with smiles and energy and love. They pick up shovels and get to work.

'I volunteered when I was in Aleppo,' volunteer Yasser al-Jassem tells the *Guardian*. 'I was an ambulance driver and helped with humanitarian rescue efforts when the Assad regime bombed civilian areas. Now, in the UK, I also want to volunteer, and so do many other Syrians who recognise the importance of humanitarian efforts like this one because of the destruction in our homeland.'

The journalist in me wants to document what is going on, and several news outlets attempt to get in touch to see if I can file reports, but all of that seems secondary when my neighbours are wading through water clutching pets and albums containing photos of their ancestors.

Soon we are all working side by side. Down at the pensioners' estate I spend several hours shovelling the raft of settled river silt that has drowned the paths and gardens. It's so viscous that as I shovel, more seems to seep back in place, like a town-sized blob in an old American B-movie. I clear a path to Maureen's flat but when I look through the window, and those of her neighbours, I see tide-lines and warped furniture, everything ruined, the walls and beds smeared with the markings of the river's dirty protest. I ring Maureen and find her at her friend's house several miles away. I tell her to brace herself: don't hurry back, most of it is gone.

There is no plan here, only scores of people turning up from across the country asking, 'What can I do to help?'

We begin to empty the flats. I find myself tearing up an elderly couple's sodden stair carpet which has buckled and jammed the stairlift, trapping them in their upstairs room for two days. I slash at it with a Stanley knife and rip it away, throw it onto one of many hundreds of piles containing household possessions.

Someone turns up with a metal urn on their back and another in their hand.

'Tea or coffee?' they ask, offering up great steaming cups of the only thing that the British cannot do without.

All is spoiled and sodden and rotten, but across the North it is a similar story. The charity the Ahmadiyya Muslim Youth Association send 350 further volunteers to thirty-eight of these towns and villages.

And people keep coming, of all stripes. We are left and right, brown and white, dyed-in-the-wool anarchists and ardent con-servatives, working in quiet co-ordination, and as I straighten and stand to drink my tea, my boots half hidden by the mulch of hillside and moor, the stinking river bed levelling everything like a rotten, acrid carpet, I am suddenly struck by the completely ineffectual nature of party politics. Sometimes – when the situation demands it – people rally. They just do. Dogma goes out of the window when flood waters rush in. There are no politicians here – they'll come weeks and months later to have their pictures taken – there are no ethical debates, ugly elections or vicious bills to be passed. Just mud, spades, laughter, tea, grit, tears, strength and sympathy. Community.

THE COLLECTIVE ENERGY generated will last for days, weeks even, but it is still exhausting. Heeding the police's warning, that night the neighbours in our terraced row leave. They pack their bags and get out of the valley somehow.

Still without power or communication, Della and I sit alone by candlelight in a row of houses behind which groans a hillside. A crack in the earth like a frown glowers up there.

Over the road, the park is still several feet beneath water too, and the toxic stench of scores of dog-shit bags and diesel stronger than ever. Over the next fortnight I will saw off and wrestle away great limbs from the fallen trees blocking our street; they'll keep the house warm for the entire next winter.

All the local shops have been ruined so we live almost entirely off fire-brewed tea and that massive panettone, the most middle-class of disaster rations.

We are dry. We still have our house.

It could be far, far worse.

BUT GOODWILL ONLY goes so far.

That night, as a foil moon settles on the chill waters and the empty streets are eerily quiet once again, there are reports of looting in the area.

Rumours circulate of men in vans – *offcumdens* – being sighted hurriedly filling their vehicles with those possessions that people have stacked on pavements to dry out, or to present for their household insurance claims.

When reports come in of the bicycle shop in Todmorden having £20,000 worth of stock stolen it becomes clear that there are cynical forces at work, small reminders that the fabric of society can quickly become unstitched. There are further tales of men appearing in houses they thought abandoned. Goods being stolen.

In response to such postings online, the following night a contingent of male and female bikers arrive to patrol the area. Many of them walk the streets on foot, their motorcycles little use in the sewage-soaked roads. They bring teabags. They are given the police's blessing.

'We saw people post on Facebook that they were trying to deter looters, and I thought who better to do that but twenty to thirty burly bikers,' Dave Cariss of the Drifters MCC from Bradford tells the *Guardian*.

The Drifters are joined by members of other motorcycle gangs – 'clubs' is the more accurate term – including Pyeratz MCC and Nuntii Mortis MCC.

'We spread out and go wherever needed,' says the Drifters' club chairman, Lloyd Spencer, described as standing at six feet five inches and weighing twenty stone, who says the area resembles 'a war zone'. 'We are not there to offer anything physical. We just show our faces. Obviously we are not vigilantes. A lot of us are quite big, chunky lads, so that helps. We don't have to really say anything, just turn up.'

Clad in their regulation leathers, for the next three nights the bikers will meet at Mytholmroyd community centre to walk the streets into the early hours, discreetly shining torches in the darker corners and generally deterring those thieves on the prowl.

MEN COME AND drain the canal ready for dredging.

Substantial banks of silt sit either side of the narrow run of water that remains. Ruffled ducks glide along it, confused and grasping for morsels.

A solitary perch breaks the oily surface with a flick of its glistening fanned tail and then darts through this emerging kingdom of dumped waste and dropped goods: a stack of road cones here, a length of wrought-iron railing there. The ubiquitous shopping trolley, from a supermarket chain that went bankrupt, practically an antique now.

The canal bank is collapsing, its sides defeated by the slow shift of earth and the weight of river water that has washed across the land. The old stones that line it have fallen, submerged like the fragments of Shelley's Ozymandias sunken in the swamp of reeking mud.

A gull hovers above and then dives, lured by gravity and hunger, its beak and head disappearing in the shallow flow, its wings angled backwards for buoyancy in the stagnant notch.

THE FLOODS BRING with them a hundred thousand stories across the North of England, where other towns and villages are underwater.

All I know is what I can see and smell from my doorstep: river mud, effluence, diesel. Refuse everywhere. Empty shells that were once homes. December frosting.

The landslide brings with it an added set of problems that will take years to address as surveyors and engineers attempt to offer solutions to secure an entire hillside and the mess it has unwittingly self-excavated. A clean-up operation begins which, as I write two years later, is still taking place. The Rock will be cordoned off behind barriers and an intricate piece of fence engineering designed to stretch and flex should the hillside crumble. The animal terrain is further shrinking and few things are sadder than a trapped young badger, skinned at the wire not yet strung last summer.

Temporary traffic lights down the main road stem the flow of traffic as houses and businesses are dismantled brick by brick as part of an ongoing plan to widen the river, replace bridges and secure the town.

But that is all still to come.

As I climb up the fresh mass of heavy mud a few days after the slip, I am alarmed to find scattered in amongst the ploughed topsoil some damp matter. It resembles wadded toilet paper, but is more fibrous and fulsome.

My neighbour, a plumber, whose house just missed being filled with soil, climbs up too and uses my dog-shit bags to take some samples to send off for testing.

We both already know what it is.

Asbestos, unearthed.

THERE FOLLOWS A long period of recuperation for the entire Calder Valley. It becomes the singular talking point, the ancient British tradition of discussing the weather conducted in a deeper, more foreboding tone, the changing sky verbally dissected in forensic detail, locked in a loop, every sign a portent, the residents stoically accepting their fate at the mercy of clouds, humour once again used as armour. Rain-talk is the only talk.

> *This weather.*
> *Isn't it.*
> *No let up.*
> *They give it more rain.*
> *Aye.*
> *They give it two weeks of rain.*

Some of those at the foot of The Rock are living miles away in temporary accommodation. For others – like Della and I, who have chosen to stay – a series of weekly council meetings take place to discuss the safety of our properties in the face of a slipping hillside. Furthermore, there is the issue of asbestos, whose origins the council has no knowledge of and – initially at least – claims no responsibility for.

Months of rancorous meetings, temporary housing, land surveys, contract tenders and workmen swarming ant-like across the hillside stretch ahead. A dull drama unfolds every Saturday morning in a town-hall meeting room and it is like living in a tedious episode of *The Archers*.

The first gathering is especially fraught: residents have been evacuated and have nowhere to live. Mytholmroyd and Hebden Bridge are totally devoid of temporary housing, and, aware of the legal implications (and the TV news crew outside), a panel of councillors, lawyers and surveyors offer conflicting opinions as to the cause of the Scout Rock slip, and who is culpable for the costs of cleaning up and securing the hillside at a potential bill of several million pounds (initial answer: 'Not us').

After what appears as an initial shirking of civic responsibility, voices become raised, and locals with a greater knowledge of the strange and tumultuous history of a hillside that has been mined, quarried and dumped upon begin to educate the experts on its geological past.

I'm only one coffee into the morning and drift off, remembering more of farmer Wendell Berry's sage words, written about a landmark as close to him as Scout Rock is to us: 'The hill . . . is a voyager standing still. Never moving a step, it travels through years, seasons, weathers, days and nights. These are the measures of its time, and they alter it, marking their passage on it as on a man's face. The hill has never observed a Christmas or an Easter or a Fourth of July. It has nothing to do with a dial or a calendar. Time is told in it mutely and immediately, with perfect accuracy, as it is told by the heart in the body. Its time is the birth and the flourishing and the death of the many lives that are its life.'

The story of the Scout Rock landslide is one chapter amongst many that tell of a valley brought close to ruin and the recovery of Calderdale after the Boxing Day floods is a book in itself, yet in the initial aftermath I find myself unable to write about any of it. Somehow I just can't face it. Because I am, in a small way, mourning for The Rock itself, whose face has been disfigured, and over the coming months and years, as trees are felled, animals displaced, wild plots tramped across, and teams of workmen arrive to set up camp, will be irrevocably changed.

My secret entrance through a covertly movable metal fence railing is bolted shut. New barriers are erected. Signs go up, trees as familiar as old friends come down.

The Scout Rock I have known for the past decade is no more. It is something else now.

Chapter Ten

After our discovery of the asbestos the landslide is covered in swathes of white tarpaulin to keep any of the carcinogenic material from becoming airborne. From a distance it looks like a huge waterfall or a sweep of simulacrum snow in a snowless landscape.

In his novel *Trout Fishing in America*, a poetic and absurdist journey deep into a changing America, Richard Brautigan recalls a search for the perfect fishing spot. Across a lush meadow, towards a grove of trees, he sees in the distance 'a waterfall come pouring off the hill. It was long and white and I could almost feel its cold spray. There must be a creek there, I thought, and it probably has trout in it. Trout.'

He heads towards the waterfall and the beautiful creek that lies at its base, but all is not quite right: 'As I got closer to the creek I could see that something was wrong. The creek did not act right. There was a strangeness to it. There was a thing about its motion that was wrong. Finally I got close enough to see what the trouble was. The waterfall was just a flight of white wooden stairs leading up to a house in the trees.'

The victim of a cruel optical illusion, the boy stands for a long time 'looking up and looking down the stairs', barely able to believe that the waterfall he was sure was a certainty is something devoid of the magic of an unfished stream. He even knocks on the 'creek' with his knuckles, the hollow rap as heartbreaking as anything in twentieth-century literature. Here domesticity has encroached upon the wildness of his mind.

I recall this story whenever I am out walking on Midgley Moor or driving along Heights Road, or simply stepping out of the front door and turning to my right, and I look across and see the covered Scout Rock landslide. On different days it become different things: a breaking wave of foam; an arid water-park slide; an industrial no-go zone; a spilled lorry-load of curdled milk or the tip of an iceberg, a ghost-echo from the form that shaped the valley and The Rock in the first place.

Following the rain and the meetings and the sodden damp void of the valley's flatlands, the land higher up is alive with the music of water for weeks.

Stone walls birth bubbling spouts and old earthen grooves return to their former purpose as filters, as repositories, pooling and flowing.

What begins as the tiniest trickle of water soon carves a miniature new ravine, leaves a black scar like a lightning bolt through the dirt.

The moraine of gravel, sand and shale up Stake Lane shifts like percussion. Soil rolls, slips and seeps the shortest route down to town.

And more buried springs become unsprung and spurt like the tips of hidden chimneys, finding relief through release. Worms of water rise, expand into snakes. Hoof prints are erased.

No terrain can contain these bold surgings as what once was porous is now overwhelmed.

A relinquishment takes place as the hills accept their reshaping, and the valley sighs to the music of fissures filled and rivulets rushing. There is a wet melody there if you care to hear it.

But the water does not stop at this transaction. It becomes power-hungry as it strips the soil, scrubs at the gritstone beneath, prises the rigid grip of tree roots, cocks a snook at every obstacle to power on through. A hundred new streams flow, and then a hundred more. They will carve their way for weeks.

The valley acquiesces.

I WALK UP through a wood towards Robin Hood Rocks.

Deer dart here. Medieval flickers of fire-red pelt.

The rocks are a jumble of tumbled gritstone boulders, atop which juts out an escarpment above the tree line. At the foot of the rocks are niches and hollows into which I stick my head, and chiselled into this finger of cold stone pointing across the valley above are the words 'R. A. Barry from Nottingham, 1893'.

Lying on it is akin to flight.

The presence of Robin Hood, perhaps the most famous figure of rural British mythology, lingers right across Calderdale, almost always without any real provenance as to the origins of the association. He's there in Robin Hood's Bed, an outcrop at Blackstone Edge, and in the boulder named Robin Hood's Penny Stone at Wainstalls. He's there too in the monument Robin Hood's Grave in Kirklees Priory, where he is said to be buried. Then a mile or so beyond these rocks is the Robin Hood pub in Cragg Vale, a homely refuge manned by landlord Roger, the dictionary definition of a Yorkshire publican, who not only sports some fine 'bugger grips' sideburns, but also serves arguably the finest hand-cut chips in Britain.

As I walk on I see Hood's avian namesake, the robin, who appeared to flee the area as soon as the waters rose, but has just returned once again. Keenly territorial, robins are fond of promenading. Years ago, when I used to swim lengths in an outdoor pool in South London, the same one would appear every day to hop alongside me, turning as I turned, length after length, day in, day out. They are impossible not to love.

Once known as the *robinet* or the *ruddock*, the bird was renamed the robin redbreast in the fifteenth century, when it was common for creatures to be bestowed human names. And though its breast is closer to orange, that word was not introduced into the English language until 1512; previously orange was known as either *ġeolurēad* for 'yellowish-red' or *ġeolucrog* for 'yellowish-orange'.

The return of the robins to their feeding and nesting places in holly bushes and hedges around Scout Rock, their ruffled, russet-coloured chests puffed out in defiance, is more welcome than ever, a reminder that nature always finds a way. In times past to kill a robin was considered a great crime and anyone who did so might suffer bad luck, such as cows that yielded bloody milk or the burning down of their houses or barns. In *Folk-Speech of East Yorkshire* (1899) it is noted that 'when a boy had robbed a robin's nest, his companions gathered round him, hissing and pointing with their fingers and chanting over and over again "Robin takker, robin takker / Sin, sin, sin!"' Little wonder that this protected creature was voted the unofficial national bird of Britain in a birdwatchers' poll in 2015.

This wood always feels particularly laden with myth, and often when I'm walking here I find myself making up fictional new myths, or bestowing new names on minor landmarks.

Occasionally I post pictures of them with entirely fictional back stories. Here is The Acorn Slab, marking the spot where Annie Sykes was 'murdered dead for corvortain nayked with a Freynchman in 1610', or there's Mandrake Scarp, 'upon which Samuel Simmins sired thirteen children by thirteen women during the English Civil War'. And – look – here is the ruined

cottage in which one Winnie S. was 'ticculd to death by brae-
cenfronds for imitaetine a cat' in 1664.

History has taught us that out of such tall tales myths often
begin, of which that of Robin Hood is perhaps the most
enduring example; and that in fact Chinese whispers form the
foundations of those folklore stories that we perceive, if not
always as fact, then at least as an intrinsic part of who we are
today. A deeper truth.

MY DAILY WALKS around The Rock alter only slightly. I slip
into a new routine. I climb the fence, scale the banks, scour the
sunken jungle.

Up top I pass a recurring symbol: a Christmas wreath fash-
ioned from pine boughs and holly sprigs, red berries and cones.
A stretch of hessian neatly bowed to bind it all together.

It sits at the same point, strung to the wooden fence that
runs the length of The Rock, just feet from where the land
falls away in a near-vertical drop. Here, I imagine, might be the
spot from which someone who has had enough of living might
choose to throw themselves.

Every winter a new wreath appears, worn by The Rock like
a miniature crown. Wreaths have been used decorously throughout Europe since Etruscan times and used in pagan practices in
England from the Renaissance era onwards, but something tells
me that its appearance is not purely seasonal. This wreath speaks

of silent remembrance, of tragedy, of something past and passed. Its position and reoccurrence tell me so.

And then when the festive time has gone, as it has now, and we face the year ahead with good intentions soon to be broken, and the promise of spring cowers in submerged snow-drop bulbs, it is still there, left to slowly rot in its clifftop eyrie, needles browning, holly leaves once waxy now devoid of sheen, pointed barbs devoid of prickly menace. No one removes it. I pass it most days, noting the loosening of its self-sustaining circle of boughs, its shape becoming uncertain as it dries and droops.

Here on the ridge I also find what my dad calls *gurgies* – regurgitated owl pellets. Two of them. I roll them over and prod them with a twig. They are still moist, recently baulked. Mashing them I discover in amongst the brown matter the perfect mechanical makings of a mouse, tiny bones like the components of an Airfix kit waiting to be assembled with glue and patience.

It is New Year's Eve when I come across a man, lost, the first non-vagrant I've seen in Scout Rock Woods in all the years I've been exploring this haunted place.

He appears more furtive then me, babbling an embarrassed explanation for his trespass: his dog has somehow descended The Rock and he had no choice but to follow, on his arse.

I put him at ease, tell him about the deer trails, the fox runs, and give a brief history of the place, and then point him in the direction of a suitably discreet exit. 'What a day,' he says. 'What a way to end the year.'

'Yes,' I reply. 'What a way indeed,' and we part, two men of the woods, the whispering polyphonic echoes of our similar passing ancestors behind us.

Later, walking home in the half-light of dusk, I see a shape up ahead, watching on the approach as if guarding a secret or squaring the root of a problem posed by the season. A black bone of winter, whose gnarled claws curl around wire, this large raven is silent keeper of The Rock.

As I come closer it does not take flight in fright but instead perches proud, as unyielding to man as the hill it protects, and only when I reach to touch it do I see that it is neither bone nor crow but a scrap of plastic, snagged, an empty bag. Flapping with laughter.

The forecast warns of more floods and thundersnow, promising travel chaos and a tidal surge towards Essex, yet the portentous icy winter silence is broken briefly by a leaping squirrel and then four plangent chimes of a church bell.

FINALLY, SNOW.

A thinly lacquered layer of it, just enough to buff the land with a gleaming new lustre. But snow nonetheless, and more welcome than dumb, persistent, callous rain.

With the settled white layers comes radiant light, and with light comes the desire for height, so I drive on up along Blackstone Edge to the moor above Cragg Vale, where the floods began.

At the highest point, where the road crests the moor, and the road is the only evidence of man, I pull over and take steps into the blur of brittle heather, and when I stop I find an opened sheep blooming like a rose, a peeling of petalled flesh whose centre sits alive with feasting maggots, 10,000 tiny components in an ancient process, glistening cogs in the death-machine.

Further on I park up and walk along the imaginatively named New Road and then take a track that is not deemed worthy of a moniker on any map, passing the last house whose views take in nothing but miles of wild grasslands, heather brush and pylons parading across the plains in a diminishing robotic procession. I think of Ted Hughes's Iron Man.

Cliff has a spring in his step as he always does when he wakes to whiteness. He skips around me in a circle, nipping at my heels.

Down in Mytholmroyd it is only just zero, but up here wind chill makes it feel more like ten below.

For a few moments the wind is a cold whistle, but then it drops away to nothing and the moor is still. The hard ground makes the walking easy, with each puddle now a frozen slate patterned with frosted geometric fractals, each a neat calligraphical exercise drawn by the steady hand of winter, smoky mirrors for the ice-coloured sky above.

I see a rare rabbit darting in the distance.

I see a helicopter over distant Halifax.

The sky rumbles like a starving stomach.

My destination is hunched on a hump of land on Slate Delf Hill, close to the highest point of the moors, way above Scout Rock. From here I can see 360 degrees, from Leeds in one direction to Manchester in the other. The dog flattens himself beneath a fence and reaches a small brick pillbox bunker known as a Special Fire, or Starfish, site.

Starfish sites were constructed as decoys for major cities following the devastating campaign of bombs that fell upon Coventry in November 1940. They were intended to simulate the bomb drops of German pathfinder squadrons via light displays and controlled fires of creosote and water. By the end of the war eighty-one towns and cities were protected by such places of choreographed pyrotechnic displays – 237 decoys in all – each co-ordinated from a small nearby bunker like the one I come across this morning, built in 1941 and now semi-submerged in the snowbound moor, and from the roof of which the dog is looking down at me curiously.

Here basket fires once burned and fire-break trenches were dug, while other Starfish sites also included anti-aircraft gun emplacements. Working in shifts, twenty RAF staff maintained this location and, in no uncertain terms, warned off any curious local who happened to be passing (a local farming family, the Sugdens, were evicted from their nearby homestead to make way for the facility, their house falling into ruin for the next half-century).

The bunker is not much to look at now: a centre entrance-way on either side of which sit two small rooms whose floor is a claggy carpet of gluey mud, beer cans and litter, illuminated only by an escape hatch in the solid concrete ceiling, which is now an open skylight fringed by the frozen grass. The left-hand space was the control room, while the other housed generators. It looks like a scene from a 1980s anti-heroin ad campaign. Out the front is a blast wall to protect the entrance. It is a sorry place and, perhaps intuitively aware that this sepulchral space was one of danger and conflict, the dog will not enter.

With numb fingertips I search on my phone and find that the main fire site was south-west of the bunker, towards Great Manshead Hill, and comprised two lines of 'flash pans' where oil was burned, where there were also lights, shadow buildings and skeleton structures.

I head in that direction following a snow line further out onto the moor, but find no scars of war or scorched circles. No bomb-blasted crates or shrapnel shreds.

Just grass, snow and heather standing stiff against the wicked rising winter wind.

DAYS PASS. WEEKS. The valley is in slow recovery and more snow swirls like the TV static that illuminated a 1980s adolescence.

When I was young I used to press my face to the screen and pretend I was in an Arctic whiteout; I can still smell it now, warm, comforting, electric. Strands of my hair rising.

I walk back up through the snow into the woods beyond Scout Rock. I am nothing if not a creature of habit and routine.

Old maps show that different parts of the wood had different names – first Hollin Hey Wood, Sutcliffe Wood in the middle, and Holderness at the upper end – but for now it feels like one entity, a wood in which I have seen more deer than people. The last human I encountered was a woman stretched out across the surface of a large boulder as if in readiness for a ritual sacrifice who, when startled by me passing by, suddenly sat up, gave a cheery wave and a hearty 'Morning!' and then reassumed the position.

I pass an old badger sett, then cross one or two small streams that are now back to being mere trickles once again.

Somewhere in the shaded centre of the trees the path rises to a level. Here is one of my favourite locations, the tumbledown remains of an old cottage whose history remains elusive.

One or two people have told me that they suspect the house to have been occupied by charcoal burners, and the woodland location and landscaped walled terraces suggest it is plausible. Historical documents show that charcoal burners certainly lived and worked in the area in the eighteenth century, including some close to our old cottage, The Stubb.

In medieval times, the valley's woodlands were exploited for their raw materials. The *Domesday Book* of 1086 suggests that 15 per cent of England was covered in trees, but here in the Pennines the proportion was almost certainly higher, each plot carefully controlled through coppicing and pollarding by the wealthy landowners. Timber from oak, willow, ash and beech served a multitude of purposes, not just as fuel but also sold on by manorial estates to be used for beams and planks in the building of dwellings and ships, plus domestic implements, fencing, basketry and furniture. Charcoal was often sold to fuel iron forges. Wood was Britain's lifeblood, a gold mine for those who owned the land. Court rolls from the 1300s show that many locals were fined for merely taking the local earl's rushes, broom, acorns and branches blown down by the wind.

Holly was another important tree in the area and was purposefully cultivated for its leaves to be used as cattle feed in winter. It's likely that this wood, Hollin Hey, takes its name from an abundance of holly trees that have grown here on this spot since the eleventh century, outlasting many moths, beetles and birds now extinct, and indeed those monarchs whose names are so synonymous with the shaping of Britain's past: Canute, Edward the Confessor, Harold II and William the Conqueror.

I consult my local historical contact John Billingsley, a folk-lorist, wanderer, author and editor of *Northern Earth* magazine, which was established above a pub in Leeds in 1979 to offer a neo-antiquarian approach to 'earth mysteries' such as folklore, megalithic sites, alignments, sacred landscapes, strange phenomena 'and other aspects at the interface of human consciousness and the land from prehistory to the present'.

John works for the local library service and is a small, neat man with sprite-like enthusiasm and boundless knowledge, an internationally respected figure in the neo-antiquarian world. He is a friend of Alan the Postman. Both having gravitated to the Upper Calder Valley several decades ago, John and Alan make for an interesting pair; a Doctor of Horror, Alan's didactic hectoring and political reading is a stark contrast to John's deep Gnostic research into folkloric traditions and his fondness for sharing stories that might loosely fall under the term 'paranormal'.

'When it comes to mythology, John knows his stuff alright,' Alan once told me, a stack of mail in his hand. 'The trouble is, he actually *believes* a lot of this bollocks about fairies.'

'Alan . . .' is all John says, shaking his head and sighing when I mention his friend's scepticism.

Though they would baulk at the observation, both are, in their own ways, very Hebden Bridge.

'There are ruined cottages like that all over the place,' John tells me when I ask him about the stone wreck in the woods. 'There's a whole hamlet in Jumble Hole, and the remains of a clump of cottages in Old Town. Sometimes they're industrial;

sometimes they're just marginal holdings that proved too marginal. Charcoal burners usually, I believe, lived in tents, but I'd recommend checking that.'

The structure now is nothing but a heap of rocks, stones, boulders, lintels, mantels, quoins and half-hidden floor slabs worn as smooth as a waxed ballroom floor.

The fireplace, so vital an aspect of any domestic life for warmth, cooking and congregation, is still there, as is a small place that would have been used as a cold store. The foundations show the division of the space into small rooms for small people. Here lives were lived in close quarters.

Through the centre of the main communal room, where people ate and laughed and cried and died, there now grow tall trees that weren't even seeds when the house was abandoned. They are the only inhabitants now, slowly pushing through the cracks of stone, and nudging aside the fallen remnants of a dwelling built when the earth was flat, the moon was a basin of curdling whey and life was something short to be endured.

I tell a lie: the trees are not the only squatters in the charcoal burner's cottage. The scent of a fox is often present here, brushed across the heather stalks and fallen cornerstones. I imagine it at night, stalking the remains of rooms and padding across the thick rot of dead leaves of a hundred winters gone.

My dog will wear the musk of it about his head, the trail stink of it carried all day, and later when he sleeps curled in on himself he will dream of the streak of rust darting through the chicane, the chase, his muffled grunts coughed into my pillow.

Perhaps the fox, like me, is attracted to this spot by the lingering presence of past lives, the residual aftermath of energy and toil in a hollow space long vacated. Perhaps we are both reaching out to the unknowable.

This sense of abandonment is tangible as further snowflakes dance all around, and the wood is still as snow blankets the charcoal burner's cottage, clinging to the holly, muting everything, and I watch with timeless wonder.

FIELD NOTES III

Woken by the Wind

Woken by the wind
in the eventide's
wailing

over The Rock it comes
like one hundred thousand horses
vaulting the drop

flexing panes
screaming
scattering the remains

of celebration
and leaving stripped trees
limbless. Landmine scenes.

Power lines reborn
as spade-cut snakes
writhe, spitting sparks.

Digging

I dig at The Deadfall stone.
Thinking that this is a game,

the dog snatches at my stick, unaware
of eighty summers ago when a fox

was found pressed flat
beneath this weighted slab,

(that someone – a farmer,
perhaps – set as a primitive trap)

and lifted from the soil
by two idol earth-brothers

camping and dreaming beneath
sagging canvas in the quarry below,

who found that in its crushed bones
and orange brush, a lifetime of poetry lay.

The Cascade

Wild is the water that washes
away the mask of the moment
and tears open the trapdoors of time
to flood the packed catacombs in
the kingdom of Cambodunum.

Finding flintheads up at Blackstone
and arrowheads at Turvin.
Scrubbing at secrets.
Gushing at graves.
Lifting history.

One Morning After Snow
When Everything Is Silent

A fresh fall.

Coating
reshaping
expanding
everything.

Removing
edges and angles,
painting the world
anew.

January blue.

Wintering Fox

The engine of the fox growls
as it dashes
grinding through the gears
into the copse
fuelled by the possibility of
the final silence.

Scout Road from the Short-Cut Through
the Woods on the Way to the Beekeeper's House,
Passing the Pond, Near to Where the Peacocks Roost

Between flood and landslide
old ways become overgrown.

It takes only two or three swift years
for the weeds to blanket the tarmac,
the creepers to strangle the street signs and
the balsam to paint the mind's eye green.

England is an idea in constant reinvention,
a concept kept fluid, an abstract Albion.
Of falling fences. Dying ideas. Arrogance,
deceit and grave delusion. Of mud flux.

In Scout Rock Woods for the First Time
in Weeks After the Workmen Have Left

Two deer
on the old town tip
disappear;

another conjured moment
from nature's bottomless
box of tricks.

While from high above
a third looks on with
long-wintered ambivalence.

Frozen Fog

Fog frozen in the night
melts by Friday morning.
Each tree is a unique
umbrella of rain –

the holly bush alone drops
ten thousand diamonds
as the weekend opens wide
to receive them

and the sun picks out a molehill
where once a mountain stood.

Infinite Night

Freefalling
through the centuries
face up
seeing the past shrink –
peony-pink
the winter sun's glow.

Left: A Mytholmroyd resident and her cat are rescued during the 2015 floods.
Right: Large, unidentified moss-covered bone found in the centre of Scout Rock.

View across to Haworth Old Road from a ruined farmhouse in Crimsworth Dean.

Sunlight illuminating the run-off from the moor.

Left: Snowfall in Scout Rock.
Right: Stepping stones over Hebden Beck in Hardcastle Crags.

PART IV

Rock

Chapter Eleven

The flood waters leave their mark long after they have left. A patina of black mould creeps across my office walls. I attack it with bleach but a week later it returns, a malevolent fungus that spreads like a diabolical shadow. The cough continues to rattle in my lungs. I'm put on antibiotics but after three months it's still there. I am put on different antibiotics, sent for X-rays.

Spring is sluggish in showing itself. It is a creature hidden. Streams still trickle through The Rock and the land is late in its blooming. The nesting ravens, carrion eaters once associated in British folklore with storms and floods (and where two seen together is a sign of ill fortune), patrol like gaolers over this strange post-industrial, semi-rural corner of West Yorkshire. It is as if the migrating birds that proudly wear their little flags of international colour on their chests have been warned away this year; only the hardy valley-born locals remain.

One morning the dog snatches a rare rabbit as it bathes in sun. The scene is like an old video tape on fast-forward; all jerky motions and grainy definition. It is a mercy killing: its matted fur is lacking lustre and its ruined eyes are already thick with globs of death pus. It is gripped by myxomatosis, a cruel disease born in laboratories and then carelessly let loose in France in 1952 when a bacteriologist infected rabbits that he saw as troublesome on his estate. Within two years, 90 per cent of France's wild rabbit population was gone. A year later it crossed the channel and 99 per cent of the British rabbit population died from this first outbreak. The poor creature is riddled with tumours. Fatigue and fever have rendered it immobile. All that is left is a little sunlight. Some still moments.

Yet still when the jaws snap it squeals and that is the worst part. It squeals for life as it meets death, the final battle, its tiny heart thumping, but it is over in the passing of a cloud across the morning sun. With a swift toss and a flick, its rheumy eyes snuffed like fading candle stubs.

The dog is doing what he does. The disease is doing what it does. And the still wood is filled with deep silence.

FINALLY FEBRUARY FORGIVES, as it always does. It sets the sins of winter aside and, if its mood is particularly beneficent, lifts the valley's lid a little to show us the sky.

The mere suggestion of sun serves as a tonic.

To see the blue sky rising above The Rock is to exhale, to breathe out. Beech leaves dead and browning on the branch cling to the breeze for a first glimpse of spring. Here they rustle, there they sing. We're not there yet but the valley yawns, stretching. And the season is born in snowdrops and birdsong.

From our house we watch The Rock's shadow recede like an oily tide across the valley, counting the days until it retreats entirely. One day I see the sun painting the windows over on Banksfield bronze, flashing there for a moment, phosphorescent. Over on that hillside was where Ted Hughes found cracked birds' eggs and carrion ripped by raptors and, looking back to The Rock, saw the valley's locked and bolted black back door, the far limit of his world.

Now there is a housing estate on that hump of hill. There are cul-de-sacs, gardens and garages. Trampolines, power tools and Wi-Fi.

The next day the sun stretches closer and The Rock appears to shrink beneath it. For two or three days the pair do battle, this stubborn lump of rock standing true against the glare of a fireball 93,000,000 miles away, a crag-faced David to a raging, roaring Goliath.

But finally it concedes and the sun's rays reach Burnley Road to flood the industrial units and workshops and bacon-packing factory with light, and fill the stagnant canal with honey, making even the dumped BMXs and deep-green swirls of goose shit look golden.

The next day the sun takes the train tracks, infuses their cold, worn steel with a solar vitality. And then it is at the trees out front, creeping across the park, and everything is amber. In just one more day it will rise one morning over The Rock and bathe our back garden entirely with joyous sunshine born from an incandescent mass of hot plasma. The light of spring will burst through the slats of our drawn blinds, refracting there, making dust dance and spiders' webs tremble, laying warm shapes on floorboards that creak like the warped galley of a galleon.

In this moment Cliff wakes by the radiator, yawns, stretches and shakes off his winter slumber, then rises onto his haunches, squinting as he surveys the landing like a war general, and then closes his eyes. Feels the warmth in his whiskers. As he tips his head back and grunts with satisfaction, the rhombus of sunlight on the rug is his kingdom for the taking.

And that night up on The Rock, his species-kin, the lone fox, finally finds a mate. On the mud-slipped slopes the two come together in violence, and a turning key finds a lock, the spark-seed of the next generation is lit. The rutting foxes detach and the male scatters, fleeing down through trees to pass dim doorways, tipped bins and railway sidings; the silent spear of him piercing the unknown, his head cocked, nose wet. Teeth bared.

WHEN THE FIRST snowdrops inch their tips through after a dormant winter I swim again.

It is Imbolc, the first day of spring in Gaelic, pagan and Wiccan traditions, and clear and bright, though as I climb the 1,000 feet up to the reservoir I can still see my breath steaming.

The wind is whipping across the water and the familiar fear I always experience begins to show itself. I meet friends Rob, Emma and Amy, all of us drawn to the shock of the cold to jolt us from a cursed winter's inertia.

As we get changed we're again joined by Keith, the reservoir's nude custodian, who tells us that the temperature of the water is 1.3°C.

'A bit nippy.'

We wade out from England's highest beach and the water is biting, my bones glass. The water is so devilishly cold there is a sense of malevolence to it that warrants respect. We each journey off in our own little worlds of sensation. Rob is wearing a wetsuit, Amy some new neoprene gloves and swimming socks, I'm just in a pair of shorts and Keith is splashing nude as a newborn baby, his cock and balls flapping about. I climb out onto the rocks to let my blood circulate, and then get back into water that is like a wardrobe of shadows, the coursing blood acting as insulator; an internal wetsuit.

For a couple of minutes there is only the water and the sky and bodies battling the shock. Pale wintered flesh tightens and everything retracts. Our sense of sound and touch and taste come into sharp focus.

We climb out exhilarated and drink flasks of hot Ribena and Yespresso, as one of us periodically peels away to run around, carving a foot-stomping circle in the coarse sand, each grain descended from the gritstone massifs, shaped by the passing of time, gathered here by the relentless wind.

Look: it is spring again.

THE SURFACE OF rural Britain is ever-changing.

The slow process of enclosure in England, which began during the sixteenth century and culminated officially with the Enclosure Acts two centuries later, did a thorough job of robbing people of common land. Prior to that, when the demand for exported English wool was great, *champaign* – common pasture land – was used for grazing sheep, or the more fertile pastures were used for growing indigenous produce such as corn, a valued and tradable commodity.

But in time such land was sold up and walled off, and the days of arable farming in open fields were over. During this reshaping, many knavish labourers and farm workers found themselves evicted from their humble properties which now sat on land annexed by unseen new owners, and the wider rural working class were irreversibly displaced, forever on the outside looking in.

Fences, walls, boundaries, ditches, hedgerows and, on occasion, moats kept them away as all across the country villages lost those shared spaces that made them fully functioning, co-dependent communities. Feudalism shed its skin, and out crawled capitalism. Subsistence for all was sacrificed for the gain of the few and the Englishman's entitlement to a shared plot was eradicated for ever, as, increasingly, was the right to roam freely.

Enclosure produced its anti-heroes and tales of riots, rebellion and uprisings abound, but most were, at best, pyrrhic victories for those who dared to take a stand for the old ways.

Never great at obeying the more pointless and petty rules of authority myself, I feel an affinity with these men, women and children. My moral compass is, I hope, correctly calibrated to the basics of goodness yet I struggle particularly with the concepts of borders and boundaries. In short, I like to trespass.

So much of our fields and woods and river banks has become inaccessible. If you don't think this is true, go to your nearest green-belt land and try walking in a straight line. You'll soon be blocked. Try exploring that wood you always drive past. You will see warning signs everywhere. Pick your own path up a mountain. Jump in a river. You will almost certainly soon be thwarted by boundaries designed to obstruct, block, stymie, prevent, discourage, redirect, herd, corral, hinder, prohibit, restrict, impede and intimidate.

And good luck if you intend to go anywhere near a moor in the lead-up to the grouse- or pheasant-shooting season. Loyal gamekeepers showing no quarter in their physical dealings with strangers are still commonplace; I've encountered them.

It is naive to assume the freedom to wander in the twenty-first century, and too easy to romanticise our rural areas, but what is the countryside if not a spark in the tinderbox of imagination?

Perhaps the spirit of Gerrard Winstanley lurks somewhere deep within me, as it does in many walkers, wanderers and watchers of wildlife of today. It was Winstanley, a writer, radical and free-thinking theologian, who in the mid-1600s led the True Levellers – swiftly dubbed the Diggers – to reoccupy those lands stolen during the enclosures, and who filled in new ditches, uprooted boundary hedges and planted crops on what had been, until recently, common land. Winstanley was uncompromising and articulate, and mastered the art of language and rhetoric at a time when few living close to the soil would have been skilled in literacy. He had a good ear for the poetry of rage too: 'Alas! you poor blind earth-moles, you strive to take away my livelihood and the liberty of this poor weak frame my body of flesh, which is my house I dwell in for a time,' he wrote in his tract *A Watch-word to the City of London, and Army*. 'But I strive to cast down your kingdom of darkness, and to open hell gates, and to break the devil's bonds asunder wherewith you are tied.'

Of course, many areas of the countryside need to be nurtured for their own survival, and species protected, with much valuable conservation work being undertaken by all manner of organisations.

It should also go without saying that one must always tread carefully and be respectful of livestock, fauna, ground-nesting birds and crops; no one wants their corn flattened, their cows rattled or their sheep attacked by errant dogs. And does it really need stating that no one should steal birds' eggs, mistreat animals, or chop down trees indiscriminately?

Yet beneath it all, the countryside is an anarchic place, and gentle trespass remains an important aspect of one's enjoyment of it. Even just stating this feels somehow subversive and I can already hear the echoes of dissent.

It's called wild for a reason, and without wildness – without spontaneity and exploration and conflict – life becomes tame. The countryside and those who pass through it become controlled. Sticking to the designated path you are only ever going to see so much.

I have ripped coats, turned ankles, skinned knees and chipped shin bones during years of clumsily vaulting gates, becoming ensnared on rusted barbed wire, pushing through holly bushes, rolling under rotten old fences and toppling face-first over stone walls into dank and sulphurous bogs, all in the pursuit of experience. And all the while my footprint is shallow, my impact minimal.

It's good to walk without thought. Recently, while ordering these thoughts during a stay in the Scottish Borders in deepest autumn, I drove for twenty-five miles in a direction that was entirely unfamiliar to me and parked at the edge of a town I had never been to.

Here I took the first path I could find round the back of

some residential houses, crossed a golf course and followed the River Tweed along perhaps the most beautiful stretch of inland water I have seen in Britain, spotting herons perched like question marks below eroded banks, and a skein of geese come crashing down upon the water. A track rich with the malodorous reek of fox led me onwards until I came to a weir, and a fish ladder, and finally a leaping salmon, one of the very last of the season as it reached its spawning grounds. That fish was on the final stage of an epic journey, one that began thousands of years ago. That fish was my reward for ignoring any obstacles in my way and following my nose. That fish was a poem written for the moment.

Perhaps life is too short to go only where we are told to go. Boundaries are changing but the beauty of serendipity is timeless.

THE FOX IS screaming.

Each night the vixen sells herself with a call that echoes off the face of The Rock. The howl is an advertisement for her availability. She is soliciting sex.

She wakes me at night, and she wakes the dogs of the street too, and when they start barking she falls silent, only to start a minute later, perhaps 200 yards away up in the trees, then what seems like only seconds later, the same distance in the other direction, the echo of her call creating its own chorus.

She is screaming for seed, and when she finds it, when she finally opens herself up to a dog once more, his penis expands and swells so that it stays inside her and she shrieks again, this time with a different timbre, singing what ancient folklore considers 'the fox's love song'.

Then in fifty or so days' time, as March greets April, four or five brown-furred cubs will slither out of the same orifice deep in the dark centre of The Rock. For four weeks they will know little but darkness and milk and the warmth of their mother in their dirt nursery, drawn to a heartbeat wrapped in fur, tree roots and birdsong above, the subterranean cellars and Oceania far below.

Then one day they will tentatively leave this sanctuary, and all the sights and sounds and smells of the wood will come rushing in, and this great citadel will harbour them in its retreating shadows.

IT IS A Sunday as dank and dreary as a Morrissey B-side and rain falls softly for hours, the sodden ground bubbling. It is spring but the birds are silent and the snowdrops bow their crowns beneath the weight of the water.

Even the dog can't be bothered, but I drag him out anyway as we have little choice – by now The Rock has become a place of constant visitation, and I trudge up like a pilgrim, without question.

There is a repetitiveness to the walk up that I must find comforting, even now with the woods in a state of post-landslide industrial transition, otherwise why else keep repeating the same pattern? What was once exploration has now become compulsion.

For five days of the week the place is no longer my own, and even when I do reclaim it from the workmen, loggers, surveyors and engineers who inhabit it, it will soon be thick with nettles, brambles and giant hogweed, and many of my routes will become an impossibility. For the weekends at least, the woods are mine and mine alone.

I visit the new drains that have been dug in, and the large black section of overground piping installed to guide the run off from The Rock. It is an impressive feat given the obscurity of the location.

The stumps of felled trees stick out from the soil like ground-out cigarette butts in a hotel-entrance ashtray, and there are great heaps of timber that had been bulldozed out of the way, including one very close to a fox den that has been there for years.

There is more stuff scattering the slope around the landslide: gloves, empty bottles and crisp packets, pieces of plastic piping. All sorts. Perhaps the work teams will take it all with them when their task of securing the hillside is complete, or perhaps they will leave it for future solitary lurkers to discover and write senseless poems about.

SIFTING THROUGH THOUSANDS of photographs archived by Pennine Heritage, a group established in 1979 to 'promote environmental conservation plus economic and social enhancement of the South Pennines', I come across three pictures of a stone named Big Rock situated somewhere in the centre of Scout Rock Woods. Photographic collections are received by donation, and I am told that these three once belonged to a man named Raymond Stell.

The first shows Big Rock to be a great hunk of boulder roughly rectangular in shape, between seven and eight feet tall and perhaps ten or more feet wide. Though not as tall as the slabs that comprise Stonehenge's iconic trilithons, it nevertheless appears perhaps as dense – certainly several hundred tonnes of ancient mass.

Sitting on top of it are one man and two women. The man is lying to one side and casually propped up on an elbow. He is wearing a suit, tie and collar, while the women are slightly more formally posed and sport their best Sunday whites. Big Rock sits in a levelled-out clearing with a well-worn path around. The ground looks dry, suggesting it is spring or summer. Undated, I would estimate it to be from around the turn of the twentieth century. The bucolic and slightly staged demeanour of its subjects reminds me of the novel and film *Picnic at Hanging Rock*, also set in 1900.

The second picture of Big Rock is taken from the other side of the stone and shows three children – boys, aged six or seven – leaning against it in sou'westers and matching rain hats, shorts and knee socks. The sepia-tinged tone of the picture and their clothing suggest that it was taken in the 1950s. The boys are smiling coyly and the one in the centre has a stick by his side. The young boys look a little like my dad, who was born in 1942, does in pictures of him from that era. Up the left-hand flank of the rock are scuffed markings, created by the metal 'segs' of generations of scrabbling climbers. The opposite side of the valley is visible through the trees.

The third photograph is captioned 'Harry Stell at Big Rock' and takes us to another era. It shows a slightly older boy, Harry, the father, grandfather or great-grandfather perhaps of the owner of the donated photographic collection, aged around twelve, in a three-piece suit, britches and stout ankle boots. He wears a flat cap, prominent collar and bow tie and stands with his hands behind his back. He is smiling, his heavy-lidded eyes hinting at the man he might become.

Here the rock is incidental. It could be anywhere, and little is seen of the background.

I would estimate the picture to have been taken around the time of the First World War, or the 1920s. I think of the novels of D. H. Lawrence, particularly that purple patch that began with *Sons and Lovers* in 1913 and reached a peak with *Lady Chatterley's Lover* in 1928.

What is remarkable about all three photographs is that, having tramped Scout Wood most days for years now, I have never once seen this unmissable slab of stone that surely peeled away from the cliff above at some point in the past 50,000 years.

So where the hell has Big Rock gone?

It almost certainly will not have been removed from the centre of the woods. There is simply no reason to do that, and it would require a tremendous amount of effort to move a boulder weighing hundreds of tonnes down a steep, densely wooded hillside. And for what purpose?

I go back to the photographs and try to detect the stone's precise location. I urge the pictures' subjects, all now old or dead, to offer a hint or give me a sign, but none are forthcoming.

So I take to seeking it out on foot instead, if only to make a connection with these past lives, to sit where they sat, to see what they saw. Once again I tramp through gorse and bramble and under slackening stretches of contemporary chain-link fencing whose holding posts have moved within the mud, rendering the slack fences useless against the entire hillside's constant shifting. I cross the old maintenance track, the giant hogweed patch and the ancient rabbit warrens once known as coneygarths.

Big Rock becomes a riddle to be solved and eventually the answer is found back in the archives: it has not been moved but yet it is not there.

Instead it sits beneath me. The magnificent monolith in the photographs predates the town tip, and in the intervening years it has been surrounded by so much dumped rubbish and household waste that it has disappeared from view. It has been buried by bits and pieces, submerged by scrap and scramble, drowned by dreck, and then laid over with the rot of dead leaves, fallen trees and the growth of mosses and weeds. Big Rock is lower than the worms. Deer dance above it and the ravens' shadows cross the soil that holds it fast.

Big Rock sees no sunshine now.

Or maybe it does, as any one of these stones poking through the earth might be a protruding corner or edge, a humped curve that is the last visible inches of a landmark that was special to some, a place of weekend pilgrimage for lazy hours of leisure, and soon, as the woodland decays around it, a single leaf will fall to finally cover it entirely.

APRIL AND THE crows are nest-building across the crooked chimneys. Two seasons they have spent living in the factory wall, their doorway a gash in the old asbestos sheet, a last reminder of the 131 poor sods who died coughing glass in Acre Mills up at Old Town.

I hear them as the drivers arrive for the six-two shift in hi-vis gilets and the sun bends beautiful around their bait boxes while up on Scout Rock, mindful of hierarchy, two ravens circle superior. It's said four fledglings hatched this winter past, doubling the woodland's numbers. Spring suggests something better: summer's song on the coming breeze, buds set to bursting, a fox cub tumbling on the old tip where ceramic shards and apothecary bottles poke up through the laminated layers of time, a carpet of dirt unrolled.

With each hour the shadow across the valley shortens; silent winter wishes fulfilled.

The next day the sky is clear and full spring bursts and I head towards the sun. My legs harbour boxing hares; I'm full of the season, I can't sit down.

Each route I take through Scout Rock Woods is signed by wayfinding markers not yet disturbed in the reshaping of the woods, the solidified sack of concrete, the storm-snapped trunk of a tree.

Walking through the upper plateau on a dry April day as the fresh batches of nettles, ragwort and knotweed are sprouting from the soil, I notice for the first time a path ahead of me at the foot of The Rock. It is a wavering line that weaves between deracinated stumps and fallen boulders, a light through-way etched across a covering of snapped twigs and flattened soil, where no weeds have taken root.

At first it seems odd that I have never noticed it before, but then the woodland's secret is shared: the new spring growth has revealed a path that I, and I alone, have carved over the years of passing through. This meandering route is one of the few regular stretches that I take without digression, and therefore is the only place where a lasting impression has been left across the soil; some call them 'desire paths'. It has taken the drying-out of the earth and the renewal of the woodland's growth to

show the markings that my footfall has made during this constant returning-to. For someone whose work exists primarily
on paper or in the bottomless vortex of the digital realm, this
sense of permanence is comforting.

In my anxiety-abating, calorie-burning, canine-exciting
excursions I have undertaken a different form of writing. I have
written a signature across the land. I have scratched my mark.
I have made a path.

It is my only lasting mark on the landscape, apart from the
Burger King I helped build at Chester-le-Street during a few days
labouring while a student, where I was bestowed the nickname
'Poet' for reading a book. It was not meant as a compliment.

Near to the centre of the woods, I pass another marker. It is
an old dustbin from the 1950s, of the type that would be hoisted
onto the shoulder of dustbin men, their thick black-rubber lids
removed and their contents thrown into the gnashing metal jaws
of the dustcarts.

This bin has lain on its side for decades, untouched by
humans during storms and heatwaves, blizzards and floods,
Amazon, Google and Twitter have all been created while this
bin lay abandoned and unseen. Functionless.

Its trunk is dented and its rim rusted, but it is without holes
and the stout handles are intact, and each day as I pass it I see it
slowly sinking into the soil as decaying plant life rises to consume it, as it does Great Rock.

A layering of soil three or more inches deep fills it now too, across which moss has spread. There also grows what appears to be *meconopsis cambrica*, a pre-flowering Welsh Poppy plant, its appearance a biogeographic quirk.

Worms turn the soil in there and spiders weave webs in the curved arch of the bin's interior. Insects hatch and die here. Mice have nested here and a curious badger has rested its claws and rolled it slightly. Sprite-like fox cubs have sniffed at the bin and puckishly bounced around it, and maybe rabbits have taken shelter in it too, shivering through violent showers. Birds – hundreds of birds – have perched here and pecked at a grub or two while passing through the valley on magnificent journeys to places I may never see.

This receptacle for man's rubbish hosts a world within a world.

And the way it lies with soil spilling from its mouth now, it is as if the bin once held the beginning of the planet itself, and was tipped by time to leak life – entire countries and continents pouring from it, before running, roaring, raging and coagulating into a brilliant sphere, a microcosmic galaxy that itself may just be an old dustbin abandoned in a still and silent wood on a beautiful spring morning.

IT'S A STILL and clear evening when I receive a text from my friend and neighbour Niall:

Peregrine perched on crag.

A keen birdwatcher, Niall is my neighbourly avian consultant and often updates me on any developments amongst the wild animals of the valley. His front lawn is a feasting place for the local badger population and, like me, whenever he has made a roast dinner Niall leaves its remains in the rough scrubland out the front for the foxes.

I grab my binoculars and head out into the street to scour the jutting upper bluffs of Scout Rock, but the binos are about as strong as my glasses and the views afforded in winter are now obscured by spring growth. I know they are up there, a perennial pair nesting in the highest reaches, though I only ever see them as shapes against the sun, black handkerchiefs winnowing on the currents.

My phone vibrates with another message. Niall again. He instructs me to head to the meadow beyond through Jerry the Beekeeper's place, where he has his telescope set up. Here I once found a deer curled trembling in the long grass. It did not flee when I approached it. Instead it slowly stood and wobbled with uncertainty as if it were a newborn fawn taking its first steps. I saw that one sessile leg hung loose, attached to its body only by skin and sinew and fur. It must have been hit by a car and limped down here.

It faltered for a moment and then collapsed, a broken, beautiful heap of life, its black eyes wide with fear like two dark worm-holes spiralling back down through the ages. At the bottom sat death.

Its nose was wet and it trembled to the bass drum of blood in its ears.

I went to tell Jerry the Beekeeper about the deer and he said he would make some calls. There was nothing else to do, so I carried on home. But I couldn't settle. All I could see were those eyes, the limp leg dangling and the final nest she had made for herself in the grass wet with morning dew.

I left the house again and returned just in time to see three men step out of a van and walk out towards the meadow. One had a cudgel, another a gun. They were country folk. Valley boys. They wore not the correct perceived outdoor gear fancied by city folk – tweeds, fancy waxed jackets and walking boots – but the actual wear of farmers and agricultural workers: layers of old T-shirts and jumpers, padded plaid outer shirts. Wellies. No coats.

Seeing them, I stopped, turned and went back the way I came.

A minute-long interregnum followed, and then after fifty yards I heard the single gunshot and the trees around me cleared themselves of crows, which scattered for the higher stone shelves of Scout Rock.

NIALL LOWERS HIS tripod and gives me instructions as to where to see the peregrine, while also explaining that Ted Hughes got it wrong in his *Hawk in the Rain* collection when he describes a kestrel, which, he explains, any twitcher will tell you is of the falcon genus rather than the hawk.

I put my eye to the telescope and find myself closely looking at a peregrine falcon in exquisite detail from over 200 yards away. It is a male. A tiercel. Somewhere in a fissure in the rock a few feet away is the female, unseen.

The peregrine's head is cocked curiously, its splayed mustard-yellow feet matching the markings of its beak. The tips of its wings reach almost down to the hem of its tail, and its pale, soft belly is dappled with dark markings. It is at ease, a magnificent creature, so compact, streamlined and self-contained.

I think then of Dominic Cooper, an English writer and horologist who wrote a series of spellbinding novels in the 1970s and 1980s in which the landscape is always the lead character, before, as he once told me during an interview, writing walked away from him.

'I ran out of words,' he said. Instead he built himself a Norwegian-style log house high on a cliff on the remote Ardnamurchan Peninsula of Scotland, two hours from the nearest town, where he mended watches and clocks, before retiring to live the life of a semi-recluse, writing poetry, enjoying the landscape and doing precisely what he wants to do in life.

'I've never done a single thing specifically for money,' he once told me. 'When I sold a film option for £25,000, I worked hard at giving it all away.'

Even an editor at his former publisher Faber & Faber con-
fesses that he hasn't heard of Cooper, a writer whose prose ranks
as some of the best of the twentieth century. Too fearful of rejec-
tion, he never sent any of his poems out until, after I wrote an
appreciation of his work for a magazine, he sent me some and
I persuaded them to publish his first ever poem, a homage to
the male peregrine falcon entitled 'From My Window, North:
Winter'. In it he describes:

> his sunburst careless form wheeling forever
> up and out of this broken, speechless world.
> Knuckled may lie this dark of earth,
> chill and crackled into clod and fist of rock,
> flux and seed held and dozing fast. Yet always
> and further, far above our pale whisperings,
> our gritted hope and set of jaw, he sails.

Through the telescope the peregrine turns its head to me.
It looks down the viewfinder straight at me. Stares. It looks
through me. Beyond me. And for a fleeting moment there is
nothing else in the world. Only us.

Chapter Twelve

It takes me nearly eight years to fully explore Brearley Wood, which sits just a mile or so further along the valley, covering the banks from the River Calder up to the hilltop village of Midgley. I have been distracted.

What is remarkable is how similar in shape and size Brearley Wood is to Scout Rock; it is as if it is a mirror Scout Rock, planted, nurtured and pollarded in the image of its slightly larger sibling just a crow's mile across the way.

Exhaustion has conspired to keep me on the down-low paths, trudging mechanically merely to exercise the dog and attempt to outrun the thoughts that are frantically carouselling around my conscious mind.

It is a prettier, neater wood than Scout Rock. Here the scars of industry are minimal and no rubbish has been dumped. There is no residual sense of foreboding and nothing pokes from the soil other than that which should be there: rock and root.

From the corner of my eye I catch sight of a movement, a gentle shifting.

It is not that of a human or an animal, but something collective.

I see it again – a sudden shifting, a flurry of activity, a flash of blue low down in amongst the densely compacted trees. I walk towards it. And again: a sweeping ripple.

Bluebells.

Hundreds upon hundreds of them.

Thousands.

They are growing in a clearing beneath a heavy canopy of leaves through which the sun's rays shine down and bathe them in shafts of ecclesiastic light.

As I approach this secreted bluebell patch a light breeze sweeps across its surface, causing the hundreds of stems to shimmer once more.

I wade into them as if they are a fresh spring bubbling up through layers of gritstone to reinvigorate an ailing stream that pours from the pen of Gerard Manley Hopkins: 'And azuring-over greybell makes / Wood banks and brakes wash wet like lakes.'

The bluebells are virginal and untouched by man. They opened up early this morning while I was wrestling with the demons of anxiety in a fretful sleep whose alarm call was the carillon of dawn birdsong. That is the magic of bluebells: they appear as if from nothing, seemingly accelerating from zero to twelve inches in the sleepy blink of a spring night's eye.

A welcome constant in the British countryside, each fresh crop heralds a turning in the inclement weather, the dawning days of the warmer season. They are a symbol of hope. Nothing bad ever happened involving bluebells.

Down the generations this wild flower has borne many names depending upon the region – Calverkeys, Culverkeys, Auld Man's Bell, Jacinthe, Ring-o'-Bells – but it always has the same face, that blue visage tilting first to the sun then silently bowing and genuflecting come sundown.

So popular and perennial are bluebells that scores of places in this country have a quiet corner nearby called Bluebell Woods, each different yet somehow the same. You only have to ask a local elder the way to the Bluebell Woods and they are sure to reply with clear and concise directions.

Bluebells are so admired that they are a protected species. To remove the bulbs is an offence, as is their removal by landowners selling their land, which might explain why in these times of creeping urbanisation, the suburbs nibbling away at our rural scapes like caterpillars at a leaf, the bluebell continues to flourish.

I wade in deeper, then fall to the floor. I let the bluebells pull me under as I lie on my back and examine the intertwining branches above that form an inchoate matrix of silhouette lines against the sky. Here I lie beneath imaginary blue water, bobbing slightly as the next incoming flicker of a breeze sweeps across this oasis, adrift on an ocean of time.

NOT A DROP of late-spring rain has fallen for days and the nightly news reports streams and becks up in the Dales and the

Lakes that have run themselves dry. They show stills of these straggling ghylls of bone-dry rocks tumbled by time.

An unexpected virus prompts a further energy crash, an unexpected landslide of body and mind. Just last week I was reservoir-swimming but now its takes every bit of energy to get out of bed and fill my sunlit bowl with bran flakes. Instead I lie beneath the duvet in a half-sleep, counting the quarter-hour bell chimes in the church turret a half-mile away.

A walk halfway up Scout Rock leaves me leaning on a wall, gasping. When I make it home a mile later I sleep for two hours, a clothed and foetal coma.

Small, easy things become big, difficult things. I recognise the signs and succumb to sleeping eight, nine, ten hours a night and then a couple more hours in the afternoon, surprised that this crash has come not in autumn but spring. Food loses its taste, and the day is so bright I can barely discern its colour.

I am in the middle of a period that will see the publication of three books in a twelve-month period and now I feel jet-lagged, flu-addled and a bit drunk. Everything is amplified but I am behind glass. A nagging pain throbs in my shoulder, neck and head and a planned day's chopping logs is cancelled; I am unable to swing an axe. I have 200 pounds in the bank and vow to give up writing (again). I take Vitamin D and paracetamol and ibuprofen and codeine and cod-liver oil and herbal sleeping tablets. I eat a lot of apples. I sleep and I sleep and I sleep.

Della is sympathetic. She has seen me this way several times before. She has seen the inertia, the loss of pep, the fretting. The wearing of the same jumper for days or weeks. She helps me retain perspective and serves me soup, and the dog still needs walking.

I watch the birds industriously flit from branch to nest as I take the same flat daily walk: past the pond, through the field, along the railway sidings. I cannot contemplate slopes so instead lose myself in the deep of the sprouting balsam, bindweed, nettles, and the sweet wild grasses that Cliff likes to nibble at like a grazing cow. I listen to the rustling and wriggling of life, and remind myself that I am but one more species whose lifespan is limited, and nothing much matters.

Nature and the animal kingdom are there for me once again.

I feel better as the day goes on, and after tea we go for sunset wanders, down to the River Calder to paddle in the shallows, noticing the new gravel banks that have risen from its beds, the fish biting at the hatching flies and the geese that come crash-landing onto the canal nearby.

One warm, still evening I step out of the house and look up to The Rock, where I see strange black sigil-like shapes hovering in the sky, like ancient hieroglyphics on an ice-cool monitor screen. They create strange and brief configurations, bastard words that make no sense.

As I blink they disappear, only to return a moment later. I am curious rather than disturbed by them. I know they are not real but instead see them as a murder of mangled crows unleashed from the cage of my frazzled mind. I watch them a while longer as they hover not far above the rocky outcrop where the peregrines live.

In her book *Tristimania* the writer Jay Griffiths describes a hallucination that she had during the early onset of a year-long descent into manic depression – 'tristimania' is an eighteenth-century word she uses to describe the combination of mania and melancholy experienced during a bipolar episode: 'I could see spirals rising, each one spinning upwards faster and faster the more I watched it, like the tiny flecks you can see with your eyes shut which fall faster if you follow them with your gaze.' Such visions she describes as 'the sick psyche's self-flowering', continuing: 'I could see unreal blooms – the idea of flowering without the actual flowers, wandering blooming, the very blossom of the mind – a rose arose, blossomed and bloomed and was blown.'

Though I experience nothing quite so extreme I take comfort in Griffiths' sentences, and recognise this as a low-level hallucination caused by too much work, too many words. Too much time spent looking inwards.

THREE WEEKS PASS before I return to The Rock, and as I climb the fence I find myself plunging into a wood in bloom. A world reborn once more.

This prolonged spell of unexpected dryness has seen the sudden growth of broom and cow parsley, plus the usual valley perennials: balsam, nettles and ragwort. The bluebells are still hanging on in there too.

Deep in the heart of the woods, the patch of hogweed is growing at a rapid rate yet by autumn they will be hollow tubers. By winter they will be spent.

I feel my spirits lifting as The Rock rises before me once more. Walls of green slide away like the sets of an elaborately staged theatrical performance as high above the two ravens circle, an advance welcoming party.

The peregrine falcons are up there too, poised in the penumbra. At the last count the female was sitting on three hatched balls of fur with screeching beaks on a tufted bracken outcrop, their father hunting further afield. Each day he brings back shredded pigeons, torn starlings, snapped jays and various songbirds that will sing no more.

Life goes on. Death goes on. And it all keeps coming back around, one feeding the other. The spinning wheel.

ANOTHER WEEK SLIPS by until a full month of inertia and chronic fatigue has passed.

I pack my essentials and force myself to Lumb Falls. I know that the shock of cold water always makes me feel better, but the physical act of getting there has prevented me straying too far from my sofa.

Today the pool has never looked more like a lost paradise. The water is low and the waterfall itself a welcoming tangle of wet white ropes thudding into the simmering cauldron below. Around it the rock walls are draped with slick algae, lichen and mosses showering a light fret of clear droplets.

The water's snap is as harsh as expected, but at least it *is* expected. A true shock is always a surprise, and I tune my breathing to work with it.

I push out and swim in small circles, shedding the anxiety and exhaustion with each slow pull of my rudimentary breast stroke.

The pool looks different now. Diminished by the turn of the seasons, the recent arid patch has revealed new jutting rocks and tempered the outflow to a tinkering dribble. Last winter Lumb Falls was a fearful place, its flow thunderous and violent, but today I am happy to drift and bob like dead leaves in the swirl of its eddy, letters posted to the sea.

I shift a few loose rocks and watch as an old, fat toad traverses a rock and then slips and plops without grace into what I see are necklaces of spawn below, each blackened orb in the chain already sprouting the limbs and tail that will soon see it wriggling its way to independence. Downstream several weeks of evaporation and little rain has formed new pools from the main thrust of the river, and in one shallow corridor I see four or five young trout dart as a tumult of hatched flies rolls across its surface like a waterwheel.

In the field above a rabbit watches on. The persistent scratching of a wasp at a bracken frond is amplified by the stillness of Crimsworth Dean. My senses have been polished, old skin shed.

And the water keeps steadily sculpting the great hollowed cup of rock, drilling deeper and deeper still into the crust of a planet revolving at 460 yards per second.

THE EARS PLAY tricks.

I'm deep in Scout Rock Woods when I hear an unfamiliar bird call.

Thring-thring.

It is loud and clear, but not being much of a bird expert I have no hope of identifying it, only that I might be able to locate its origin and catch a glimpse of its shape or colouring.

Thring-thring.

The bird call is full-throated and consistent. It appears not as a call of distress or desire, harrowing or hunger, it simply *is*. To describe it on the page, or transcribe it phonetically, I'm faced with the same dilemma of twitchers the world over: it is impossible. Perhaps it is a croak, pitched somewhere between a post-coital toad and a harried crow. Or maybe it is a reedy thrum; a fleshy yawp.

Thring-thring doesn't do it justice.

Thring-thring doesn't come close.

All I know is it is emanating from higher up on Scout Rock, from a place I can reach if I scramble and claw my way up there.

The call falls silent but as I continue the ascent, my lungs scorched and hair already matted from the exertion, Cliff skipping ahead and lost in the heather stalks, it starts up again. I'm above the trees now and I can see all of Mytholmroyd below me. The school, the shops, the churches. The estates. The lines of transport that run in parallel: river, road, canal, train tracks.

Here the bird's call appears louder still, though I am no closer to reaching the area from which it is coming. Is it below me now, down somewhere in the thick cluster of trunks?

Thring-thring.

Or above me, where my favourite crag juts below the high peak of The Rock?

Thring-thring.

Or perhaps it is over to the right, down a tight deer run that passes precipitously close to a drop I have never dared navigate.

Thring-thring as an echo.

I cannot see the feathered creature, yet still it calls.

Thring-thring as poetry in the season of rebirth.

Thring-thring amplified by the arena of stone.

Then I realise.

And I laugh.

I laugh at my idiocy, and The Rock's neat deceit.

The garage where I take my car for its annual MOT, where men confuse me with technical words about oil sumps and brake pads, sits at the base of the valley. It is housed in a large warehouse in the heart of a modern industrial estate, whose doors open right out onto one of the best views of Scout Rock. Whenever I am down there I notice how the dark cliff appears to hang from the sky like drapes and wonder if the mechanics marvel at its rugged structure, and get the desire to down tools and scale it. Or has this visual familiarity bred indifference?

The garage people have their phone rigged up to speakers so that even when laid beneath a car or deep in the inspection pits, or outside blowing smoke rings from roll-ups, it always gets answered by someone. The digital trill of the ringing landline bounces around the cavernous metal space of the MOT depot and out across the forecourt.

And right up The Rock.

For it is not the call of a bird that I have been tracking, but a regularly ringing phone.

Between the new world of the industrial estate and the old Ice-Age world of The Rock – between wires and metal and stone – the sound has become amplified, distorted, reshaped as something new.

Thring-thring goes the phone far below me, and I can picture one of the lads picking up the receiver and reaching for a pencil from behind his ear. Taking down a booking.

'Tuesday morning is fine, love. Yep, MOT and full service. We'll see you then. Bye now.'

THE WAY THAT the stone face of The Rock traps and echoes sound is the same as the sound mirrors erected during the 1920s and 1930s, which can still be found along the coastlines of Kent, Essex, North Yorkshire and the East Riding today.

Cast from concrete in the shape of either curved walls or parabolic concrete slabs (with half a sphere scooped out to create a basin effect), sound mirrors were installed with collector heads – state-of-the-art microphones – and used as early warning systems to detect the growling engines of incoming aeroplanes. Their usefulness was limited, though, and they were soon redundant in the face of more sophisticated detection technologies, specifically radar.

The sound mirrors that remain today are Brutalist objects, with the appearance of having fallen from the skies of another era. Their curves and lines are sculptural, the substance from which they are made cold and functional.

The Rock, itself a senescent relic, also draws sound and holds it there. In certain spots if you stand still and listen closely you can hear every chime, clink, clang, buzz, hum, jingle and jangle of the surrounding area.

On weekends a cry of dissent or howl of pain is amplified from a Sunday League football game and carries across the valley, so that when I am at the base of Scout Rock, or up on its meadowed peak, it is as if I am watching from the touchline.

Or in summer the creak and crack of an unseen leather ball on a linseed bat, the anguished bowler's bellow and the group call of *howzat* seem so close, even though the cricket club is a twenty-minute walk away

The Rock is not only the valley's ears, hearing all that goes on in its lap, but its mouthpiece too, the way it speaks back the sounds of traffic-jam horns, a lone car alarm, or the siren from a Lowry-esque factory signalling the end of a lunch break. It resonates with an announcement from the station that '*The next train to arrive on platform two will be the . . .*'

In the depths of one damp December day Della and I drive for two hours to visit a sound mirror at Kilnsea, in the East Riding, trudging through a field until our boots become weighted with the heaviest of Holderness mud.

The Kilnsea sound mirror sits in the agrarian flatlands and avian wetlands, tilted out towards the sea and a Europe that sadly today feels further away than ever, the North Sea now less a connecting waterway to the Continent and more of a moat to shut it out.

We touch its contours and see the lichen that grows across it. I splay myself in the cold concave of the mirror's mottled parabola and press my face to it. The grey salt-broth of the sea is behind me, and somewhere beyond that the first spit of land where Holland meets Germany. A deep-dug ditch of water sits nearby, a reminder that this edge of England has more in common with the lowlands of the Netherlands and Belgium that it was once a part of. What, I wonder, will this place look like 1,000 years from now? Or 50,000? A million?

Will this sound mirror be found sitting in the sea bed, a relic to be pulled up and viewed with curiosity – and will there even be a sea, or anyone around to extrapolate false meaning?

SOON THE TRUE scent of summer arrives: pig shit, freshly spread across the top fields. Strong and sweet, it descends in warm, wafting waves.

The farmers have already had one grass harvest, their baling machines *put-putting* along until sunset, as great black balls bound in stretched plastic silage wrap are deposited across the meadows like the droppings of a mechanical beast slinking towards the horizon.

And now they spread fresh fertiliser across the stubbled fields for stealth growth. The air is dry and dusty as the machine steadily sprays the effluence and the smell of it drapes itself across everything.

Once the trucks that carried the muck were known as honeywagons because of the amber-coloured liquid that dripped from them; still today it is a term used in the film business for the blocks of portable toilets used on set.

A cocktail of pig shit and piss makes for the finest manure. Gardeners used to refer to it as 'black gold' as it aerates tired soil and allows new roots and shoots to grow through it. It helps retain moisture too, adding nutrients that in turn intensify growth.

It is a clinging smell though. Acrid. It gets everywhere. Lingers. It sneaks into houses through open windows, scents clean washing, gives the air an acidic, urine-like tang.

Here the natural resources are being used, and reused, just as they always have been. Food creates waste, from which new food is grown, and out of it comes the milk that makes the milkshakes and the beef that shapes the burgers to be eaten by the people as they drive through the fast-food outlet, hastily winding their windows back up again to escape the rural funk.

I breathe it in now – it is impossible not to – and know that I am experiencing nature's dire perfume, as generations of valley folk have before me.

RECENT YEARS HAVE seen our book shops swell with works that consider the rural landscapes of Britain. Often their authors are people like me, blindly staggering around trying to make sense of the world and their place in it. I am acutely aware of the privilege of being able to do so, and forever grateful.

But so many of these accounts veer towards the romantic. They are escapist representations, bucolic wood-cut renderings of a modern rural world one step removed from the reality. Beautifully written, but over-precious. Few seem prepared to tackle the more insidious side of the landscape – the blood and guts of it, and also the actions of those individuals whose negative influence can define a place for decades or centuries.

As a society we have a persistent need to demarcate. It offers a chance to exert power over our habitat, a conquering of wildness. For centuries pioneers, planners and landowners have enjoyed nothing more than unrolling blueprints, surveys or maps and continually reconfiguring the land into new interpretations of ownership. And with each new field, wood, housing estate, park, alleyway or scrubland created, a new history is imprinted upon it by the human activity that takes place there.

But to what extent does a place dictate people's behaviour? Can the contours of a county determine the actions of its residents?

West Yorkshire has an undeniable toughness about it. Historically it is represented as masculine, a land of grit and spit. Meat and bone. Beer, industry, rugby. In her 1986 book *The Streetcleaner: The Yorkshire Ripper Case on Trial*, the writer and academic Nicole Ward Jouve identifies a demarcated 'West Yorkshire quadrangle' roughly formed between Leeds, Bradford, Halifax and Huddersfield (and extending beyond to Manchester) in which the majority of the attacks on women by Britain's most notorious and feared serial killer – 'the type that Anglo-Saxon countries produce' – Peter Sutcliffe, took place between July 1975 and his arrest in January 1981.

Jouve reprints a 'Geography of Terror' chart from the *Sunday Times*, which maps out the locations where Bingley-based Sutcliffe's thirteen murders and seven maimings took place. Somewhere in the centre, unsullied by his presence, sits the raw and beautiful landscape of Mytholmroyd. Somewhere in the centre sits Scout Rock.

Of the moors Jouve writes: 'In the eighteenth century people called them "bleak". Bleak: stark. That wonderful hard "k", that has something hard about it. The surface is bare like high mountain slopes where the tree-line stops. Their colour too makes you think of high mountains. Darker hues though: bog brown, rust brown, purple as well as the whitish shimmer of dry grass. Their appeal comes from this illusion of sudden, magical heights: you haven't climbed much, you can see the patchy green dales at your feet. And yet you'd think you were on the roof of the world. You feel violence in the wind.'

Jouve's insights are especially valuable as being both French and female – and an academic – she offers an outsider's views of a landscape whose facets have been traditionally represented in figures of masculinity, from Heathcliff to Ted Hughes and on to Sutcliffe.

'You couldn't help wondering what connections there were between the socio-economic dereliction which much of the geography expressed, and the type of violence which was at work in the nooks and crannies of those landscapes,' she writes. 'I, as a French woman, had settled in Yorkshire because myths like the Brontës, spaces like the moors, had appealed to me as deeply nurturing, promising freedom and scope. Now, other places and a new myth that were uncomfortably close to those I loved, were threatening murder. The place was spelling death to me as a woman. It was willing you dead.'

Jouve's account of the West Yorkshire stalking ground of Sutcliffe, his crimes and the attendant trial, is noteworthy for its reclamations of these landscapes, a feminist/intellectual counter-punch to a case that was so predominantly male on both sides of the law, where females were reduced to mere footnotes, either as faceless victims dismissed because of their lifestyle circumstances (some were prostitutes) or guilty through association (Sutcliffe's wife Sonia). It is an attempt to wrestle back these valleys, moors and industrial towns from becoming for ever 'Ripper country'.

Through West Yorkshire today there runs a corridor of towns, which if travelled along could give the impression that it is an entirely built-up county of conurbations, retail parks and agribusinesses, yet it is flanked on either side by semi-wild, weed-choked spaces, farmlands and a barren vastness. Sutcliffe often attacked on the edges of the West Riding's towns and cities, crossing demarcated boundaries to lurk in darkened corners like the original Jack the Ripper of Victorian London. He lived in the Aire Valley (his first victim was in Keighley, close to the moors), through which the fictional Heathcliff may well have wandered during his missing three years in *Wuthering Heights*, when he left as a boy and returned a man.

Before him, the surrounding Pennine uplands that Jouve calls a 'secret moorland cemetery' had been desecrated by child murderers Ian Brady and Myra Hindley; their burial ground, Saddleworth Moor, was part of West Yorkshire until boundary changes in 1974. 'I felt sullied,' she writes of her moorland experiences. 'What had always meant cleanliness and expanse had been violated. Then time and the wind and the heather won. The silence washed over the sickness.'

'The landscape is a dream,' Jouve adds. 'Dream-like, too, the sudden ease of access to all the towns: Leeds – Bradford – Dewsbury – Halifax – Huddersfield – the Pennines, and then Manchester and its drove of worker towns . . . All these towns: places where murders are taking place.'

When a recording believed to be the voice of the Ripper dubbed the infamous 'Wearside Jack' tape was played at a Leeds United home game in an attempt to flush out the killer, the crowd drowned it out with chants of *'Eleven – nil!'*. Meaning: the Ripper had killed eleven women, and still the West Yorkshire Police had nothing.

West Yorkshire: historically – stupidly – masculine.

A land of grit and spit. Meat and bone.

This place.

THERE EXISTS SOME old Super 8 footage – you can view it on YouTube – of former nightclub promoter, disc jockey and children's TV presenter Jimmy Savile on one of his many visits to the Upper Calder Valley.

It dates from the late 1960s and looks washed out, expressing only the faintest hint of colour. It is silent too, and has that slightly jerky effect that heightens the impression of nostalgia and reality once removed.

Leeds-born Savile had strong ties to the area. He kept a motorhome up at Cragg Vale, one of the many boltholes that he had scattered around the country like a feral creature who consistently needs to go to ground. There were flats in Scarborough and Leeds, the caravan out the back of King's Cross depot, the private rooms at Broadmoor and, later, Stoke Mandeville.

He had status around here. Locals still remember him turning up at Cragg Vale in the middle of a dark, stormy night and banging on the vicar's door to pick up a key for the church, St John the Baptist in the Wilderness, that sits tucked down in the hollow, halfway between Mytholmroyd and the stark and barren moorlands. St John's is the only Protestant church in the village, and the old stone bridge outside is cut by the Greenwich Meridian. Savile is remembered as wearing circular pink-tinted sunglasses and a floor-length lime-green floral hooded cape; the same get-up he would periodically sport, and was still wearing when he visited decades later.

'I first came down here to help the church find a vicar and soon after was appointed churchwarden for my effort,' he told the *Halifax Courier* at the time. 'There has been no better pull for me to keep coming back.'

Though the Super 8 footage features a younger and leaner-looking Savile rather than the crusty, nicotine-stained golem of later years, and his trademark electric-peroxide hair has been temporarily replaced by a dark bob kept hidden beneath an ersatz deerstalker hat, it's him alright. You can tell by the saluting, the gurning, the eye-rolling. The craven mugging for the camera.

There is snow on the ground as he leads a procession of local children, faces flushed with the winter cold and the excitement of the occasion, Pied Piper-like along the same incline that Daniel Defoe wandered, and where the notorious Cragg Vale Coiners ran their forged goods under the cover of eighteenth-century darkness, and up which the Tour de France cyclists powered, and down which the great wrathful flood waters of a Christmas night ran with fury.

The future knight of the realm passes the old gritstone cottages that remain unchanged a half-century later – indeed it could be any day from the past 400 years were it not for the parked cars. Marching purposefully with stick in hand, he turns onto Scout Road, and here the street is reduced to base shapes of grey buildings, patches of snow, the moving forms of figures wrapped in woollen hats and worsted overcoats. Only the sky has a hint of colour. He walks towards the camera, his cretinous face first looming, and then filling the screen.

Just as he reaches my house we're afforded a fleeting glimpse of Scout Rock watching over it all. A dark stain over the 1960s. It is seen for only a second or two as Savile passes.

Then the film cuts dead. He's gone, just like that. A ghost from the past, vanished on my doorstep.

SAVILE IS THE new bogeyman of the North, a person of no discernible talent and the vilest son of West Yorkshire since Peter Sutcliffe, whom Savile met in Broadmoor and formed a friendship with. One of Sutcliffe's victims, Irene Richardson, was found just yards from Sir Jim's penthouse in Roundhay Park and a year earlier the Ripper had attacked another woman, Marcella Claxton, at the very same spot. A cast of Savile's teeth was even taken during the widespread hunt for the Ripper to see if they matched bite marks on some of his victims. (Years later a note in a police file, made public by the Freedom of Information Act, revealed that 'Savile, Jimmy [the famous one]' had offered his services as an intermediary, 'should the Ripper wish to make contact'.)

When Savile died in 2011 his body lay in state in a gold-coloured steel coffin in the Queen's Hotel by Leeds train station. Five thousand mourners queued up to pay their respects to the man they called a West Yorkshire legend.

Are these men, raised from the sod to live in the shadows – mythical figures of their own monstrous making – products of their environments then?

Could all the elements of history and landscape in this county that the writer David Peace renamed 'Red Riding' have conspired to produce a Sutcliffe, a Savile? Must we admit that these men, who may remain notorious throughout the forthcoming few centuries, are as West Yorkshire as rain, curd tart and real ale?

On dank and lingering days of little light, a wandering imagination certainly wonders, and Della and I discuss the subject often, so much so that we cogently tell ourselves that Scout Rock might be the very centre around which some of the worst crimes in recent history revolve, renaming the landmark as 'the Craggheptonfax Axis of Evil', in homage to the compound name bestowed on another local demarcated conflation of 'Clreckshuddersfax', an area of mile upon mile of unbroken post-industrial urbanisation.

We're over-thinking it, of course, but when we dig a little deeper more occult history is unearthed. Why, for example, did Britain's most prolific serial killer, Harold Shipman, murderer of 215 people, choose to begin both his career as a GP and his killing spree after moving to Todmorden at the top end of the Calder Valley in 1974? Just two months after joining Abraham Ormerod Medical Practice Shipman signed his first death certificate and was later suspected of killing five of his patients by lethal injection in that year alone. Several more on the same day in January 1975. Twenty-two in Todmorden in all.

Today his surgery has been levelled and there are plans to build a supermarket where 'Doctor Death' once played God with the sick and the vulnerable of Calderdale.

Sutcliffe. Savile. Shipman.

There's more. Five miles beyond The Rock in the valley village of Northowram, John Reginald Halliday Christie, the infamous strangler of 10 Rillington Place, was born. For his crimes he was executed by Albert Pierrepoint, last state executioner who, by coincidence, was born just a few miles away in West Yorkshire. Hapless burglar turned multiple murderer Donald Neilson (real name Donald Nappey), dubbed 'the Black Panther', grew up nearby too.

Like TV detectives, we take out a large map of the area on the floor and pin the numerous crime locations, birthplaces and haunts that form the Craggheptonfax Axis of Evil, to see if a pattern emerges. A pentagram or a goat's head, perhaps. An occultist formation to confirm The Rock's true powers.

'I see . . . a sparrow on a perch,' says Della.

'I see . . . a cheeseburger.'

'Or maybe Yasser Arafat.'

We fold the map away. The sun is shining.

We step out into the green-chequered swathe of harvest fields. I see a hawk hovering for mice on the move.

The valley has never appeared more beautiful.

Chapter Thirteen

E arly summer and the trees create a corridor, and the night comes alive with bats.

Dusk is the best time for being amongst them, when the moths they feed upon are tricked by the draw of the waxing moon and the mosquitoes seek the hot liquid of mammals, and all is consumption.

The bats of The Rock leave their hollows to flit the incline, brilliant black shapes against the circle of light along the arboreal tunnel, where the trees end and the future begins.

They bomb and flicker and I stand amongst them, feeling their flitting as they brush past my hair. The click of their echolocation is pitched at too high a frequency to register in human ears but I know it is steering their passage, preventing them becoming entangled. They always bank away at the final nanosecond.

It is a myth that bats are blind. In fact, their strength of sight is comparable to that of humans, but it just so happens they hunt under the cover of fading daylight or darkness so rely on hearing instead.

We come here on summer nights to watch them as they each devour up to 3,000 insects per feed.

One night, late, a car pulls over just beyond the tree tunnel and a woman jumps out. She runs round to the front of her vehicle and crouches in the white beam of the headlights.

Della and I cross the road to see if she is OK.

'I think I just hit a bat,' she says, unnerved.

I squat down beside her at the front of the car, and there it is, clinging to the front grille, a small pouch of fur just above the registration plate, its tiny digits curled around wire, its wings only partially folded away. It is a common pipistrelle.

'Is it hurt?' asks the woman.

'It's hard to say.'

I gently the prise the bat from the warm grille and cup it in my hands, aware that it is a delicate and complicated machine of bones and veins, sharp teeth and finely tuned senses. Beautiful too. I can feel its pulse, the blood of it.

I remove my woollen hat and carefully place the bat inside. It is nearly weightless; the average pipistrelle weights about five grams, the same as a 20p coin. The woman leaves the creature in our care.

We find out the number of a national bat-line. They advise us to put him in a shoebox, so we make a bed for Vlad – as we inevitably call him – and add a small saucer of water to it, then put his makeshift home in the cellar, where it is cool, dark and quiet.

In the morning when I check on him there are some tiny bat turds on my hat, so I know that Vlad is alive and functioning.

It takes us two days to locate the bat man, a recently quali-
fied volunteer at the local bat rescue branch called Nigel.

He arrives that Saturday morning wearing a full morning
suit. Top hat, tails, necktie. Buffed shoes. We shake hands.

'I can't stop too long. My daughter's getting married.'

'Great,' I say. 'Congratulations.'

He looks at his watch.

'At midday.'

'Today?'

'Aye. In Huddersfield.'

'But that's forty-five minutes away.'

He shrugs.

'And it's eleven now,' I say.

'I'll be reet,' he replies in that brusque West Yorkshire way.
'Now, where's this bat at.'

I take Nigel down to meet Vlad, who has drunk more of the
refreshed water and decorated my hat with further minuscule
brown baubles.

He peers into the box and then carefully lifts him out. He
studies him.

'Well, you did the right thing. He looks in decent nick.
Probably just got a fright, is all.'

'What will you do with him?'

'I put them in the attic for a bit of R&R,' he explains. 'Rest
and relaxation. I'll monitor him and if he can fly alright we'll
release him back into the wild.'

Nigel gently strokes Vlad's fur.

'Is this your job?' I ask.

'More of a hobby. I've only started a couple of months back. This is my fourteenth rescue so far. Ten have survived.'

I look at my watch.

'It's quarter past you know, Nigel.'

'Is it,' he says, still gently stroking the bat in a manner that suggests he is in no hurry whatsoever.

Two weeks later there is a knock on the front door.

It's Nigel the bat man back again, though I barely recognise him now that he is not in his nuptial fineries.

'How is he?' I ask. 'How is Vlad?'

Nigel holds up a clear plastic box with air holes in the top.

'He's in fine fettle. Been feeding him up. I thought it best to release him back to where he came from.'

We walk up the road and into the trees at the foot of The Rock where the bats roost. Three-quarters of Britain's bat populations live and hunt in such woodlands. Unable to bore holes or create nests, they instead find homes in natural cavities in trees or crevices left by other creatures such as woodpeckers, while the rest live in man-made structures – houses, barns, bridges, churches – or in underground roosts in caves, cellars, mines or tunnels.

Field surveys done over the past two decades show an increase in population of the common pipistrelle, yet at the same time roost counts register a significant decrease, though this may simply be down to this species' tendency to switch roosting locations frequently, making it extremely difficult to monitor numbers.

Past the bend in the road where we first found Vlad clinging to the car we stop and Nigel hands me the box.

'Here you go.'

I lift the lid and pick up the bat. Perhaps I'm imagining it, but he feels more dense somehow, as if his sojourn at Nigel's has been one spent idly gorging himself as one might at an all-inclusive holiday resort.

He sits in my palm and his tiny five-fingered hand is human-like the way it rests upon mine. His ears are pinned back and his wet snout sniffs at the afternoon air.

Beside us the trees rustle and sway. Above them is The Rock, whose cracked face must surely harbour a thousand similar creatures.

'That's it,' says Nigel. 'Gently as you like.'

I lift my arm, and hold my hand out.

The bat's mouth opens then, and I see its pink interior as it tastes the day, and watch as it unfolds wings that have been efficiently packed away, and they are large as they spread wide – so much larger than I thought, so much wider than I expected – and it takes flight, and for one short moment the sun shines through the thin membrane of its wings, and the scaffolding of tiny bones are held there, and then the bat is gone, away into the trees.

I will think of him every time we come out bat-watching,

wondering if he or his descendants are amongst the colony that devour the quiet hum of the static night.

FRIDAY AND THE sun is spilling treacle across the moor.

It is the hottest day of the year so far and all feels still.

The evening smells of freshly sliced celery.

Dylan Thomas called May 'the cuckoo's month' and as I drive bare-chested and uncaring the five or six miles up above Cragg Vale I hear from my open window a cuckoo call from down in the cleft of clustered trees where someone thought to leave a village. Its song is an illusion, first heard far away, and then close by, and then from the other side of the road. 'So quick it flies from wood to wood / 'Tis miles off 'ere you think it gone,' wrote John Clare. 'I've thought when I have listening stood / Full twenty sang – when only one.'

My back sticks to the seat and a through breeze lifts the litter of parking tickets and sweet wrappers in the back of my car.

Where civilisation ends and the vastness of moor begins I park up in a stopping place and walk a short distance along the roadside, glad of the warming air-thrust of the occasional passing car commuting from Manchester back to the valley for a long bank-holiday weekend that lies ahead. It is an evening of endless potential; no time for work or worries.

I recall once again the words of Glyn Hughes, whose book *Millstone Grit* has begun to take on a sort of talismanic significance for me. In it he writes of the subtle seasonal shifts that register across the moors, where the hills are 'an archipelago of islands in the wandering fog. In March, when the old grass, whinberr and heather are burnt so that their ashes might fertilize new growth (they call it "sweeling") whole hills are dramatically on fire; and in autumn the hills are turned the duller, more resonant red of the decaying herbage. In late summer, the sunlight strikes purple heather mixed with white grass.'

I see the same heather now as I cut into a field busy with sheep and lambs, soporific in the heat. The lengthening shadow of a wall offers a refuge for some, and they begrudgingly unfold themselves from it as I approach. The lambs are rounded things, their soft faces not yet indolent or dumb, but full of delight and their throats are tremulous as they call out. The field of lush grass is clipped to a gamekeeper's perfection as it rolls away to the beginnings of the same narrow clough that fed those great floods of a winter that now seems like an old film I once saw. Memory already turning sepia.

THE FOLLOWING DAY the summer hum of the garden deepens to a reedy timbre; a rising anger.

I straighten, look up and see: wasps. A pother of them like a dust cloud kicked up by an off-screen disturbance. There must be a million or more of them rolling in from under The Rock. A homeostatic army scoping new terrain.

My first thought is: fight or flight (or film?).

But it is too beautiful a sight to move. So I stand amongst them, perfectly at ease as they swarm, flitting black petals against the sun.

Then they are at my ears, across my shoulders and in my hair. I do not care.

Wasps aren't so bad. No wasps ever offered tax breaks for the wealthy or stirred up racial tension for their own political ends. No wasps ever threatened to build a border wall between countries, only the beautiful paper lanterns that they call home.

I am in the eye of the storm now and the wasps sense that I am no threat, only a totem of the clan.

The noise they make is as immense as a phalanx of pylons, an orchestra of blood.

A drowning menagerie.

A holocaust of wolves.

I stand stock-still as they pass on through.

HIGH SUMMER AND the humming days drift through pools of sunshine.

The prolonged dry spell feels like a gift, overdue compensation for the long, dour months of dreich days.

Meteorologists mark it the hottest June day since the heatwave of 1976 – at Heathrow they record 34°C. (Like Gatwick, whose name *gāt wīc* derives from Old English for 'goat farm', the

lingering presence of the rural in these most modern construc-
tions has always struck me. The Middlesex hamlet of Heathrow,
demolished to make way for the sprawling airport through
which 75 million passengers travel each year, was once *Hithero*,
Hetherow, *Hetherowfeyld* and *Hitherowe* – all meaning a 'row of
houses on the heath'.)

Up above the reservoir levels drop to reveal shores that have
not seen sunlight for years. Scarves of algae are left there, stranded.

The sky is a blue band and rain, when it comes, is furious and fleeting. Afterwards the valley feels refreshed; the wild
grasses more lush than ever, the birdsong heartier.

In the pastures above The Rock cows pause mid-mouthful
to stare as I pass, their tails reflexively swatting like a lazy ring-
master's whip at the halo of flies that gather around their rears.
The cows occupy one field, sheep dot another. When the
thermometer pushes thirty they are brought down closer to
shade and water sources.

And the woods of Scout Rock become denser, darker, more
impenetrable even than during that first summer that I explored
here – how long ago was it now? Eight years? Nine?

I stroll up a few minutes shy of 10 p.m. I've reconnoitred a
flat, rectangular rock slab set fifty feet up the lower hillock below
the rock that looms majestically like a battered ziggurat. It is the
perfect proportion for lying on and offers a view across a hollow
that is perhaps 200 feet across.

If I twist my body I can see a full 360 degrees.

I laid a stick there earlier to help me when I leave later on in near-total darkness and have to pass over fallen boulders and perilous potholes deep beneath the rug of grass and bracken.

From here in my royal box of warm rock I stretch out and listen to the closing bird calls. They are a series of songs, like the strings of violins and cellos being unwound. Notes are traded in a manner that suggests, to my anthropomorphic understanding at least, a sense of contentment. I think of the closing scene of the 1970s TV show *The Waltons*, where the wholesome down-home clan bid each other goodnight from the comfort of their bedrooms. 'It's not that [birds] sing because they're happy, and it's not even that singing *makes* them happy,' writes Richard Smyth in his recent study of bird song, *A Sweet, Wild Note*. 'I think that perhaps the singing is the happiness, and the happiness is the singing.'

Soon the various avian species settle into sleep, and I let my breathing fall into step with the slowing pulse of the wood. Beads of sweat gather at my temples, and then trickle. I blink the salt from my eyes. The warm stone is cooling beneath me.

Midges. Many midges.

I train my eyes on an owl box that was lagged to an old tree split two winters ago during a violent storm, and which I helped my neighbour Niall clean out of moss and dust and bones last year after it was vacated by the previous tenant. I hear a final kazoo-like call of a roosting peacock down in Jerry the Beekeeper's house.

I feel the sigh of the earth as the day's dimmer switch is slowly turned.

The trees are unmoving statues turning black, reminders that the British land mass was once almost entirely covered by trees which took root during the first great tree migration across Europe when the Ice Age ended over 10,000 years ago.

This was after towers of ice in the swamplands of what is now northern France had melted, and salt water sluiced the last of the land away to create the English Channel, so that a newly formed island became exiled from the rest of the continent, cast out like a bad son to slowly nurture a resentful outsider's mentality.

First came birch, then Scots pine. Latecomers to the party, as the land became wetter and warmer like a large, dirty sponge, were the trusty oak and reliable alder. They clustered into little copses, then grew into woods and forests, all merging into an ancient arboreal maze. And in amongst them, the badgers, red squirrels, hedgehogs and grass snakes arrived too.

There was no tea or tobacco or potatoes but there were plenty of trees.

Trees from sea to sea.

And then man harnessed fire and man created hammers and blades and man got busy.

Trees were felled. Stumps burnt. Clearings created.

Modern farming began in earnest, and by 2000 BC the woods resounded to the *chock* of the swinging blade. The great British tree cull had begun, and the attendant Bronze Age saw its acceleration. *Swish* went the falling trunks, their rustling limbs spread wide, the sky a mosaic of fleeing birds. The soil was turned and pigs were set loose to feed on acorns. And on it went.

Pruning, burning, digging, hacking.

Wood as fuel, wood as tool.

Plotting, dividing, colonising.

The screech and scratch of axes being sharpened on primitive grinding stones.

Sparks.

Down through the centuries the trees continued to fall.

In the age of Enlightenment, while man pondered the question, 'If a tree falls in a forest and no one is there to hear it, does it really make a sound?', they just kept falling and it seemed for a time that Britain was to become a balding land with a grim future, whose remaining trees would be kept in reservations away from the cities. Forgotten curios, neglected relics.

By 1919, when a generation of young men were killed, maimed or irrevocably changed by the Great War, and the psyche of a nation perhaps forever changed too, England was down to a 5 per cent covering of trees, and there was a surplus of pencils.

Thankfully in 1919 the Forestry Commission was established and finally the trend was first halted and then reversed. By 2017 England was back to over 10 per cent coverage, the highest level since circa 1350, and 13 per cent in the United Kingdom as a whole.

Perhaps it has always been this way, and that in fact trees

come and go like the tide. Perhaps there have always been times of plenty followed by leaner days of bare screes, barren clearings. Dead spaces.

And perhaps our perception of our natural habitats is a victim of our tendency to endlessly romanticise times we have never known, and that as a nation – a species, even – we collectively suffer from what the travel writer Hugh Thomson calls, in an essay of the same name, 'Sherwood Syndrome'. This, he explains, is:

> the need to believe that much of England – most of England – was both wild and wooded until modern history 'began' in 1066, or indeed stayed so until much later; and that these ancient forests were the repository of 'a spirit of England', the Green Man, that could be summoned at times when we needed to be reminded of our national identity; where Robin Hoods of all subsequent generations could escape, where the Druids gathered their mistletoe from the trees, where the oak that built our battleships came from. The myth panders to our need for a sense of loss. There is an undercurrent of regret running through our history. A nostalgia for what could have been.

AS FULL DARKNESS falls the trees begin to merge, and I see not their leaves or branches but the spaces between them, the shifting diamonds of dying light created by the overlap.

Once again in these woods perception distorts. The mind plays tricks but the eyes never lie. I watch and wait for something living to cross these final shards of sun that dim like fading glow-worms.

Everything slows and settles and I tune into the new frequency. Another soundtrack emerges and the night shift begins.

I hear the slow crackle of something nearby as it crawls through fallen leaves. I hear the dry squeak of insect wings as thin as Japanese *Tenguchoushi* – paper so thin you can read a newspaper *through* it – being rubbed together. A slick and gluey slithering sound of something becoming unstuck. A distant sibilance. Licentious squelching. One snapped twig.

Footsteps?

I hold an exhalation.

No. No footsteps.

It is as dark as a high-summer night gets now, and, robbed of the ability to see anything but the barest outline of trees and the black mass of bracken across the hollow, other senses come more strongly into play. I experience a heightened awareness of my own body. The click of the left side of my jaw, the grind of my stiffening neck when I roll my head. The touch-points of heels and elbows as I recline on the slab.

The point of a pin-like proboscis piercing my skin, and then beginning to draw blood.

Far below me something passes across the clearing, treading carefully.

With each passing moment I feel less an observer and more

a part of the wood, but always aware that out there, despite my best attempts at utter silence, creatures are listening to *my* movements. The awkward shifting of limbs, the scratching of my scalp and the sudden slapping-away of whatever succubus is feeding on my hot blood.

Minutes pass this way. Hours. Maybe even centuries of night. Here 'time is measured', wrote J. A. Baker, 'by a clock of blood'.

As my joints ache and the edges of night become charred black like a burning newspaper I sit and dangle my legs over the edge of the stone.

Only now do I turn on my torch and sweep its beam across the hollow. Almost immediately I see two blue-glass eyes staring back at me.

They stare and stare, and then disappear briefly in the blink of a neatly split second.

Fox.

With my walking stick acting as a fifth limb and torch turned off, I pick my way down through the darkness. I move as quietly as possible, which is not quiet at all. The gap between myself and the fox closes.

I stop. Stand. Wait. Point the torch again. This time I see three, four, five sets of eyes staring back at me. Ten starlit dots boring through the dropped veil of summer.

Neither I nor they move.

Only the planet moves.

SUMMER SIGHS AND stretches like a yawning cat, and I find myself over a pool in a feeder stream.

Leaning over this gurgling rill I see young trout like lightning bolts, silver bullets hammered flat by the dropping of the levels, the passing of time.

The way they dart from pool to pool via copper-toned runnels and held fast by stone corridors so shallow you wouldn't think it possible to pass through them holds my gaze for an hour or more. The young fish are mesmerists, illusionists, and when one leaps lightly I resist the urge to applaud its tenacity in crossing borders and boundaries between worlds. There is no smoke and mirrors here. For a moment I believe in magic.

And beneath their skin a million pulled strings. Folded feathers.

Muscle memories.

And summer drifts.

Summer sings.

The workmen return to Scout Rock to continue their sculpting and securing of this slumped hillside. Weeks become months become years and with them they bring drains and rods and steel girders and clamps and steamrollers and generators and lengths of pipe and diggers and drills and an oversized corkscrew for creating boreholes and a towering teal-green metal silo for mixing concrete. They bring portable cabins and offices and temporary toilets and warning signs.

And in and around them work tree surgeons, further felling trees that block their path.

The valley echoes to the sound of sharpened teeth chomping through ancient wood once again. More men arrive with chainsaws and ropes, and we are awoken to the crack and splinter of timber at first light. The lungs of the valley are being lifted out. Stumps dot the hillside and new spaces appear.

The felled trees feel like a kind of heartbreak, or worse, because broken hearts are mended by time, but these trunks are merely dragged up the slopes and roughly shoved towards the centre of the woods into a pile the size of a house. Discarded.

Many have marked my point of entry into The Rock for years, but then one Friday evening they are gone, and the tree surgeons too, and though they have taken all hefty limbs and shredded the branches into a large pile of woodchip and sawdust, they have left behind several dozen cross-sections of trunk.

Snagging my coat on the KEEP OUT sign, I vault a temporary metal fence. Where once there were trees and roots, crows' nests and badger setts I find new patches of dumped concrete, hardened into artless piles of grey vomit. The plastic ribbons of tape like those used at crime scenes are still here from last winter, but they are sagging in places and torn in others, flapping in the breeze like snagged tails detached from flyaway kites. Further patches of wild thicket have been levelled by the caterpillar treads of machinery, a new track carved through, with anything in its way removed: trees, boulders, tiny ecosystems.

But for now, on weekends when the workmen down tools, The Rock belongs to me once more as I wander with a bow-saw slung over my shoulder to scavenge, saw and stack wood in secret stashes, erecting tall teepees of timber in the remote hidden corners that only I know about, ready to be reclaimed once the workmen have left, each log, limb or branch to be carried out one at a time on my shoulders through bogs and down slopes, to be stacked again, each pile a little closer to home.

It's an energy-inefficient and time-consuming practice that few people would ever bother with these days when heat is available at the flick of switch, but I enjoy the physicality, the feel of dirt and moss about me, the weight of wood in my arms. And later, there will be the ache of the effort in my muscles, and, come winter, the pop and crackle of the burning, the glow of them held in the dog's eyes as he stretches on the rug before another blaze, The Rock's gift to us as I warm my splintered palms, and wonder how I ended up here.

The old countrymen's adage has it that wood warms you thrice: when you cut it, when you move it, when you burn it. I have heated our house for several years this way. On a writer's wage I have often had to.

I dismantle one of my secreted woodpiles and find many fat slugs and knots of wriggling worms squeezed into the small rotting spaces between logs. There are spiders and slaters – woodlice – and a large toad staring back at me. I find a fat newt in this micro-menagerie too, and the eggs of either a slug or snail, slick and glistening like mustard-coloured sturgeon roe or spilled cod-liver oil tablets.

The rest of the weekend is spent wrangling the dense, sap-heavy circular slabs of wood into my car boot, and then driving them 100 yards down the road. Each is as heavy a piece as I can lift up the back steps into the garden, where I methodically fraction them, the crack of my sledgehammer on the old axe-head that I use for a splitter echoing off The Rock like gunshot.

In one of his lesser-known observations, Albert Einstein identified a simple pleasure when he remarked that 'people love chopping wood – in this activity one immediately sees results'.

Logging requires a sort of unthinking focus, where body and mind lock into one shared goal, and a combination of tactics and brute force yields the best results. There are similarities to boxing: one must strike *through* the wood as a boxer punches through their opponent. You are aiming for something beyond. It is not the hardest hammer blow that achieves the deepest cut, but the truest one – that which comes from somewhere deep in your centre, and aims for the bullseye of the earth.

LIKE THE ROMAN army that colonised this country all the way up to the Border lands through force, cunning and guile, the balsam that chokes the valley commandeers an empire entirely.

The river banks and the rail-side gulches, the sunken woodlands and the mulched bogs; all belong to this popping plant.

A dominant disciplinarian and martinet of a species, this weed reigns supreme, brawny and dumb, forever seeking safety in numbers and imposing itself *everywhere*. As summer progresses it wears its purpling flowers proudly. They appear late in the season to provide succour to the bees drawn to the musk, which is as aromatic as a spice-rack. Bees are of course one of the natural world's true wonders, like small, brilliant shards of sun falling to the earth – 'The keeping of bees is like the direction of sunbeams', wrote Thoreau – so any friends of the bees should be a friend of ours. But such is the allure of the balsam, like the invading army it is all-conquering, indiscriminately colonising all it sets foot on, the bees their unwitting foot soldiers. The pink flowers, I have been told, can be used in jam.

'It is such a good source of nectar that often bees will visit [it] in preference to native plants,' reports a website entitled Himalayan Balsam Wales. 'This means that native plants get a double hit by not being pollinated well, and also by being out-competed by the balsam. This can lead to thick stands of Himalayan Balsam, with lower overall biodiversity, which die down in winter and leave areas prone to erosion.'

All empires crumble under their own weight and by late summer this tumescent army of invidious invaders – this *Übermensch* of the weed world that stealth-grows as if it has been skin-popping steroids and pushing iron all summer long – rapidly withers.

Their claw-like roots, in June so certain and full of entitlement, will gradually loosen their grip, their green leaves, waxy and full, will turn jaundiced in pallor as they concede defeat in the battle for the sun's affection, and the reedy stalks that only six or eight weeks ago crunched so satisfyingly – like a forest of snapped cucumbers – and whose tubers sound sonorous when swung about one's head or flung blindly into the stagnant, black, sulphurous Pennine mangroves, will soften and fall apart in sad, wet strings until this irascible weed is utterly emasculated by the onset of the season of rot and mourning.

Spring's child and summer's victor become victims once more to the wheeling cycle of life, their seeds long since ingeniously flung into a future that awaits them, cast to fortune, each tiny seed set unseen in the soil to wait out another winter, biding its time, plotting, planning, bursting with brutish photosynthetic potential.

My friends and neighbours Steve and Gayle, who run an architectural practice and had to evacuate their house following the landslide, know a great deal about the history and topography of Scout Rock; living in its shadow, they have had to. They tell me that a consultant geologist told them that when the old town tip in Scout Rock was capped in the 1980s thousands of tonnes of soil were brought into the woods, in which was inadvertently carried the seeds of Himalayan balsam. Before then the plant had minimal presence in the valley, but in the three decades since it has spread like a moorland fire with the breeze at its back, aggressively filling every spare space, so that in the summer months the wastelands become transformed. The Calder Valley balsam problem began here, then – right on my doorstep.

IT IS A dismal late-summer afternoon and the plant is at its most virulently pungent when the men appear.

For weeks I have been wandering amongst the towering tubers that grow at the foot of The Rock, lost in this jungle of stalks and shaking their heads so that each spring-loaded seed pod dispenses its cargo for up to seven yards. The great irony of balsam is that in pulling them up, one is aiding their dispersal. It always makes me think of the ironic line from The Specials' 'Too Much Too Young' that Alan the Postman is fond of quoting: 'I'd love to spread manure in your bed of roses'.

Because it is dogged in its dominance over other native plants – some of which are practically slothful – balsam is viewed with contempt as an outsider. It is the foreigner who has found its footing on this isle.

The disruption balsam causes in each short life cycle may contribute to river-bank erosion and chokes all other plants into submission, but I am drawn to its exotic otherness, and the way its flamboyant, blazing rise is matched equally by its sudden and tragic downfall. Balsam is the glam rock of the weed world – proudly peacock-ish and aggressively aspirational, but short-lived and doomed to falter, collapsing finally under its own inflated sense of self.

The afternoon is fading through a blear of damp grey light when I see from my window police and medics gathering over the road by the balsam in the gloom. Luminous jackets dot the undergrowth like fireflies, and they appear to be in no hurry.

Close by, the factory siren signals the end of the working day and scores of employees file out just yards away. I wander over and ask one of the workers if they know what is going on.

'They found a body,' he says.

A local man around my age has been missing for several days and his friends and relatives have been out looking for him. There have been reported sightings, but he has not been located until now, draped in tragedy deep amongst the purple flowers.

He is believed to have taken a lethal dose of heroin. The needle is still in his arm as the heady scent of summer's end leaves the valley on a westerly wind.

A few days pass before I gingerly walk into the balsam and see the coffin-shaped space that he had made from himself during untold torment, just yards away from the footpath.

It is a bedded rectangle of ultimate silence. A sad spot that will be erased by the balsam's own passing over the coming weeks. The breeze is set to turn, and autumn will soon crawl across the land. I find flowers and messages. Notes of sorrow and remembrance.

They will still be there when September sheds its skin to become October and when October rots into November too, but the balsam will not.

Yet in the shallow soil the seeds sit, waiting, and on the wheel turns.

FIELD NOTES IV

Imbolc Sun and Birdsong

Imbolc sun and
birdsong at dawn births
spring like an uncertain
foal, slick and wet.

And this afternoon up
on the ridge we'll see
silhouettes of stag horns
piercing the old blue net.

Sighting in the Top Fields

In the chorus of the day
a rare black rabbit sleeps
like an old photograph
in the attic of forever.

Scout Rock from Daisy Bank

The scarp
awaits the sculptor's chisel
and the words within
his weary muscle.

Spring melodies split the valley
as his mallet splits the song.

The Accidental Jetty

Pylons stand as soldiers, strung,
the westerly wind in their wires.

Summer has settled on the moor
and the waters of Whiteholme are low.

The sky reveals a foreshore
of new tussocks and ancient algae

and an accidental jetty made of
red rock, goose shit and shale.

The surface steals a cloud or two
as I walk across them, whistling.

Scout Rock from the Garden

Perhaps garlic is the smell of spring
mint and balsam is summer
rosemary autumn
smoke winter

and resin all seasons
as I blunt another blade
and the sledgehammer
strikes the chock that splits the forest.

Future Fires

Up in the creak of it –
enough felled wood for
ten hundred winters,

each chainsaw–chewed
slice a wonderful wound
drying in the dusk.

Resting in the cathedral
silence of its aching spaces,
I summon future fires.

Muggy June Afternoon

April-spawned perch
snatch at
May-hatched flies
in slow brook water
as deep as a hand,
as ancient as the harvest,
as certain as
the oxblood sky.

Sitting in the Woods After Dark in June

Night recognises not
the shape that
reality takes
but a need for
sunless dreaming.

Heron

A sprung bough bent
and shaken by a squirrel
sends a shower down

and a great heron up,
rising from its
reed bed

(its name comes from
haigiro, hairo
eron and *hairon,*

but some just
call them
shitepokes.)

Here by the old stone crossing
where the clough bubbles
sour cream

it is July
in the heart
of all things.

Unheard

My goal in life is
to walk the
hills unheard.

Stone slab in Scout Rock: the perfect spot for some nocturnal fox-watching.

Work begins to secure the lower portion of the landslide.

Left: Cliff sniffing the air during a snowstorm.
Right: Weaver's cottages at The Stubb near Mytholmroyd, built *c.* 1641. 'Stubb' refers to the tree stumps in what was once a woodland clearing.

CODA

Beyond

Chapter Fourteen

Winter comes around once more, and the first fresh snow falls through daybreak's seeping – cloying, wet, exhausted by the calendar.

Outside in the unreal world, snake-oil sales rise, borders are redrawn. There have been elections, new leaders. The world appears angry.

In the barren Scottish Borders, in an annual retreating from the valley shadows, I take the dog to the top field, the last before the moor rises to the forged and bolted silver November sun. Two days ago he caught a rabbit here.

Set-traps line the heather. I have to watch out for them, and watch for the sadistic flame-haired gamekeeper too, as branch-bound, over-fed pheasants sit like targets on the firing range of the horizon, and my mind is elsewhere. I've been up all night following worldwide political events via an erratic internet connection.

The news tells me that hope is crumbling like the trunk that harboured that resting rabbit, whose dead form sits there still beneath snow, like something turned out from a mould. An idea.

The dog slow-stalks the bank that houses the warren but the rabbits have got wise – wiser than the people elected to lead us wandering barefoot onto the burning plane.

DEMAGOGUES AND DESPOTS come and go, and I try to ignore political discourse. It all seems too myopic and fleeting.

I watch the seasons overlap. They layer on top of one another. Winter becomes spring and spring is summer and memories merge and meld, and the flood evolves from fact to myth, a recent history that is still being relived through stories on the tongues of all who witnessed them.

Nature does not stop. It never shies away from the task at hand: perpetual growth and death, growth and death. Survival – that is all. Of plant species and creature alike. Feeding, mating, birthing. Dying. On and on it goes. The fox screams and the deer stomps a hoof. The raven croaks with delight as it feels the first warm rays on its hellish-blue wings.

Only humans reach further, filling their time with false desires, delusion and distraction from the self. Turning away from news media, I find myself instead considering the wider environment, at a deeper level.

ANOTHER DAY BACK at The Rock. Another week or month or year.

Here I stand.

Feet planted. Neck cricked. Eyes squinted. What do I see?

I see a place. A small place.

A place long molested.

Once raked and blasted and quarried; dug up, cordoned off and dumped upon. A place demonised and still home to rock-falls and landslips thanks to man's terminal tinkering.

To some it is barely seen at all, passed by in the blink of an eye. It's just wallpaper. A backdrop. A flash of green, then gone.

They do not realise it is the centre of the universe.

I see bees gorging and a woodpecker hole, and a deer that's as close to peace as it can get, ambling across the open pages of this book to dip a head to a cool trickle of water that drips from the corner of the cover. I see a narrative and a continuity.

No map could truly know this place, for its clefts and con-tours are ever-changing.

The Rock is a clock. Time passes across it and through it.

It measures moments and celebrates them, then discards them.

IN RECENT YEARS there has been a growing argument in favour of the rewilding of our urban, suburban and rural spaces.

The emerging 'edgelands' of recent cliché. Rewilding encourages the increase of natural habitats in which indigenous species can feed, nest and breed, and the reintroduction of those creatures whose populations have suffered, or disappeared entirely from Britain, during the jackboot-stomp of progress.

It is about acknowledging that the natural world is a system, or a series of systems, that do not exist in isolation but in fact co-exist, complementing each other in symbiotic relationships established over thousands of years in a harmonious food chain, or series of life cycles. Animals such as the wolf, the beaver, the wild boar and the lynx are the most commonly cited examples of those whose reintroduction might benefit Britain's wild systems. It is not just the animal chain that needs deeper consideration either, but the varying environments that sustain it too. Nan Shepherd put it best when she wrote: 'The disintegrating rock, the nurturing rain, the quickening sun, the seed, the root, the bird – all are one.'

On paper, rewilding sounds like a step in the right direction, a recognition of human responsibility to embark on reparations for the damages caused.

Yet part of me worries that rewilding is merely the latest trend, and just one more set of arbitrary rules and focus-group ideals imposed upon a natural world that should not be subjected to rules at all. The radical in me wonders if rewilding – true rewilding – requires the complete removal of humans from the equation and that nature should, wherever possible, be left entirely alone, so that paradise can recreate itself in peace, and nature might assert itself as the only religion once more.

Perhaps humans should have no say in the matter.

Before the workmen, surveyors and asbestos-testing scientists arrived at The Rock I saw perhaps two or three people in this overgrown plot of ten wooded acres in a decade of exploring it. The dark mythology of Scout Rock has its benefits: people stay away, and in the absence of external interference nature has been given free rein to embark upon its cycles of life untouched.

Plants rise and fall, and I witness their struggle for dominance over both terrain and sky, and then their downfall, their remains pulped down to nourish the soil, seeds scattered for next year's corresponding season.

Most are weeds and viewed as invasive or poisonous or ugly, yet I find them fascinating and beautiful, each as valuable as a wild orchid, if not quite as rarely seen. I have watched storm-split trees waver and fall and then, over time, find new purpose as micro-metropolises; ecosystems for the tiniest insects whose role in the worldwide matrix is to recycle the rotten, irrigate the soil, process death. I have seen birds and mammals flourish down the generations, heard the rutting of foxes and the howls of the cubs that these violent congresses produce.

I have seen the explosion of life, the inevitability of death.

Here in a valley where people live and work, where all things great in the modern Western world – technology, medicine, travel, an abundance of food – are being enjoyed, I have seen true rewilding at work at a microcosmic level, and barely a stone's throw from schools and houses, pubs and petrol stations. It has been completely accidental, and has happened *despite*, rather than *because of*, humans. (My own intrusion is, I hope, minimal. I take nothing from the wood but newly felled timber, my only mark a faint new path.)

The rewilding of Scout Rock is born out of neglect, and is nature's fight-back against the centuries of industrialisation. It makes me believe that once we, the planet's custodians, find our future numbers drastically reduced and living artificial existences due to the destruction of our natural resources – or perhaps destroy ourselves entirely – earth will slowly repair itself and begin all over. Rain will fall, its acidity chipping away at the rock to form new sea beds, new deserts. Cells will evolve. Seeds will take root. New species will emerge. A version of humans, perhaps.

Maybe next time we'll do things differently.

Maybe we'll do things exactly the same.

But life will sing its song again.

STILL, WATER CONTINUES to define this place – the mood and shape of it.

But this water is only ever passing through. The rivers, streams, reservoirs, ponds and canals may be the veins of the valley, but they are not self-contained. They all lead elsewhere, and here 'elsewhere' means to the sea, taking everything else not tied down with it.

Even the *aqua pura* that seeps through The Rock one squeezed drop at a time joins an ocean eventually, and I must remind myself that there is a world beyond.

Della and I drive across the plains of the East Riding on the day of the winter solstice, the shortest of the year, to see where the water that begins in the mossy bogs of the Pennines uplands, and that drowned the Calder Valley, culminates.

We are here to chase the low-skulking silver sun, walk the frosted sands at the end of a year, and mark the closing of another calendar.

Spurn Point, the natural three-mile-long sandbank that curves out into the North Sea, is our destination. To reach it we pass farmed fields and I find myself unnerved by the views afforded by the flatlands. My valley-formed sense of depth perception is unused to seeing twenty miles or so in any direction without first climbing to a good height. (Unlike the other Yorkshire counties named for the three other points on the compass, the eastern flank of Yorkshire celebrates its difference by favouring the name the East Riding. East Yorkshire does not technically exist.)

We pass through more villages, and see signs for curiously named outposts across perfectly flat fields that rustle with wheat in the summer but now are ploughed acres of dense, rutted winter mud.

Swine, Paull and Sunk Island.

Roos. Hollym.

Once marshland that was drained in the Middle Ages, Holderness offers rich agricultural land and a complex network of old ditches, and streams still run the water away into the River Hull now.

The soil is good here, the sky wide. Rainfall is relatively low. It is the antithesis of the undulating, sodden Calder Valley landscape where weeds have the whip hand, and the wool of hardy fell creatures is one of the few worthwhile products.

The birdlife is diverse out here too, and draws visitors from across Britain.

We reach the village of Holmpton, where Ted Hughes was despatched in 1949 to undertake two years of National Service. Just as the future poet departed Holderness in October 1951, the military embarked upon a much bolder venture down the road in Holmpton, when they began constructing a grand subterranean early-warning radar station, which was later repurposed as a nuclear bunker, and that is now a museum that perfectly captures the paranoia that permeated the strange and fearful Cold War era.

Such monuments to war still litter the landscape now, each a reminder of a time of past conflicts.

A hundred yards or so from the lower edge of Scout Rock there sits a small Second World War air-raid bunker. It is not one of the makeshift corrugated bow-shaped shelters that were erected over hastily dug holes in the back gardens of London housing estates, but a small, solid concrete structure with a curved roof, and dug into the bank side. Though blackened by rain and moss-coated, it remains sturdy beside a marshy puddle, and is largely hidden from view behind the screens of balsam in the summer months. It is sculptural and mottled, and proto-Brutalist in style.

The black mouth of the shelter leads down a set of concrete steps into the dirt bank beyond a neighbour's back garden, and then takes a right turn into a subterranean corridor about ten yards long. It is gated and padlocked now, another neglected relic of a conflict, its floor a stagnant pool of rainwater containing the usual pieces of broken wood, plastic, beer cans. Inside suggests a place of foreboding; it was searched by police when another young man went missing some years back.

I pass by it most days and often imagine that it is not an air-raid shelter at all, but an entrance to the underworld, a portal to a place deep beneath The Rock.

The vast bunker at RAF Holmpton in the East Riding is a few hundred yards inland from where the sea is steadily chipping away at the clay of the coastline. Erosion is an ongoing concern, as this edge of England is continuously diminished.

Amongst the hardy ruderal vegetation that grows on the clifftops we stumble across two further concrete look-out bunkers. One of them has sunk into the sand, tipped like an exhausted wedding cake, so that the only things that can be viewed from the narrow slits of its windows are the stars.

An estimated five feet of land is lost along this stretch each year, the marlstone and mud swept away along with silt, sand and shingle by longshore drift. Some of it is drawn down to the long spit of Spurn Point, where we are headed now.

We can see wind farms on the sea's horizon, but once there were villages out there on the low flatlands too. At least twenty-three of them, and three miles of land are believed to have been eaten up by the North Sea since the Roman occupation, the most notable of which village was Ravenspurn, which appeared in several of Shakespeare's plays.

Beyond the erected sea walls and rock-filled gabions built in nearby towns such as Withernsea, not a great deal has been done to prevent further disappearances continuing, the hypnotic pull of the undertow drawing away the earth, forever altering our physical borders, erasing history. Central government seems a universe away.

We are a shrinking island.

We head south to Spurn Point, and onto the spit that reaches out over the mouth of the Humber.

A long, narrow and arching topographical oddity, Spurn looks out across the tidal estuary towards the distant Lincolnshire coastal towns of Grimsby and Cleethorpes in one direction, and the North Sea and Holland in the other.

Spurn was inhabited for centuries; the earliest reference to a lighthouse existing here dates back to the early fifteenth century. People lived and worked on the dunes, and in the twentieth century a railway line delivered a stream of day-trippers. Ralph Vaughan Williams even composed a piece of chamber music in its honour. But now it is a carefully managed nature reserve, under continuous threat from the elements.

The road that until very recently allowed us to drive out onto it was first breached and then destroyed during the Boxing Day floods, and is now reduced to little more than a 'washover' bank of sand and smooth pebbles at the mercy of the perilous tides, the sea encroaching at either side, a foaming mocha swell topped with fizzing briny cream. Aside from Yorkshire Wildlife Trust vehicles, the two lighthouses at the far end can now only be reached by a long walk on foot.

We arrive at 10.44 a.m., at the exact moment of the winter solstice.

The shale beaches and sparse sand dunes whistle with marram grass and host all manner of birds and mammals that have made a home on this coastal reach which, on a short, biting winter day like today, seems to float like a ghost ship adrift.

Information boards inform us that there are roe deer and grey seals, and birds including wigeon, fieldfare, knots, snow buntings, brent geese, curlews, short-eared owls and yellowhammers. In the spring and summer there can be seen pipistrelle bats, brown hares, foxes, grass snakes, dragonflies.

On the foreshore eelgrass peeks from the distant shallows and worm casts spiral upwards from lacquered-looking sand that reflects the bright midwinter sun. In the far distance, across a great, broad, unnerving abyss of a bay are the discernible signs of industrial Lincolnshire.

There are signs of past lives here too. Old buildings, half-hidden foundations. Shattered stone barracks. Broken bricks.

Everything has a salt-worn, wind-bitten feel. We are at the very edge of everything.

HERE IS THE true conclusion of the River Calder. Anything washed down our valley and not snagged on river-bank roots, weirs or overhanging branches is likely to end up delivered into the Humber estuary, slowly bobbing out to the North Sea, or, as is evident now, up onto the beach of the Spurn peninsula.

The air is sharp and invigorating like a hit of smelling salts.

As I walk the Point the ebbing morning high tide reveals lines of gnarled black groynes leading out across the wet sand – and the fresh cargo left behind, almost all of it man-made and man-dumped.

Once more I make a note of the detritus deposited around me. There are tyres with their treads worn away, knots of frayed blue rope, plastic containers, a shred of a tattered Union Jack, a yellow workman's helmet. There are small bows of polystyrene used for packing parcels and further larger pieces smoothed into more abstract shapes, plastic bottles – so many plastic bottles (a million of them are bought every minute worldwide, and only a fraction recycled) – a life jacket, a single phallic-looking finger ripped from a rubber glove, a balloon from a party long since passed, a metal dustbin, cross-beams from a building, several yards of black rubber-coated cable, trunks of bone-like timber of varying lengths, footballs, golf balls, a tangle of tennis-court fencing.

And scattered amongst the sand that has been combed clean by winter wind and the pebbles that once were mountains are further pieces of glass, rubber and plastic, worn down, broken, their edges bevelled away by the foaming, rolling water.

All are the trappings of a downward ecocidal spiral.

The level of rubbish is staggering. Volunteers regularly congregate to clear Spurn Point, but it keeps coming back, more trash with each tide. A global analysis of plastics by

US academics reported in July 2017 that since the 1950s the world has produced over *eight billion* tonnes of plastic, half of which becomes waste within four years or less, and the majority of that ultimately ends up in landfill sites or in the oceans, threatening a 'near-permanent contamination of the natural environment'. Projections forecast an increase in plastic production over the coming decades, a growth trajectory on course to produce an estimated 34 billion tonnes by 2050.

Where will it all go?

Here. There.

Everywhere.

To remote Arctic beaches miles from inhabited areas, or tangled around the feet of puffins and the gills of basking sharks, and inside a third of fish caught in British waters too.

With each passing day the world appears more amazing, yet ever more in need of our protection. Or perhaps it is in need of nothing but our complete removal. I have been thinking about the finality of extinction a lot.

We walk on. I see something up ahead, slumped. It is a grey seal that has dragged itself up from the water and now lies resting. It has dark, expressive eyes and a cluster of whiskers, a single wavering trail across the sand behind it. It resembles our dog, who is curled up at home in his bed, and I make a note to alert the first Yorkshire Wildlife Trust worker that we see to its plight.

Reaching the lighthouse, we stop to eat sandwiches. A robin settles on the sign beside us. I hold out some crumbs and this lovable symbol of England hops onto my hand and pecks away, unperturbed by our presence.

Here the three of us sit in the centre of winter. Beyond us is nothing but water, and the curve of the earth, and strange and beautiful things unknown.

Sources

The following texts were referred to in the writing and research of this book.

Alexander, Marc, *British Folklore, Myths & Legends* (Sutton Publishing, 2002)

Baker, J. A, *The Peregrine* (Harper Collins, 1967)

Barker, Paul, *Hebden Bridge: A Sense of Belonging* (Frances Lincoln, 2012)

Bate, Jonathan, *Ted Hughes: The Unauthorised Life* (William Collins, 2015)

Bell, Richard, *Yorkshire Rock: A Journey Through Time* (Earthwise Popular Science Book, 1996)

Berry, Wendell; Paul Kingsnorth (ed.), *The World-Ending Fire: The Essential Wendell Berry* (Allen Lane, 2017)

Billingsley, John, *A Laureate's Landscape: Walks Around Ted Hughes' Mytholmroyd* (Northern Earth, 2007)

Billingsley, John, *Aspects of Calderdale: Discovering Local History* (Wharncliffe Books, 2002)

Billingsley, John, *Folk Tales from Calderdale Volume I* (Northern Earth, 2007)

Billingsley, John, *West Yorkshire Folk Tales* (The History Press, 2010)

Boswell, Geoff, *On the Tops Around Todmorden* (Delta G, 1986)

Brautigan, Richard, *Trout Fishing In America* (Picador, 1967)

Brautigan, Richard, *The Toyko-Montana Express* (Picador, 1980)

Brennan, Ailis, 'Is Jimi Hendrix responsible for London's parakeet population?' GQ online, 10 February 2016

Coleridge, Samuel Taylor, *Coleridge's Notebooks: A Selection* (Oxford University Press, 2004)

Cooper, Dominic, *Waymarking* (self-published, 2016)

Cope, Julian, *The Modern Antiquarian* (Thorsons, 1998)

Crowdy, Terry, *Deceiving Hitler: Double Cross and Deception in World War II* (Osprey, 2013)

Davies, Caroline 'Bikers patrol flood-hit Yorkshire towns to deter looters', *Guardian*, 29 December 2015

Defoe, Daniel, *A Tour Through the Whole Island of Great Britain* (Penguin, 1971 edition)

DeSilvey, Caitlin; Naylor, Simon and Sackett, Colin (eds), *Anticipatory History* (Uniform Books, 2011)

Dickens, Charles (ed.), *All Year Round* (Chapman & Hall, September 1885)

Drayton, Michael, *Poly-Olbion* (Nabu edition, 2012)

Dugdale, Dorothy, *The Annals of Todmorden, 1552–1913* (Self-published, 2002)

Elmet Trust (Lesley Alston, Donald Crossley and Nick Wilding), *The Ted Hughes Trail in Crimsworth Dean* (The Elmet Trust, 2008)

Gammage, Nick (ed.), *The Epic Poise: A Celebration of Ted Hughes* (Faber, 1999)

Garner, Alan, *The Voice That Thunders* (Harvill Press, 1997)

Gifford, Terry, *Pastoral* (Routledge, 1999)

Gifford, Terry and Roberts, Neil, *Ted Hughes: A Critical Study* (Faber, 1981)

Gill, Adi; McCue, Andy; Nicholson, Andy and Troilett, Matt (eds), *Yorkshire Gritstone Volume 2: Ilkley to Widdop* (Yorkshire Mountaineering Club, 2014)

Goddard, Christopher, *The West Yorkshire Moors* (Jeremy Mills Publishing, 2014)

Goddard, Christopher, *West Yorkshire Woods – Part 1: The Calder Valley* (Christopher Goddard, 2016)

Griffiths, Jean 'The curious case of Tom Bell and his cave at Hardcastle Crags', *Yorkshire Journal*, Issue 3, Autumn 2014

Harrison, M. John, *Climbers: A Novel* (Victor Gollancz, 1989)

Hopkins, Gerald Manley, *Poems and Prose* (Penguin, 1953)

Hoskins, W. G., *The Making of the English Landscape* (Little Toller, 2013)

Hughes, Gerald, *Ted and I* (Robson Press, 2012)

Hughes, Glyn, *Millstone Grit* (Victor Gollancz, 1975)

Hughes, Glyn, *Best of Neighbours* (Sunderland Arts Centre, 1979)

Hughes, Ted, *The Hawk in the Rain* (Faber & Faber, 1957)

Hughes, Ted, 'The Rock' in *Worlds: Seven Modern Poets,* Geoffrey Summerfield (ed.) (Penguin Education, 1974)

Hughes, Ted, *Season Songs* (Faber & Faber, 1985)

Hughes, Ted, *Wodwo* (Faber & Faber, 1967)

'Jimmy Savile back to see old friends', *Halifax Courier*, 2 December 2007

Jouve, Nicole Ward, *The Streetcleaner: The Yorkshire Ripper Case on Trial* (Marion Boyars, 1988)

Lewis, Wyndham, *Blast 1* (Thames & Hudson, 2009)

Monbiot, George, 'The age of loneliness', *New Statesman*, 21 October 2016

Mort, Helen, *No Map Could Show Them* (Chatto & Windus, 2016)

Murty, Steve, *Summat A' Nowt* (Steve Murty, 2009)

Nicholson, John, *Folk-Speech of East Yorkshire* (Simpkin Marshall, 1889)

Pearce, Fred, *The New Wild: Why Invasive Species Will Be Nature's Salvation* (Icon Books, 2016)

Pero, Thomas, 'Poet, pike and a pitiful grouse', *Guardian*, 8 January 1999

Pidd, Helen and Halliday, Josh, 'How the floods united the North – from chefs bearing curry to refugees with sandbags', *Guardian*, 5 January 2016

Piggott, Mark, 'Dust storm', *Daily Telegraph*, 6 October 2007

Radford, E. and M. A., *Superstitions of the Countryside* (Hutchinson, 1948)

Sagar, Keith, *Ted Hughes and Nature: Terror and Exultation* (Upfront Publishing, 2010)

Shaw, George, *The Sly and Unseen Day* (Baltic, 2011)

Shaw, George, *My Back to Nature* (The National Gallery, 2016)

Skelton, Richard, *Beyond the Fell Wall* (Little Toller, 2015)

Smith, Julia, *Fairs, Feasts and Frolics: Customs and Traditions in Yorkshire* (Smith Settle, 1989)

Smyth, Richard, *A Sweet, Wild Note* (Elliott & Thompson, 2017)

Sprawson, Charles, *Haunts of the Black Masseur* (Vintage, 1993)

Summerfield, Geoffrey (ed.), *Worlds: Seven Modern Poets* (Penguin Education, 1974)

Tegner, Henry, *Beasts of the North Country* (Galley Press, 1961)

Thompson, E. P., *The Making of the English Working Class* (Penguin Modern Classics, 2013)

Thomson, Hugh 'The Sherwood syndrome', Aeon.co, 17 September 2012

Thorpe, Adam, *Ulverton* (Vintage, 2012)

Thoreau, Henry David, *Walking* (Arc Manor, 2007)

Turner, Luke, 'Stoodley Pike', *Somesuch Stories*, Vol. 2, 2016

Tutti, Cosey Fanni, *Art Sex Music* (Faber, 2017)

'Valley's darkest secret', *Halifax Courier*, 31 October 2003

Wainwright, Alfred, *Wainwright on the Pennine Way* (Michael Joseph, 1985)

Walder, Dennis, *Open Guides to Literature: Ted Hughes* (Open University Press, 1987)

Warner, Judith and Simon, *The South Pennines and the Brontë Country* (Town and Country, 1984)

Warner, Simon, *Discovering West Yorkshire* (Dalesman Publishing, 1999)

Welsh, Stephen, *Cragg Vale: A Pennine Valley* (Pennine Desktop Publishing, 1993)

Whone, Herbert, *The Essential West Riding* (Smith Settle, 1987)

Websites

The Northern Antiquarian (megalithix.wordpress.com)

Malcolm Bull's Calderdale Companion (www.freepages.history.
    rootsweb.ancestry.com/~calderdalecompanion)

TV and radio

Alice: A Fight for Life, Yorkshire Television, 1982

The Matter of the North, Episode 5: 'Lakes and moors: the
    power of Northern landscapes', presented by Melvyn
    Bragg, Radio 4, 2 September 2016

'The dust at Acre Mill', *World in Action*, Granada Television,
    1972

Acknowledgements

This book partly came about after a conversation about Scout Rock and the Calder Valley with the poet Zaffar Kunial, who encouraged me to write about the place. It reached the hands of Elliott & Thompson after the writer Melissa Harrison published some of my work in her series of anthologies of seasonal writings. Thank you to both of them.

I extend gratitude also to friends, fellow wanderers and swimmers alike. Amy Liptrot. Rob St John, Emma Cardwell and Eily. Nick Small. Steve Ely. Kevin Lord. Christopher Goddard. Luke Turner, John Doran and all *The Quietus*. Jeff Barrett and all at *Caught by the River*.

For input, information, introductions, opinions and general encouragement: John Billingsley at *Northern Earth*. Steve Gittner and Gayle Appleyard. Niall Roche. Melvin Burgess. Elliot Rashman and Michele Rashman. Alan Rogers. Colin Robinson. Helen Mort. Dominic Cooper. Francesca Glenn. Paul Buck. Andrew Wheatley at Cabinet Gallery. All at Hebden Bridge Library. Mal Campbell and everyone at the Trades Club. All at the Book Case, Hebden Bridge. Kevin and Hetha Duffy and all at Bluemoose Books. Claire Malcolm and everyone at New Writing North. Susie Troup for the Hadrian's Wall commission. Carol Gorner and all at the Gordon Burn Trust. Rob Cowen. Jenn Ashworth. Delaney Jae. Richard Dawson.

Thanks also to Rich and Helen Myers. Kathryn Myers and Stephen Carney. My parents, Geoff and Dorothy Myers. Emma Stripe. Ian Stripe. Katy and Matt Calveley. Davey James and Anna Barker. Anthony Luke. Lisa Cradduck. Heathcliff of Howarth.

Special thanks to my agent Jessica Woollard, and also Clare Israel, Alice Howe and all at David Higham Associates. And to Jennie Condell, Pippa Crane, Alison Menzies and everyone at Elliott & Thompson.

And especially to my wife Adelle Stripe.

A considerable amount of information for this book was gleaned during conversations with people I met while out walking. I am indebted to the knowledge, opinions and stories freely shared by familiar faces and strangers alike, and to those who contacted me online to share any related information or stories. For the sake of discretion some names may have been changed.

Users of Instagram can access an archive of photographs featuring locations and subjects explored in this book by searching for *#undertherockbook* or following www.instagram.com/benmyers76.

Index